No. 1469
$17.95

149 ONE-EVENING FURNITURE PROJECTS

BY MIKE & RUTH WOLVERTON

TAB BOOKS Inc.
BLUE RIDGE SUMMIT, PA. 17214

FIRST EDITION

SECOND PRINTING

Copyright © 1983 by TAB BOOKS Inc.

Printed in the United States of America

Reproduction or publication of the content in any manner, without express permission of the publisher, is prohibited. No liability is assumed with respect to the use of the information herein.

Library of Congress Cataloging in Publication Data

Wolverton, Mike.
    149 one-evening furniture projects.

    Includes index.
    1. Furniture making. I. Wolverton, Ruth.   II. Title.
III. Title: One hundred forty nine one-evening furniture
projects.
TT194.W64   1982   684.1′042   82-5915
ISBN 0-8306-2469-4   AACR2
ISBN 0-8306-1469-9 (pbk.)

Cover illustration by Keith Snow.

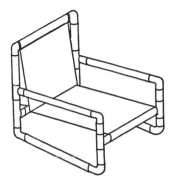

Contents

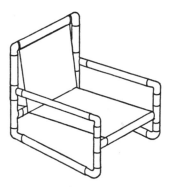

Introduction

Most furnishing and home improvement projects are designed for people who are master craftspersons at heart. You know the kind—they think nothing of spending hours painstakingly sanding and resanding, varnishing, tole painting, decoupaging, and the like. Precision and perfection in their projects are these people's goals.

We decided to develop projects for people who will settle for less than perfection but like attractive well-constructed furnishings. These projects were easier to come by than we anticipated.

You will be working with clean simple lines, few details, prefinished or easy-to-finish materials, and simple construction methods. In addition, you will use prefabricated items, incorporate available items as subassembly parts, and utilize "found" objects. You will farm out any work that is time-consuming; the lumberyard can precut any lumber needed to your specifications. An upholsterer can cut foam, and a professional can strip old furniture.

You are left with the fun parts—design, materials selection and assembly. These projects can be completed with minimal time and effort.

Ready? Let's begin.

Other TAB books by the author:

No. 1349 *How To Build a Lie Detector, Brain Wave Monitor &
Other Secret Parapsychological Electronics Projects*
No. 1381 *Draw Your Own House Plans*

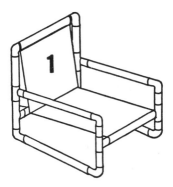

Work Sequence

If you leaf through the book, you will notice that the projects are set up in the same general format so that all projects have the same basic organization or series of steps. It doesn't matter whether you are going to make a pin cushion, shelves, doghouse, or an addition to your home; the basic steps will always be the same. First, you must plan the project. Then obtain the necessary materials and tools. Cut the material into appropriate shapes and sizes and fasten the pieces together. Finally, finish your project by painting, trimming, polishing, or other means. We will look at these steps in detail.

PLANNING FOR SHELVES

Before you can do anything, you must have an idea or plan of action. Perhaps you need shelves. Take a sheet of paper and write down the following:

● Where you will put the shelves.
● What kind of things you will put on the shelves.
● How much ready cash or credit you want to spend on the project.
● How urgent the need is for the shelves.
● The time you will have to work on the shelves in the next two weeks.

Let's say that you answered living room, pottery, as little as possible, desperately, and hardly any. For pottery, you need sturdy shelves so they won't collapse under the weight of the ware. Most pottery doesn't look good above eye level. You want some sturdy, low shelves.

See if you have room for some low shelves in your living room. Don't overlook unlikely places like beneath a low window. The shelves could cover the very lowest part if that doesn't interfere with opening and closing the window. Another possibility is along a wall in a traffic aisle—which means that the shelves would be narrower than usual—or between two chairs where the shelves could actually double as a table.

If you can't find room for low shelves, you are faced with two alternatives. You can move some article of furniture out of your living room and replace it with low shelves, or you can put the pottery and shelving in another room.

It is tough to find very short standards for low shelves. If you go the below-the-window route, there would be no way to attach the standards. You would need to support the shelves well because of the pottery's weight. The studs in the wall never seem to be where they are needed most to anchor a standard. Ignoring the studs and relying entirely on molly bolts is a bad idea. Your choice is either self-supporting wooden shelves or shelves of wood and other materials.

MATERIALS FOR SHELVES

Because wood is expensive, you may not want the shelves made solely of wood. Ready-made items like bricks and boards will make sturdy, low shelves that are inexpensive, easy to assemble, and attractive. *Ordinary common brick, Roman brick,* and *modular brick* are available in various sizes. There is the matter of color. The term *red brick* covers a large range of shades from the pale pink to deep oxblood. There are bright white, ivory, cream, chocolate brown, gray, and coal-black bricks. *Glazed brick* is coated with ceramic or glassy material before it is baked or fired in a kiln.

Your next decision is the finished appearance of your boards. What will look nice with your furnishings? What will set off your pottery best? Natural finished wood and painted surfaces work equally well if the shelves are a light neutral color.

If you want to finish your wood naturally, you will need grade A boards. White pine is probably the least expensive wood. If you paint your boards, particle board is ideal.

When you compare the labor involved in finishing versus painting, the odds are heavily in favor of painting. When you finish a wood naturally, you have to sand it smooth. Fill it (if necessary), stain it, seal it, and finish it with clear varnish. There are products that combine staining, sealing, and varnishing, but they are difficult to handle. You might finish the boards with *linseed oil*. Rub the oil in after lightly sanding the surface. Apply the oil 10 to 20 times to get a surface that is easy to care for and attractive.

If you paint, you can use a *latex* paint that dries in two hours. Paint will cover particle board nicely if you seal the boards first.

Each project in the book has materials and tools lists. Enter the items needed on your shopping list for materials and on your tools list (Figs. 1-1 and 1-2). Decide how you want to execute the project.

Let's get back to the brick and board shelves for pottery. You have decided to put the shelving under the living room window. Measure exactly how long the shelves can be. Options are illustrated in Figs. 1-3 through 1-6. For the sake of the shopping list, let's settle on the one in Fig. 1-5. These shelves extend for 2 feet on the left of the window and 1 foot on the right. The total length is 8 feet.

The next decision concerns the width of the proposed boards. If you have several large bowls, a 12-inch board will set them off better. Boards of 8 and 6-inch widths should be considered if your collection has small pieces. These decisions have to be made before you can make a shopping list. When you are sure about the dimensions, enter the needed materials.

The next decision concerns the size, color, and number of bricks you are going to use. Because you are going to use heavy particle board, you must support the boards adequately

Materials	Dimension	Number	Store, Address	Price	Remarks
Plywood ¼"					
Plywood ½"					
Plywood ¾"					
Hardboard					
Pegboard					
Particle board					
1×2s					
2×2s					
2×4s					
1×4s					
1×10s					
Other's					
Fabric					
Plastic					
Paint					
Adhesive-backed					
Vinyl					
Wallpaper					
Molding					
Findings					
Hardware					
nails					
screws					
braces					
supports					
Rope					
Cord					
Adhesive					
Other:					

Fig. 1-1. Shopping list.

Tools	On Hand	Acquire	Borrow/Rent	Remarks
Hammer				
Tack-hammer				
Saw (hand)				
Drill (hand)				
Drill (electric)				
Pliers				
Screwdriver				
straight				
Phillips				
Wrench				
Level				
Yardstick				
Tape measure				
Scissors				
Straight edge				
Dropcloth				
Needles				
Pins				
Paint roller				
Paint tray				
Brushes				
Applicators				
Other:				

Fig. 1-2. Tool list.

4

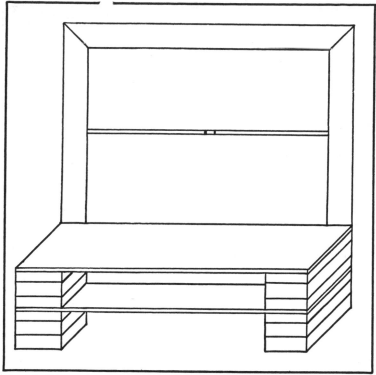

Fig. 1-3. Brick and board shelves.

to keep them steady and prevent any unsightly sagging. You will want to raise the lower board off the rug so that you can clean under it and, more importantly, so the shelving will be balanced. Usually one brick stacked along the long surface will raise the board sufficiently, though two bricks often look better if you have deep napped carpeting (Figs. 1-7A and 1-7B). You will need four stacks of bricks for your bottom shelf whether you use one 8-foot board or two 4-foot boards. Regarding supports for the upper shelf, the size of your ware is a factor, as well as the distance from the windowsill to the floor and the actual window area you are willing to obscure with your shelves. You have a choice of stacking your bricks the way we did for the bottom shelf or setting them upright in blocks of three, four, or more (Fig. 1-8). You will need four stacks of whatever arrangement you prefer. Add up the bricks needed and enter that number on your sheet. There will be a

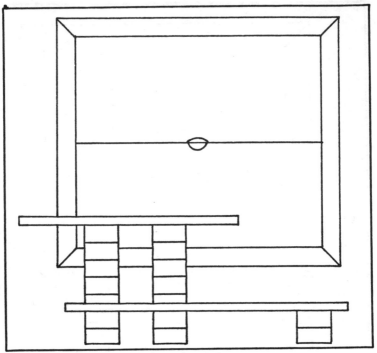

Fig. 1-4. Bricks and boards in front of a window.

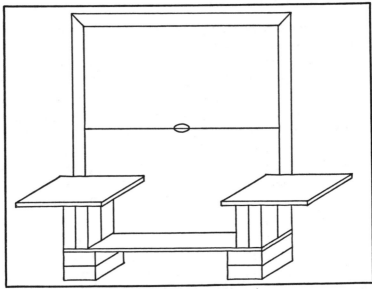

Fig. 1-5. A different arrangement of bricks and boards.

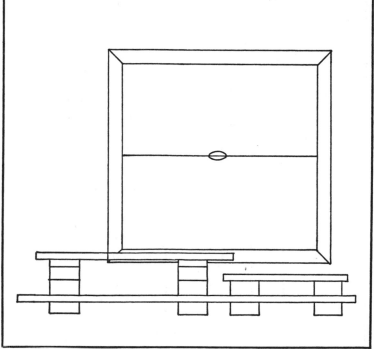

Fig. 1-6. Bricks and boards low under the window.

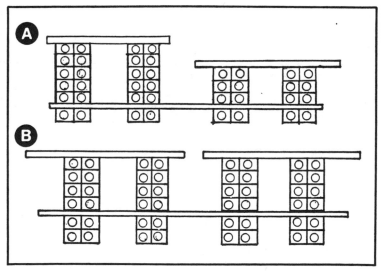

Fig. 1-7. (A) Raising the bottom shelf off the floor. (B) Raising the bottom shelf off the rug.

7

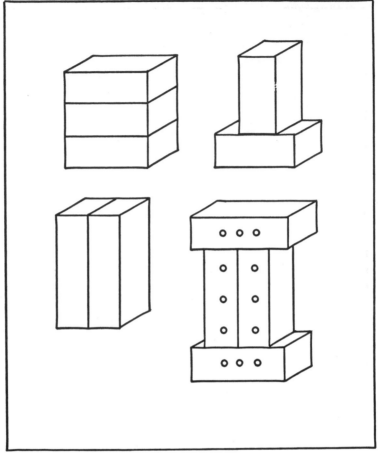

Fig. 1-8. Various ways of stacking bricks.

difference in the finished size of stack according to the kind of bricks you use.

FINISHING ITEMS FOR SHELVES

Let's turn to finishing materials. You have decided to paint the boards, so you need sealer and paint. Some people say you do not need sealer with latex paint. We recommend sealer to save time. Latex paint will cover a board, but it will take three or four applications. If you seal, you usually need only a basic coat and a light touchup. This takes less time for application and drying. You will need some clear polyurethane varnish for a hard finish that will not be easily marred by the pottery. Handmade pottery often has rough bottoms, and they will scratch paint even if felt strips are put on them.

For tools, you will need a paintbrush or two. A *drop cloth* will protect your floor from paint drips.

SHOPPING TIPS

Whenever you have a few minutes take out your list and turn to the local telephone directory's yellow pages. Look up whatever category you need, say, brickyards. Call three brickyards and ask for the kinds of bricks available and the color, size, and price. Find out when they are open and whether they deliver. Enter your information on your shopping sheet in the proper column. Call lumberyards and paint stores. Ask about the availability of boards, paint, sealer, polyurethane varnish, and paintbrushes.

If the brickyard people will deliver let them do so. Trundling bricks around is heavy work and takes time. Waiting for the truck to turn up can also be a waste of time. Don't buy your bricks sight unseen.

Particle board usually comes in 3, 4, 6, and 8-foot lengths. The 8-foot length might be harder to find. You can settle for the 4-foot length and usually save a couple of dollars or more on each board. The only difference is you have four extra edges to paint. There will be a crack where the two boards join, though this is not noticeable.

PREPARATION FOR SHELVES

You should have all bulky materials professionally cut to size, but you will have to do some minor adjusting and cutting on some projects. You must measure where to put the screws or other fasteners and where the joints will be. Measure the material for covers.

Drill starter holes for screws and cut slots if they are needed for assembly. Smooth out any particularly rough places on lumber. Cut and mark covering materials.

Regarding the brick and board shelving, measure and place the bottom row of bricks. Experiment with different arrangements of the bricks between the shelves until you

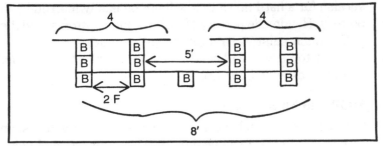

Fig. 1-9. Sketch of possible brick placement.

achieve a pleasant design. This is recorded in measurements on paper, because the structure will have to be disassembled again so the boards can be finished. A sketch will be a helpful accompaniment to your measurements (Fig. 1-9).

FINISHING SHELVES

Finishing includes preparation of the surface, final trimming, and application of the desired finish. Select those finishes that are readily available, easy to apply, and give good service. There is nothing quite so exasperating as the kind of finish that looks good when you first get through with the job but shows signs of wear and tear in a few weeks.

For particle board, run the dusting brush of a vacuum over the boards on both sides. Wipe the boards, including all edges, with a damp, clean sponge. Apply a coat of sealer to all surfaces and allow for drying. When you finish boards, set them on a drop cloth on one end and prop them against a wall at the other end at a pretty steep angle. A tiled wall is the best choice. Any paint that inadvertently gets on the wall can be easily wiped off. If your bathroom has adequate space, consider it as an emergency paint booth. You can even set the boards inside the tub to insure that no paint will get on the floor.

When you have propped up the boards and insured against spillage and splatters, proceed by painting the surface of the board, as well as one long edge and one short edge. When dry, you flip the board and paint the other surface, plus the other long and short edges. Next, apply a second coat. Take care to catch any thin places or spots that have been missed entirely the first time around. Apply a polyurethane coat and allow for overnight drying. With the brick and board shelving, you then build up your shelving according to your sketch and put your pottery on top.

For small projects, a card table is ideal. You can work on the tabletop. When quitting time comes, you can throw a drop cloth or tablecloth over everything. You can work on a piece of cardboard or plywood on top of your card table. When you are ready to stop, simply set the plywood or cardboard on the floor with all your work on it.

WORKBOARDS

Workboards need not be huge. They will be used primarily for subassembly operations and storage. When you are working on assembling large projects, you will use a very large table or the floor. *Workboards* are hard surfaces on which you can do assembly work. This surface can serve as temporary storage for your work.

Decide whether you want to store your workboard under a piece of furniture or overhead. Again, this depends on your living conditions. If you have a bed that has some room to spare between the floor and the spring or platform, you also have a potential area of roughly 3 feet by 7 feet for a single bed and 4½ feet by 7 feet for a double bed. Granted, the space probably only has clearance of 4 or 5 inches, but you can use several boards. A couch, sideboard, or any other large piece of furniture that is high enough off the floor will also work.

Plywood Model

The size for this workboard is up to you. A 3×3-foot model or larger is suitable, again depending on the size of your bed and what else takes shelter underneath it. A 3×3-foot board is the size of the average card table. A 4×4-foot board is nice and offers an excellent work surface. You will need at least a double bed under which to store it. You can also go to a 3×4-foot model or even a 3×5-foot model if you have a large enough table to set the workboard on when it is in use.

The workboard itself can either be a piece of plywood ½ inch thick, cut to correct dimensions by a lumberyard worker, or a piece of particle board of the same size. If you use particle board, you may have trouble finding the right width. You can acquire a full sheet of 4×8-foot paneling with a particle board base. Let your lumber dealer cut the panel to the appropriate size. Paneling backed with particle board is the least expensive paneling on the market. The paneling also can be cleaned easily, because the panel side is actually plastic. The disadvantages are that particle board is heavy to carry, and it tends to crumble around the edges.

materials and tools

One piece of plywood cut to desired size (3×3, 3×4, or 4×4), eight number 9 screw eyes, four small glides, small can of polyurethane varnish, one piece of fabric or heavy plastic, Stitch Witchery (optional), nail polish, glue, metal eyelets, ¼-inch cord, sewing machine, drill, pencil, paintbrush, scissors, eyelet setter, ruler, needle and thread.

shopping

1. Have the man at the lumberyard cut your plywood to the size you want.

2. Buy screw eyes, glides, cord, and varnish at the hardware or discount store.

3. Buy a small foam brush for varnish.

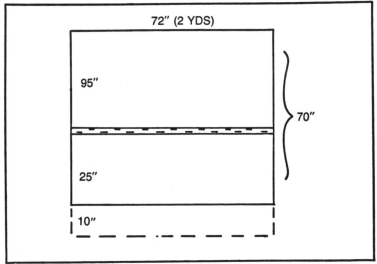

Fig. 1-10. Piecing fabric 45 inches wide for a 3×3-foot board.

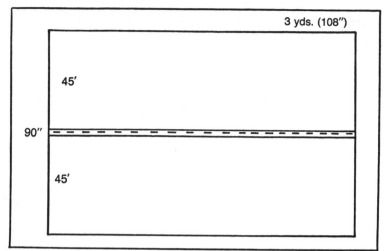

Fig. 1-11. Piecing fabric 45 inches wide for a 4×4-foot board.

4. For a fabric cover, you can use an old sheet or shower curtain. If you want to buy new material, get the widest width you can. For a 3×3-foot board, the fabric can be up to 54-60 inches wide. For the bigger sizes, you will have to piece the fabric as shown in Fig. 1-10. If you want to use narrower fabric, you will have to piece for the sizes shown in Figs. 1-11 and 1-12. The quantities then will be for a 3-foot×4-inch board, 2¼ yards of fabric 54-60 inches wide; for a 4×4-inch board, 4¼ yards of 39-48-inch fabric; for a 3×4-foot board, ½

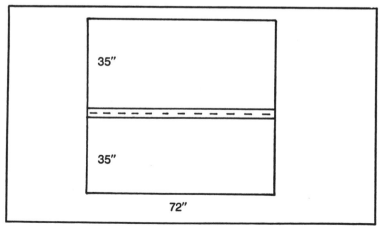

Fig. 1-12. Piecing narrow fabric (35-36 inches) for 3×3-foot board.

yards of narrower fabric; and for a 3×3-foot board, 4 yards of fabric 35-36 inches wide.

5. Get a cheap eyelet setter. Sometimes you can get a set of eyelets that has a little gadget included. You won't be setting all that many.

6. If you buy the cord by the foot, you will need 22 feet for a 3×3-foot board, 28 feet for the 3×4-foot board, and 36 feet for the 4×4-foot board.

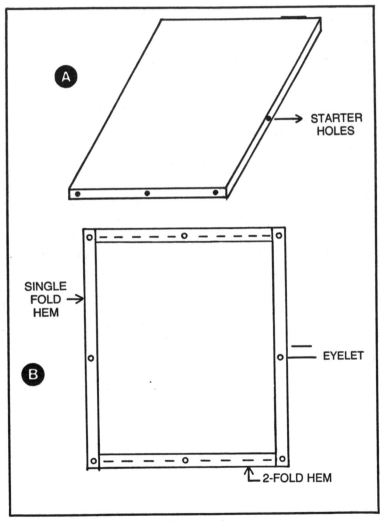

Fig. 1-13. (A) Marking board. (B) Preparing the cover.

preparation

1. Mark the center of each side of your board.

2. Drill a starter hole on each mark and in each corner (Fig. 1-13A).

3. Screw in screw eyes.

4. Mark centers on the fabric.

5. Mark off 2 inches from cut edges on both ends of the fabric (Fig. 1-13B).

assembly

1. Turn up 1 inch on cut edges, press, and turn up the next inch. Sew or fuse in place. Turn up 1 inch on the selvage. Sew or fuse in place for the fabric. Sew or glue for plastic.

2. If you need to piece the material, follow Figs. 1-11 or 1-12 for the cutting. Then sew together with a double seam. Hem.

3. Set in eyelets in the corners and centers of each side.

4. Cut the cord to required size.

5. Coat ends of the cord with nail polish for at least 2 inches.

finishing

1. Varnish the board. Let it dry for the required time.

2. Varnish both sides of the board if you like. Two coats are better than one.

3. Attach glides to corners.

4. Lash the cover to the board (Fig. 1-14).

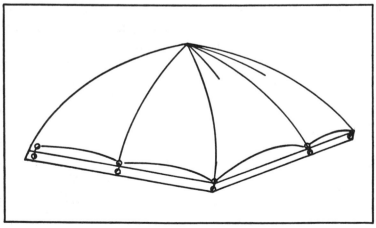

Fig. 1 .14. Workboard and lashed-on cover.

Particle Paneling Workboard
materials and tools

They are the same as for the plywood model, except that you substitute the paneling for the plywood. Have it cut to desired size. Aluminum tape is needed.

shopping

Instructions are the same as for the plywood model, except you need to get the aluminum tape at the hardware store or discount center.

preparation

1. Cut four strips of aluminum tape the length (one for each edge) of the board. If your board is square, all four pieces will be the same length. If the board is oblong, you will have two strips as long as the long sides and two strips the same size as the short sides.

2. Bind edges of the board with tape (Fig. 1-15).

3. Follow steps 1-5 for the plywood model.

assembly

It is the same as for the plywood model.

finishing

1. Varnish the unfinished side of the paneling only.

2. Attach glides.

3. Lash the cover to the board as in Fig. 1-14.

Simple Version of Covered Workboard
materials and tools

One piece of particle board paneling or plywood cut to size, varnish, cord, aluminum tape for particle board, sewing machine or needle and thread, scissors, paintbrush.

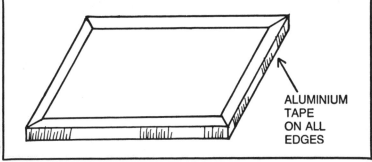

ALUMINIUM
TAPE
ON ALL
EDGES

Fig. 1-15. Workboard with aluminum taped edges.

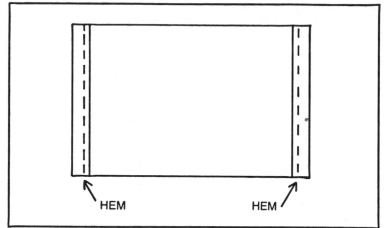

Fig. 1-16. Hemming both ends of the cover.

assembly

1. Tape sides of the board if you use particle board.

2. Turn up the hem on the narrowly hemmed end to match the wide hem on the other end. Stitch down (Fig. 1-16).

3. Fold the sheet in half and stitch up the sides. Leave hems open.

4. Run the cord through hems (Fig. 1-17).

finishing

1. Varnish the board and let dry.

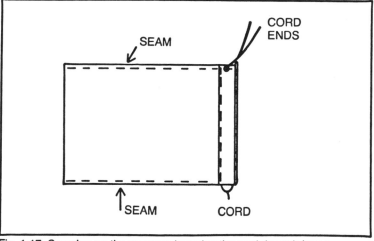

Fig. 1-17. Seaming up the cover and running the cord through hems.

2. To put on the cover, slide the board inside the sack and pull the cord taut (Fig. 1-18).

STORAGE AREAS

Look at your hallway and bathroom. You probably have 1½ feet above doorways that can be used for storage. The space directly above your tub would accommodate extra storage space.

Overhead Hallway Storage Area for Workboards

Measure the width of your hallway and decide at which end you want the new storage area to be. Most hallways are between 3 and 4 feet wide, but be sure to get precise measurements of yours. If you have a long hallway, you may want to put storage at both ends.

Let's say your hallway is 3 feet 6 inches. Decide how large you want that storage area to be—3 feet deep if you have a 3×3-foot board or 4 feet if your board is a 3×4-foot one. If your hallway is 4 feet wide or more, then you can go with the 3-foot section and still come out with room enough for a 3×4-foot one. We don't recommend a larger board for this type of storage. It is tough to hoist a 4×5-foot board up over your head even on a stepladder, and the same is true for removing the board from its hiding place.

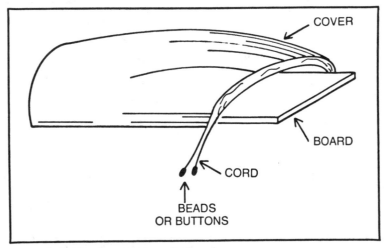

Fig. 1-18. Putting the cover over the board.

You will end up with a storage area of 3 feet 6 inches by 3 feet or 3 feet 6 inches by 4 feet. No matter what size board you have, opt for the latter size. You will have to use plywood or particle board, both of which come in 4×8-foot sheets. One sheet will make your workboard plus the storage area, and you will have scraps left over.

materials and tools

One sheet of ½-inch plywood or particle board, two pieces of 1×2 as long as the storage area will be deep, sandpaper, sealer, paint, ¾-inch flathead screws 1 inch long, medium-size molly bolts, drill, screwdriver, paintbrush, ruler, pencil.

shopping

Have the man at the lumberyard cut your plywood into two pieces: one 3 feet 5 inches by 4 feet and the other 3×3 feet or 3×4 feet for your workboard. Ask for the scraps. There should be a large piece that you can use for a door on the storage area if the wood is cut according to Fig. 1-18. Have the 1×2 cut into two pieces each 4 feet long. Get medium fine sandpaper. Buy 10 molly bolts for walls from ⅝ to 1¼ inches thick.

preparation

1. With your ruler, measure down from the ceiling to where you want your shelf to be. Mark in the corner and again at the end of the shelf as in Fig. 1-19. Draw lines.

2. Mark your 1×2s at each end on the 2-inch surface and again at each 12-inch interval in between (Fig. 1-20). Mark both sides.

3. Mark a plywood piece 3 feet 5 inches by 4 feet along the shorter sides, starting 1 inch in from each end every 13 inches in between.

4. Drill holes at marked places.

finishing

Note: this is a case where it is easier to finish first and then assemble.

1. Sand all wood surfaces.
2. Seal all surfaces.
3. Paint all surfaces. Allow for drying.
4. If necessary, apply a second coat. Allow for drying.

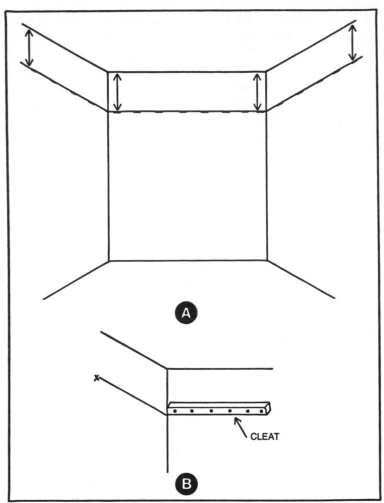

Fig. 1-19. (A) Marking the wall for the shelf. (B) Attaching the cleat.

assembly

1. Starting in the corner, attach a 1×2 to the wall through predrilled holes using molly bolts.

2. Slide a board 3 feet 5 inches by 4 feet on top of the 1×2 cleats. Fasten in place through predrilled holes using your flathead screws.

3. If you have trouble getting in a molly bolt, that means you have hit a stud. In that case, use a regular screw instead of your molly bolt.

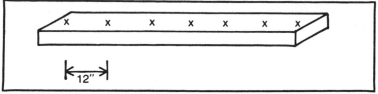
Fig. 1-20. Marking 1×2s.

4. Finish your workboard as indicated for plywood workboards.

5. Slide in place atop the shelf.

Variation
materials and tools
Plywood and 1×2s as specified earlier, molly bolts and screws, 7 yards of adhesive-backed vinyl, your choice of color and pattern, sandpaper, ruler, pencil, drill, screwdriver, scissors, paint roller or rolling pin, straight pin, sponge.
finishing
This is a case when finishing is best done before any of the other basic steps.

1. Sand wood surfaces lightly. Wipe well with a damp sponge.

2. Cut adhesive-backed vinyl to fit the plywood and cleats.

3. Cover plywood with vinyl on both sides. Cleats are on one 2-inch surface only. Cover the front edges.

4. Use a paint roller or rolling pin to smooth the covering. If you have neither, roll up some magazines tightly (Fig. 1-21).

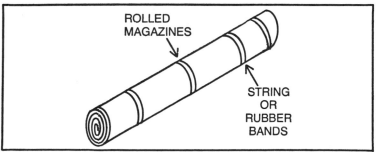
Fig. 1-21. Making a magazine roll for smoothing vinyl.

5. Use a pin for persistent bubbles.

preparation and assembly

Proceed as discussed earlier.

Overhead Hallway Storage Area with Door

If you want to be economical, your board can be 2 feet 10 inches by 3 feet. The shelf will be 3 feet 5 inches by 4 feet. A door can be cut 14 inches by 3 feet 6 inches.

materials and tools

Materials are about the same as for the overhead hallway storage area, but substitute a board 2 feet 10 inches by 3 feet for the 3×3-foot one. Add a piece of plywood cut to 14 inches by 3 feet 6 inches. You also need a wooden knob plus a screw and a magnetic catch or latch, and three butt hinges 1½ inches long and ¼ to ½ inch wide. Tools are the same as for the overhead hallway storage area.

shopping

Follow the instructions for either version.

preparation

Follow steps 1-4 given earlier.

5. Mark the door for knob and hinges as shown in Fig. 1-22.

6. Mark the ceiling and door for the magnetic latch.

7. Drill starter holes in the door at marked places.

8. Mark the shelf for hinges along the edge.

finishing

If you want to use adhesive vinyl, do your finishing before the marking and measuring.

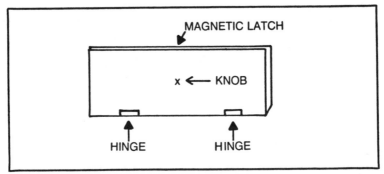

Fig. 1-22. Marking the door.

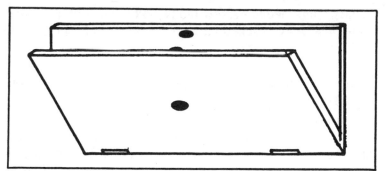
Fig. 1-23. The door showing the catch and knob.

1. Follow instructions for desired finish.
2. Finish the door in the same manner.

assembly

1. Follow steps 1-3 given earlier for the overhead hallway storage area.
2. Fasten the knob to the door.
3. Attach hinges to the shelf on marked places.
4. Attach other ends of hinges to the door on marked places.
5. Attach a magnetic catch on the ceiling and door.
6. Finish the workboard. You can omit the cover and add extra cord to lash the materials in place.
7. Slide in place and close the door (Fig. 1-23).

Above-the-Tub Solution

This is a slightly different version for those of you who don't have hallways or prefer a larger storage place for your work. This extra room allows you to stash your tools and leftovers in a space you will never miss unless you are more than 6 feet 8 inches tall.

materials and tools

One piece of marine plywood, ¾ inch thick and 22×60 inches, two pieces of 1×2 60 inches long and four pieces 20½ inches long; a curtain or shower rod, 60 inches long, with brackets; 16 corner braces 1½ inches by ½ inch; eight corner irons 2 inches long; either 2 yards of 48-inch-wide fabric or plastic or a ready-made valance to contrast or match a shower curtain at least 14 inches wide; ¾-inch flathead screws 1¼ inches long; medium-sized molly bolts; sandpaper; sealer; paint or adhesive-backed vinyl; plywood 3 feet by 4 feet by ½ inch, drill, screwdriver, pencil, ruler, measuring tape, paintbrush, sponge, paint roller or rolling pin (optional), straight pin (optional), iron (optional), sewing machine (optional).

shopping

Have the man at the lumberyard cut all lumber to the specifications given in the materials section. You can substitute regular plywood of the same thickness for marine plywood, or you can have a 2×4-foot or 2×5-foot workboard cut out of the extra marine plywood. The board will be a tad heavier, but it will work well. The same is true for the ordinary ¾-inch plywood. You need the oblong size because you can't store a 3×4-foot board on a 22-inch shelf without much of that board projecting out.

If you are painting, use enamel—either latex or acrylic. Acrylic paint takes a long time to cure. You may prefer to line the shelf with adhesive-backed vinyl or shelf paper for the first month rather than scratch the paint every time you store your work. Latex will cure in about two days. You can also seal the paint in with some polyurethane clear varnish on top; one coat will do. You will need about 4½ yards of the adhesive-backed vinyl if you cover both sides and 2¼ yards if you only line the shelf with it.

preparation

1. Mark the 2-inch side of the long 1×2s ⅜-inch in from each end and again 15 inches from each end with an oblong (both sides).

2. Using a different mark, note six more positions on one of the long 1×2s (both sides) (Fig. 1-24).

3. Mark the short 1×2s on the 2-inch side ½ inch in from each end and again at 7½ and 15 inches (Fig. 1-25).

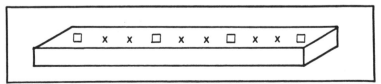

Fig. 1-24. Marking the long 1×2.

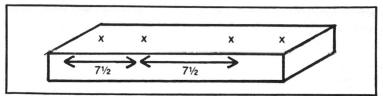
Fig. 1-25. Marking the short 1×2.

4. Drill on marks all the way through. Starter holes are on oblongs.

5. On the wall above the tub, measure 14 inches down from the ceiling on all three sides. Draw a line all the way around. Transfer marks to the wall. Drill holes for molly bolts.

assembly

1. Line up the long 1×2 with the most marks against the back or long wall on the pencil line. Fasten to the wall at predrilled holes with molly bolts, but leave oblong marks at 15 and 30 inches free.

2. Fasten the two short 1×2s to the end walls in the same manner, butting the ends against the 1×2 on the long wall.

preparation

1. Using one of your corner braces as a guide, mark places for screw holes on the long and short 1×2s on the wall (Fig. 1-25).

2. Mark the other long 1×2 in the same manner (Fig. 1-26).

3. Mark the short 1×2 pieces that you haven't marked yet.

4. Using your corner irons for guides, mark the bottom edges of your wall-hung 1×2s (Fig. 1-27).

5. Mark your free short 1×2s and your long one in the same way.

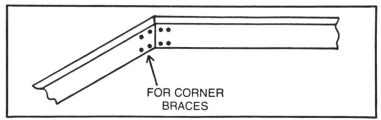
FOR CORNER BRACES

Fig. 1-26. Marking for corner braces.

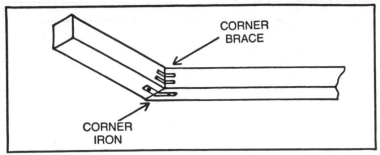

Fig. 1-27. Attaching corner braces.

6. Drill starter holes.

more assembly

1. Reinforce the rear corner with your corner braces—two to a corner.

2. Attach the short pieces to the rear 1×2 at oblong marks with three corner braces on each side (Fig. 1-28).

3. Attach a long 1×2 to the front end of the frame with corner braces. The braces will be on the inside of the frame.

4. Fasten the two short pieces to the front piece with corner braces as you did in the back.

5. Reinforce the frame with corner irons at the bottom of the frame at each corner and at the joints of the two supporting members.

6. Predrill starter holes in plywood at 3-inch intervals all around.

7. Screw plywood to the top of the frame. (Fig. 1-29).

8. On walls ½ inch down from the ceiling and 2 inches in front of the board, or just in front of and above the shower curtain rod (whichever insures a 2-foot-wide enclosure), mark the position of brackets for curtain rods. Drill starter holes and fasten the brackets to the walls.

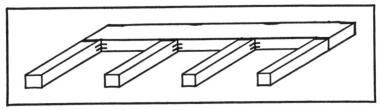

Fig. 1-28. Framing detail.

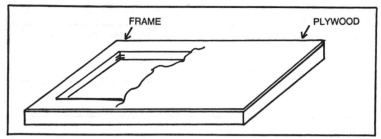

Fig. 1-29. Putting plywood on the frame.

9. For the valance, cut material into three 20-inch-wide, 48-inch-long strips.

10. Sew strips together along the short ends as in Fig. 1-30.

11. Fold under ½ inch along both long edges and press.

12. Fold down 2 inches on one long edge. Stitch in place. Stitch again ⅝ inch from the top (Fig. 1-30).

13. Turn up another ½ inch on the other long edge. Press and stitch in place.

14. Put the valance on the curtain rod and hang it after the platform is finished.

finishing

1. Lightly sand all wooden surfaces.

2. Wipe with a damp sponge.

3. Seal all surfaces and allow for drying.

4. Paint all surfaces. Allow for drying.

5. Put on a second coat of paint if needed.

or

1. Cut adhesive-backed vinyl to fit the top and bottom of the plywood and cover the board before attaching to the framing.

2. Seal and paint framing before attaching the board. Hang the valance from the curtain rod (Fig. 1-31). If you use a ready-made valance, omit steps 9-14 under assembly. Finish the workboard as before and stash behind the valance on the shelf.

The L-Shaped Solution

This idea is for those of you who have no halls and would

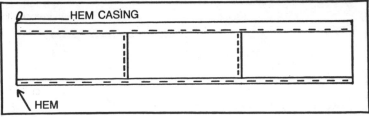

Fig. 1-30. Valance details.

rather place your work areas elsewhere. Basically, the L-shaped solution is not as sturdy as the others. It should not be made any longer than suggested, and the space should not be loaded with heavy items in addition to the workboard.

materials and tools

One piece of ½-inch plywood 4 feet by 2 feet, one piece of plywood 2 feet by 14 inches*, one piece of plywood 3 feet by 2 feet for the workboard, two pieces of 1×2 2 feet long, one piece of 1×2 47¼ inches long, one piece of 1×3 48 inches, one piece 14", sealer, ¾-inch flathead screws 1¼ inches long, medium molly bolts, 3d finishing nails, 2-inch corner braces, paint, sandpaper, wallpaper or adhesive-backed vinyl (optional), ruler, pencil, measuring tape, sponge, screwdriver, drill, miter box (optional), rolling pin or paint roller, paintbrush.

shopping

Before you go shopping, measure the distance from the ceiling to the top of the door frame if you are going to locate your L-shaped solution above it. If there is no window or door on either wall, you may go as high or low as you like. Generally, the L-shaped solution looks best when it conforms to the window frame or door frame. This is usually a distance of 14 inches. In older buildings, though you may have as much as a 2 or 2½-foot distance to the ceiling. Have the man at the lumberyard cut the wood as indicated. Allow for adjusting if your ceiling to shelf distance is larger or smaller than 14 inches on the pieces indicated with the asterisk.

You might like to cover the L-shaped solution with wallpaper. Adhesive-backed vinyl in a color that matches the background of your wallpaper or the paint on the wall will also do a good camouflage job. You will need 5¼ yards of 18-inch

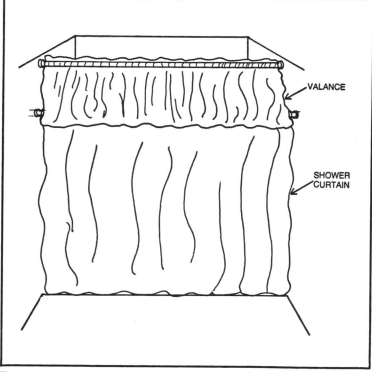

Fig. 1-31. Valance and shower curtain.

width and 3 yards of 24-inch width.

preparation

    1. Measure down from the ceiling to the top of the door or 13½ inches in the corner where your L-shaped solution will be. Mark.

    2. Measure 48 inches along the long wall. Mark again, 13½ inches down from the ceiling.

    3. Measure 13½ inches down for 2 feet along the short wall.

    4. Draw lines connecting marks.

    5. On the ceiling at the 48-inch mark, draw a line 2 feet long.

    6. Mark 1×2s every 3 inches along the wider side about ½ inch down from the top edge. Mark walls to match.

    7. Drill holes through 1×2 on wide sides. Drill holes in walls.

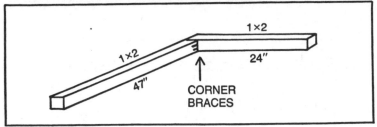

Fig. 1-32. Corner construction detail.

assembly

1. Attach one of the shorter 1×2s along the short wall with the bottom edge of the 1×2 even with the drawn line. Holes are matched. Use molly bolts when possible. Otherwise, use screws.

2. Butt the long 1×2 onto the shorter one and attach to the wall in the same manner. Reinforce with corner brace (Fig. 1-32).

3. Screw the remaining 1×2 to the ceiling (Fig. 1-33).

4. Mark and drill 14-inch-wide plywood ¼ inch from both long edges every 3 inches.

5. Screw plywood to the ceiling cleat.

6. Mark a large sheet of plywood every 3 inches along one long and one short side as in Fig. 1-34. Predrill starter holes.

7. Attach a plywood sheet with screws to the lower edges of the wall-hung 1×2s.

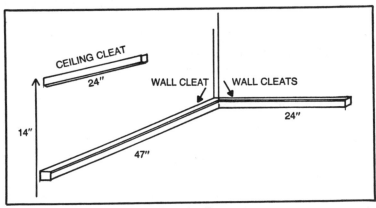

Fig. 1-33. Attaching 1×2s to walls and ceiling.

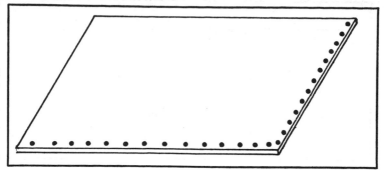

Fig. 1-34. Plywood detail and starter holes.

8. Attach the large sheet to the small sheet of plywood with screws as in Fig. 1-35.

9. Reinforce with two corner braces at 8 inches and 16 inches from the edge.

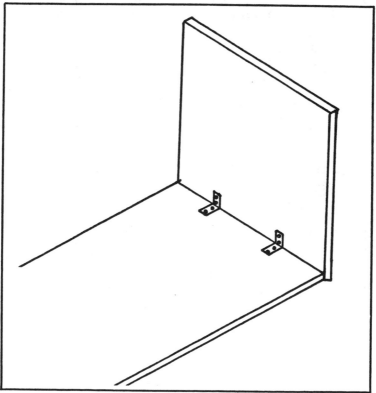

Fig. 1-35. Plywood detail and reinforcing joint with corner braces.

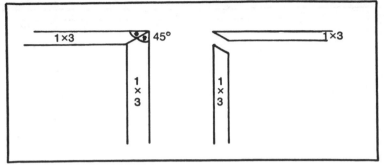

Fig. 1-36. Mitering 1×3s.

10. Miter 1×3s at 45 degrees (Fig. 1-36).

11. Nail in place with your 3d finishing nails (Fig. 1-37). If you use wallpaper or adhesive vinyl, cover the plywood with the paper or covering before marking it and attaching the pieces to the cleats, i.e., the 1×2s and the 1×3s.

finishing with paint

1. Sand all surfaces lightly.
2. Wipe with a damp sponge.
3. Seal and let dry (Fig. 1-38).
4. Paint and let dry.
5. Apply a second coat if needed.

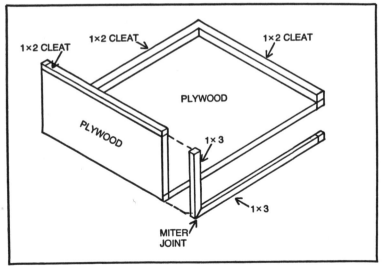

Fig. 1-37. Overall construction sketch.

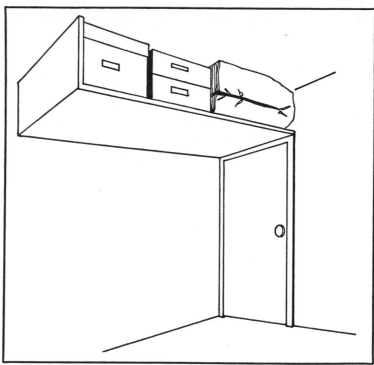

Fig. 1-38. Finished L-shaped storage.

finishing with paper or vinyl

1. Sand all surfaces lightly.

2. Wipe with a damp sponge.

3. Seal and let dry.

4. Cover both sides of both pieces of plywood with the covering.

5. Paint 1×2s and 1×3s as discussed earlier.

6. Complete assembly when the paint is dry. For the workboard, follow instructions for the plywood workboard and cover.

CLEANUP

You will want to clean up quickly and efficiently. Here's how:

● Remove work in progress from the workboard. Wipe the board with a damp sponge. Dry with a cloth or paper towel.

- Stack the workboard with work in progress. Put on the cover.
- Wipe off tools and return them to the tool caddy or box. Power drills and other tools should be put in the appropriate boxes. Cords should be looped loosely around the tools.
- All hardware should be stashed in the appropriate drawers or compartments. Discard any hardware that can not be used again such as bent nails and sprung molly bolts.
- Put paintbrushes in a piece of aluminum foil and wrap tightly. Wipe the rim of the paint can and the lid with a paper towel. Close the can tightly. Wrap the stirrer in aluminum foil.
- Fold tarp or drop cloth in toward the work area, so you won't track any dust or paint through the place.
- Put away the workboard and tools.
- Pick up the tarp or drop cloth. Shake it out outside. Fold and store.

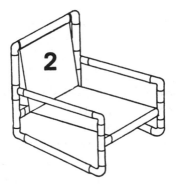

Tools

Pretend that you know nothing more about tools than their names and read the following thoroughly even if you do have previous knowledge. Some specifics given apply particularly to our way of working on these projects.

ELECTRIC DRILL

For these projects an electric drill is vitally important. You will use it to drill starter holes for screws, holes for molly bolts in walls and boards, and other holes needed for the projects. You will also use it to drive in the screws into predrilled holes, to mix paint, to sand projects, and to buff, brush, grind, polish, and even saw.

If you want to use an electric drill effectively, you have to know the tool's limitations and stay within them. Home-use drills come in ¼-, ⅜-, and ½-inch sizes. The measurements used for sizing are the maximum size straight shank the drill's chuck will hold.

The ⅜-inch drill is your best bet. It delivers enough torque for most drilling jobs and accessories at the top speed of 1,000 rpm. Remember to slow down the drill on big jobs.

Many electric drills are available with a trigger switch that lets you control the speed of the drill by the way you pull the trigger (Fig. 2-1). It's absolutely the greatest. You can start slowly when the drilling is difficult and keep the drill from jumping around. You can also use the slow speed to drive screws and tighten nuts and bolts.

Another useful feature is *reversing*. This will let you loosen nuts and bolts and extract screws, as well as drive them in.

Always buy a power drill that is "double-insulated" or so-called shockproof. The cases of shockproof drills are plastic that will not conduct electricity. Plastic has high impact strength. Furthermore, handling a plastic case is more pleasant than handling a metal one. When cleaning this plastic case; care must be taken. Those nifty household detergents that cut through grease usually contain ammonia that can dissolve your plastic. Use ethyl alcohol or kerosene when you want to shine your plastic drill. Never use gasoline, gasohol, or any chlorinated cleaning agents.

The *chuck* holds the tools to be driven by the drill motor. You tighten the chuck around the tool with your hand, an allen wrench, or a geared key (Fig. 2-2). The last alternative is best. Tape that key for tightening or opening your chuck to the

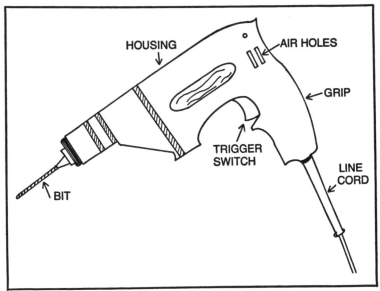

Fig. 2-1. The power drill with trigger switch.

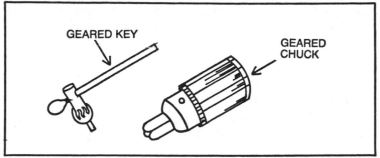

Fig. 2-2. Key and chuck.

power cord of your drill—near the plug. This keeps the key from getting temporarily misplaced and forces you to unplug the tools when changing bits. It also insures that the key is removed from the chuck before the drill is plugged in and started. If a drill is started with the key still plugged, that key can be expelled with considerable force and, like any metal object at high speed, can cause serious injury.

Bits

The bits most often used in electric drills are called *twist drills.* There are bits that will drill holes into metal, glass, ceramic, masonry, stone, wood, or plastic. These twist drills are made from high-speed steel (alloyed with tungsten, chromium, and vanadium) or from carbon steel alloys. High-speed drills are expensive, but they can work without coolant. The carbon steel drills are soft, inexpensive, and work quite well when used on wood, plastic, or soft metal. Be careful when drilling soft metal, though, because the carbon steel bits will require a coolant—water, light machine oil, or kerosene—to guard against burning. You can either keep the coolant dripping or flowing into the hole while you're working or withdraw the drill bit from the work every couple of minutes and dip it into cold water. The twist drills come in sizes ranging from 0.0135 inch to ½ inch.

Regarding screwdriver bits, you have a choice of sizes like in regular screwdrivers, plus the option of slotted or Phillips-head blades. You can also get a bit specially designed to make pilot holes for these screws. Many screwdrivers have

37

a spring-loaded metal sleeve that helps you find the slots as you press the drill down onto the screwhead. The sleeve will help keep the screw bit in the slot for both Phillips-head and slotted screws.

Using the Power Drill

Use both hands on the drill. It will help you hold the tool firmly at the correct angle. Don't feel self-conscious or awkward because of your two-handed grip.

Mark both sides of your work whenever possible. You can't do it when you mark a wall, because you don't want your molly bolt to come out in the other room. It is also not wise to drill through the bottom of the board to which you are fastening a small piece.

Drilling from both sides prevents the wood from splintering even when you drill fairly close to the edge. When you are halfway through the board, flip it over and start over again until you finish the hole.

Clamp your work down if possible. This is particularly true for small pieces.

Before you start to drill, make a small punch mark or layout hole by tapping a nail on the mark. It doesn't need to be deep—just an indentation for the bit's point. Place the bit's point into the layout hole and turn on the drill. Feed the bit into the work with gentle pressure applied in a straight line right along the bit's shank.

Brace yourself against the twisting motion of the drill. If you push too hard, you may deflect the bit or stall the motor. If the motor stalls, it is overloaded. Stop the drill, remove the bit from the work, and determine the problem. Perhaps some cuttings are jamming the bit. Clean them off and begin drilling again.

When you are drilling deep holes, withdraw the bit several times from the hole to clean off the cuttings. You can also overload the motor and stall it if you apply too much pressure to get the work done quicker. Let the tool do its work in its own time.

Always work with sharp bits. The drill bit sharpener takes from one to four seconds to sharpen a bit to its proper angle. There is a precision angled grinding wheel inside.

You need a double insulated electric drill with a trigger handle and variable speeds, plus reversible drilling action, so you can remove and set screws and bolts. Montgomery Ward sells one with a plastic casing guaranteed not to rust, chip, peel, crack, or dent. An excellent drill bit sharpened made by Black and Decker works much like an electric pencil sharpener. It will keep your bits sharpened at the correct relief angle.

Stanley Works manufacturers a fine drill guide. This device will enable you to drill perfect right angles. The drill guide protects your work from marring by a skittering bit. The guide holds the bit during drilling. It will accommodate 13 different bit sizes—from 1/16 to 1/4 inch.

HAMMERS

The *carpenter's hammer* is used primarily for driving and pulling nails. Drive the nails with the striking surface and pull or remove nails with the claw at the hammer's other end. The striking surface is called the *face* of the hammer (Fig. 2-3). There are plain-faced and bell-faced hammers. The bell-faced hammer makes it easier to drive the head of a nail flush with the surface of the work without making hammer marks.

Carpenter's hammers come in sizes from 7 to 28 ounces. A 7-ounce hammer is for light-duty work like driving in brads.

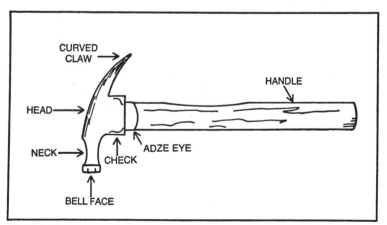

Fig. 2-3. The carpenter's hammer.

The 13-ounce hammer is used by cabinet and furniture makers. The 16-ounce model is standard for carpenters and ideal with larger projects.

The *upholsterer's hammer* is used for small construction work and upholstery work. It has a magnetized end that is very handy for driving tacks. The long thin claw on the other end of the hammer is wonderful for pulling tacks and lets you get those tacks that are in tight corners (Fig. 2-4).

Keep your wrist loose and relaxed when driving nails in with a hammer. Grab the handle so its end is flush with the lower edge of your palm. Most people will hold a hammer too far up the handle—near the head.

Hold the nail with your thumb and forefinger in the hand that does not hold the hammer. Put the point of the nail into the exact spot where you want it to go. Hold the nail at the angle you want it to go through the wood. You will hold it straight or perpendicular to the surface in most cases.

Rest the head of the hammer on the nailhead and give the nail a few light taps, square on the head, using a good loose wrist motion. This not only gets your nail started a bit but gives you practice in lining up your target.

Strike the nail harder and harder. Take away your fingers as soon as the nail no longer needs their support. If the nail doesn't go in straight, pull it out (with the claws of your hammer) and discard it. Don't waste time trying to straighten out the path of a nail.

If you have to go through a knot in the wood, drill a very tiny hole through the obstruction. Your nail will then go in straight and true.

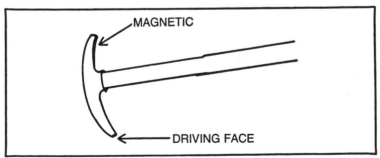

Fig. 2-4. Tack or upholsterer's hammer.

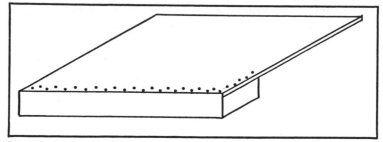
Fig. 2-5. Staggered nailing is stronger.

Hardwood can be quite stubborn about not letting nails or even brads through. The hole-drilling trick is often a great time-saver. Another trick is to dip the nails in paraffin before driving them through hardwood.

For a tight hold and to prevent splits in your wood, nail in a staggered pattern (Fig. 2-5). A few staggered nails are much stronger than many nails in a straight line.

To pull a nail, slide the claw of the hammer under the nailhead and pull on the handle. If it is a really large nail, you might have to slip a block of wood under the hammer head when the handle is nearly vertical. Then finish pulling the nail free with the help of the block. Never try to pull a nail bigger than 8d with a hammer. That nail is a job for a crowbar or wrecking bar.

SCREWDRIVERS

There are basically two types of *screwdrivers*, the standard or straight blade screwdriver that you use for slotted-head screws and the recessed-head or Phillips screwdriver (Figs. 2-6 and 2-7). The part of the screwdriver that you grip in your hand is the handle. Extending from the handle is the shank of the screwdriver, and the tip of the shank is the blade. The two kinds of screwdrivers differ at the blade. The blade is designed to fit the screw—a flat tip to fit the screw that has one slot across its head or the pointed tip with recesses to fit a Phillips-head screw.

Screwdrivers come in sizes ranging from 2½ to 12 inches. This refers to the combined length of blade and shank. The blade sizes range all the way from 3/32 inch up to ½ inch.

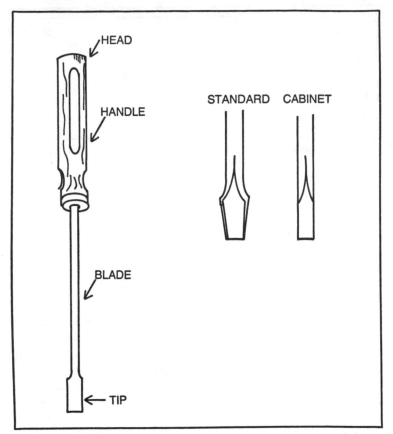

Fig. 2-6. Types of screwdrivers.

A good collection will include a 3/32-inch tip with a 3-inch shaft, a ¼-inch tip with a 4-inch shaft, 5/16-inch tip with a 6-inch shaft, and a ⅜-inch tip with a 10-inch shaft. There are many uses for a stubby 1½-inch shaft screwdriver that has a ¼-inch tip.

While the tip is the most critical part of your screwdriver, the handle is important, too, when it comes to proper use. Most handles nowadays are made of plastic, and they are getting thicker. The thicker the handle, the more leverage you can apply through it. Some people even advise slipping a rubber sleeve over a handle to increase the leverage.

Select the screwdriver of the proper length whose tip fits the screw slot of the screws you plan to use exactly. If the tip is too thin, it will slip out of the screw's slot and often mar your work. Also, the blade will have room to twist and shave away fine slivers of steel from edges. Because screws are made from soft steel, the edges of those slots can be worn down in a jiffy.

The width of the tip is just as important as its thickness. If the width of the tip is wider than the screw and extends over the edges, that tip will cut into your work when you drive in the screw, especially when it is a flathead one that you want to set in flush. Make sure that the screwhead and blade match.

The Phillips screwdriver is the most common of the recessed-head screwdrivers. The head of a Phillips-head screw has a four-way slot into which the screwdriver fits. This is a boon because the screwdriver never slips out of the slot—never, that is, if you apply more downward pressure on

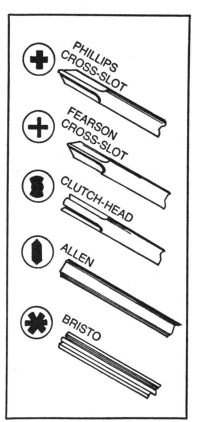

Fig. 2-7. Recessed-head screwdrivers.

the screw than you would on the slotted-head kind, and provided the screwdriver is fairly new and not worn along the tip.

You don't want to apply too much pressure when you first start driving screws. You need a starting hole. Without one the screw tends to meander around, following the grain of the wood and refusing to be driven in straight. To make a starting hole, use a nail or a bradawl for a small screw or a drill bit for a larger one. This starter hole insures easy, straight driving and prevents your wood from splitting if you drive a screw near the edges or ends of the wood. Here are some guidelines for driving screws. For starters:

● In softwood such as pine, drill your starter hole half as deep as the threaded part of the screw.

● For hardwoods like oak and maple, make the hole as deep as the screw. The hole should be slightly smaller in diameter than the screw. If you are putting large screws into hardwood, drill a second hole the same diameter as the upper unthreaded part of the screw on top.

For driving the screw:

● Use the longest shank that is handy for the job and a tip that fits the screw slot exactly. A long screwdriver gives you more power with less effort.

● Place the screw on the tip of the screwdriver and hold it on with the fingers of one hand. Put the screw in the starting hole and turn it *clockwise* to drive it in.

● A plastic drinking straw makes a handy gadget to hold a screw onto the tip of a screwdriver. Cut your straw about 1 inch shorter than the screwdriver's shank and slide it onto the shank, then slide the straw over the screwhead.

● As soon as the screw holds firmly to the wood, move your fingers up to the blade and let the blade slip between them. Keep the tip centered in the screw slot.

A lot of effort can be avoided in setting screws if you rub the threads of the screws with wax or paraffin before driving them in. Do not use soap or oil on your screws. Soap will cause the screw to rust, and oil will stain the wood over a considerable area around the screw.

If you are replacing a screw, you might have to fill the old hole with some wood putty or a plastic plug to provide a firm gripping surface. You might also simply use a larger and/or longer screw as a replacement.

When it comes to removing old screws or tight ones, use a screwdriver blade with parallel sides that fits the slot exactly. Turn the screw slightly clockwise and then counterclockwise. Alternate back and forth between clockwise and counterclockwise until the screw can be backed out easily. The application of oil or WD-40 will also be of help.

PLIERS

Pliers are holding and cutting tools. Slip-joint pliers have grooved jaws fastened together with a screw or pivot that moves to either of two positions (Fig. 2-8). Most slip-joint pliers have a wire cutter at the junction of the jaws for cutting soft wire and nails or similar materials. With or without the wire cutters, slip-joint pliers are available in sizes from 5 to 10 inches in length and with jaws from ¼ to 1¼ inches thick.

To open the jaws of the slip-joint pliers, spread the handles open as far as possible. That slip-joint will then move to the open position. To close the pliers, spread the handles apart as far as possible and then push the slip joint back into the closed position.

When you want to use the cutter, open the jaws until the notches are all lined up. Put the wire, nail, or whatever you want to cut as far back as possible into the cutter opening. Squeeze the handles together. If you haven't made your cut, you might have to use both hands. It depends on the thickness of the material to be cut and the strength of your hands.

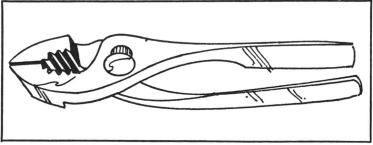

Fig. 2-8. The slip-joint pliers.

SAWS

Saws are indispensable cutting tools. *Ripsaws* and *crosscut saws* differ in the shape of the teeth. Because of the special shape of its teeth, a crosscut saw will cut across the grain of the wood. A ripsaw will cut or rip the wood with the grain (Fig. 2-9).

A *backsaw* is a crosscut saw with a rigid blade (Fig. 2-10). It works especially well when you need to make straight cuts across small pieces of wood.

Any handsaw consists of a steel blade with a wooden or plastic handle at one end. The end of the blade nearest that handle is called the *heel*; the other end is the *toe*. One edge of the blade has teeth that bend alternately from one side and form two rows of cutters. That's what makes the cut or *kerf*

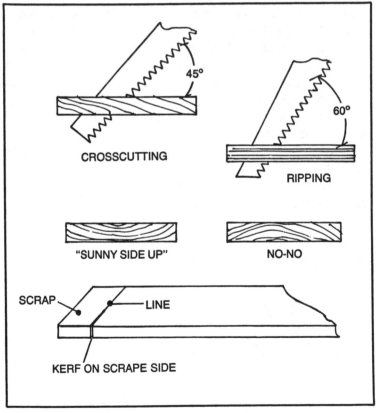

Fig. 2-9. Tips on sawing.

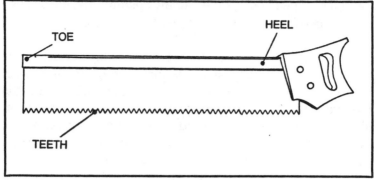
Fig. 2-10. A backsaw.

wider than the blade used to cut it. The angle at which the teeth are bent is called the *set* of the teeth. Saws are described by the number of tooth points per inch. That number is usually stamped on the saw blade right under the manufacturer's trademark.

Always mark your cuts with a straightedge or ruler so you will have a straight line to follow. Put the board to be cut on a sawhorse or in a vise to hold it steady. Pick up your saw with your dominant hand extending the first finger along the handle. Your cutting angle should be about 45 degrees with a handsaw but parallel to the surface with a backsaw.

Keep the saw in a straight line with your forearm. Pull it toward you to start the cut. You might have to do this several times to get a nice groove. When you have started that groove, use full strokes back and forth. Keep that saw straight and perpendicular to the cutting surface, not leaning right or left. You might use a try square to give you the feel of the saw in the right position to the cutting surface.

Don't watch your saw exclusively while you are cutting away. Instead, keep your eye on the cutting line you drew so accurately and neatly. Operate the saw with only one hand and don't force the tool along. If your saw is sharp, the weight of the saw is all you need to make the cut. If your saw binds or sticks, the blade is dull or the teeth have not been properly set.

Blow sawdust away from the line. Clamp a piece of scrap material cut straight and true next to your line and use it as an extra aid. When you are cutting plywood panels, always use those guide boards—one clamped to the top and one to the bottom of the panel.

If your saw begins to wander from the line, give the saw handle a very slight twist in the direction of the line to get back on course. Shortening your strokes while doing the twisting will also help. When you get near the end of the cut, slow down for the last few strokes. Hang on to the waste material with your free hand, so the wood won't split from the drag of the waste material at the last stroke.

It makes a difference which side of your wood is "up" when you saw. If you use a "sunny-side up" position, you will avoid splintering the last resin ring.

Keep your saw on the waste side of the line that you are following. Don't try to cut on the line.

STAPLE GUN

With a staple gun you can attach wood to wood, plastic to wood, fabric to wood, and other combinations. Most staple guns will only take one kind of staple—that made by the gun's manufacturer.

Staples are wire bent into an upside-down U-shape. The ends of the "U" are pointed. There are standard sizes for staple legs that run in length from ¼ up to 9/16 inch. When buying staples for a job, choose the size of staple that will penetrate the bottom layer but not go all the way through it. When you are using a plier staple to staple two very thin pieces of material together, you will use staples that go all the way through on both pieces of material. The ends of the staples are bent in a closed position, just as the legs of the staples, when you use an ordinary stapler on paper. This plier stapler can only be used when you have access to both sides of the material.

Here are the four basic steps of successful staple gun operation:

● To open the tool, lock the operating lever—which is part of the handle—and push the loading latches forward. Push both at the same time—one on each side of the tool. Pull out on the staple channel with your free hand.

● Turn the tool upside down and pull back on the staple channel until the feeding bar is far back as possible. The staples will now drop right into the staple pocket. Make sure the "legs" are pointing up.

● Pull back on the loading latches and snap the staple channel securely into place. Release the latches and then test to make sure the channel is locked in.

● Release the operating lever by releasing the handle lock. Place the base of the staple gun on your work with the area you wish stapled directly under the staple ejector. Squeeze the handle and operating lever together. Hold the tool steady and, if necessary, use both hands to steady the tool and depress the operating lever (Fig. 2-11).

MEASURING TOOLS

At this writing, there are two measuring systems used in the world. Most countries use the *metric system*. The United States is the sole user of the *English system*, although a conversion to the metric system is in progress.

All your rules and measuring tapes should read down to 1/64 inch or to ½ millimeter. Your rules should not be too

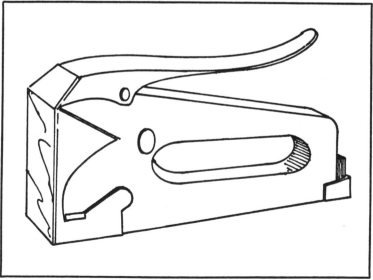

Fig. 2-11. Basic staple gun.

thick. Thin rulers allow you to mark more accurately because the division marks are closer to the work. Always hold the rule so that its edge is against the surface to be measured. You thus rule out any error due to the thickness of the measuring device. The hook at the end of the rule or the eye at the end of the tape is included as part of the first inch. On your tape rule, you will have to add the width of the case to your measurement.

You will need a *yardstick*, a *tape rule*, and a cloth or plastic *tape measure*. You will use your yardstick to measure soft goods, lay out short lines against the walls or on wood, and as a straightedge to make true lines to connect two or more measurements. The flexible steel rule is for accurate measuring tape is mainly used when you need to determine the circumference of something. When you use the cloth tape, hold it firmly and bring it around to the 2-inch mark as your beginning reference point instead of the tape's front edge. That end tends to get frayed and is therefore not too accurate. Remember not to stretch the tape as you measure, because both cloth and plastic have some give to them. Don't forget to deduct the 2 inches from your measurement before recording it.

Be sure to verify each measurement. The order of measuring then is to measure, record, remeasure, and compare. If there is a discrepancy, measure a third time.

When you are measuring lumber, write the measurements you need directly on the board. When the measurement is for cloth, pin a note to the material.

Keep your pencils sharp and mark your points with a cross instead of a line. A line has a certain width, particularly if your pencil point is blunt. This can be as wide as ⅛ inch. If you have a cross, you have also established the other dimension of your measurement (Fig. 2-12).

SEWING MACHINE

A *sewing machine* needed to make some of the projects in this book. Machine stitches are usually stronger than stitches sewn by hand. If you don't own a sewing machine, rent one for

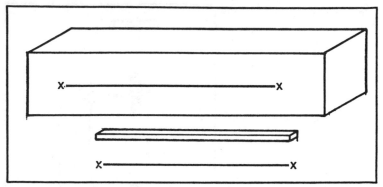

Fig. 2-12. Marking accurately.

the projects you intend to make. Obtain a complete instruction book with the machine.

If you are a novice, have somebody show you the simple operations of threading, winding a bobbin, and sewing a straight seam. Operating a sewing machine is quite simple. The sewing for these projects consists basically of straight seams.

Most of the newer machines offer stitches other than the regular straight stitch. You might try zigzag stitching.

Sewing machines need needles and thread. When selecting the needle, consider the kind of fabric you wish to join. The size of the needle will determine the size of the thread you use with it. Bigger needles take heavier thread; smaller ones use thinner thread. The needle will need a large enough eye to allow the thread to pass through without breaking or fraying it. It should be thin enough to penetrate the fabric you are working on without making large holes.

Sewing machine needles come in sizes that range from number 9, very fine, to number 18, very heavy. A number 9 needle would be used for a very light fabric, while a number 18 needle would be best suited for a heavy one. For general sewing, numbers 12 and 13 are usually fine. Needles also come with different points: regular sharp, ball-point, and wedge-point. Regular sharp ones should be used for all types of woven fabrics. They will give you even stitching with little or no puckering of the fabric. Ball-point needles are great for

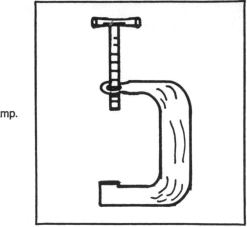

Fig. 2-13. C-clamp.

knits or elastic fabrics, because the ball point pushes in between the fabric yarns and never pierces them. Leather and vinyl should be sewn with wedge-point needles, because these needles make holes that close upon themselves. For sewing heavy or multiple layers of leather or plastic, be sure to use a large wedge-point needle like a number 18. A number 11 may be used on the kind of leather or plastic that is soft, pliable, and relatively thin. Bent, burred, nicked, or dull needles should never be used, because they will damage the fabric on which they sew.

Thread comes in many sizes and fibers. The fiber and color should be matched to the fabric; the thickness is matched to the needle. The higher the number on the thread, the finer the thread is. Number 50 is best for general use. For sewing heavy vinyl and upholstery weight fabrics, you will need a size 40. Always use thread one shade darker than the fabric. If the fabric is a print or plaid, use the dominant color for your thread.

OTHER TOOLS

Eyelet pliers or *setters* are a must for setting eyelets—those round metal or plastic reinforcements you put around holes in fabric or plastic. These eyelet setters are easy to use. Insert an eyelet into the eyelet setter, put the fabric over it, and squeeze shut. The eyelets come in various sizes to match your fabric and can be bought, along with the eyelet setter, at your nearest variety or discount store.

C-Clamps

Clamp your work with a handy C-clamp. C-clamps affix one piece to another and hold on to let glue dry and set. The smaller C-clamps, light or medium weight, will be best for the work in this book. C-clamps come in sizes from ⅝ to 12 inches and in light, medium, and heavy service weights (Fig. 2-13).

Try Square

A *try square* is useful for checking the squareness of things. You can also check right angles with it, measure sections, and use it as a straightedge to score, scribe, or mark on a workpiece (Fig. 2-14).

Miter Box

This gadget enables you to miter corners like a master craftsperson. Miter means to cut at an angle. You can miter or angle different degree angles. The question of whether to miter or not is up to you.

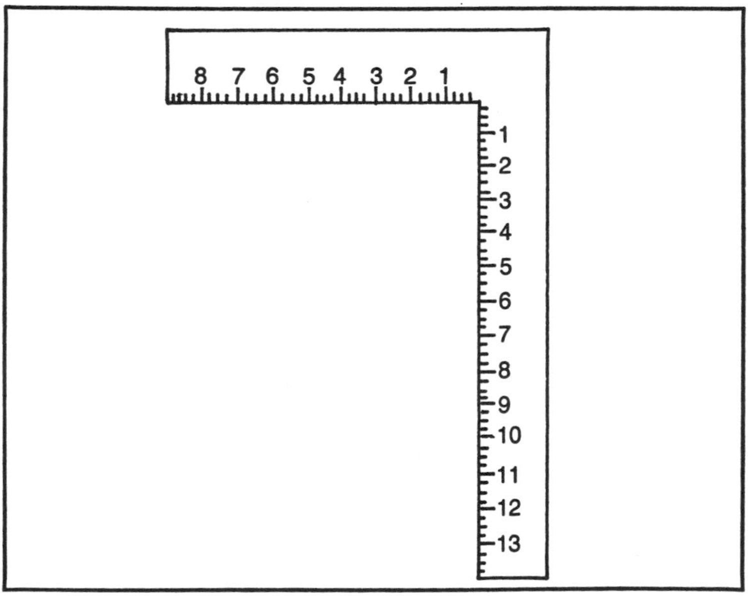

Fig. 2-14. Try square.

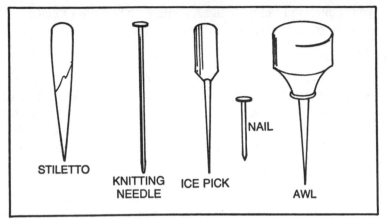

Fig. 2-15. Extras are nice to have.

Scissors

Electric *scissors* are nice if you have to cut through heavy fabric, leather, plastic, foam, or cardboard. Some people prefer ordinary scissors. Small, accurate cuts have to be done with small hand scissors.

Use paper scissors for paper, fabric scissors for fabric, and so on. Embroidery scissors are just the right size for cutting corners, trimming and making accurate notches, and clipping curves.

Electric Knife

An *electric knife* is ideal if you have to deal with foam thicker than 1 inch. It is an easy tool to use. The electric knife is useful for special fitting or trimming.

Extras

A *stiletto* or *awl* can punch holes into plastic, leather, or fabric. You can just as easily use a knitting needle of the required size, an *ice pick*, or a finishing nail (Fig. 2-15).

If you are interested in making lamps and other light fixtures, wire strippers are handy. The wire strippers will cut the insulation off the wire without cutting or even nicking it.

Materials

This chapter is an overview of the materials and methods with which you will be working. An understanding of what materials can and cannot do is essential.

WOOD

Wood is divided into two categories—*softwood* and *hardwood*. Hardwood is not necessarily physically harder than softwood, though this is often the case. Hardwood is more expensive. It will take a natural finish better and is often tougher to work. Nailing hardwood can be difficult. We will recommend softwood, although plywood is also suitable.

Grades and Grading

The grading standards for softwood and hardwood differ. These grades are as follows:

Grade 1	clear wood	no visible defects, knots, or splits
Grade 2	number 2	has knots
Grade 3	construction	least expensive and most flaws

Let's look at the subcategories within this grading system.

A- and B-Select or Number 1 and Number 2 Clear.
These grades are the highest quality lumber you can buy.
They will take finishes perfectly and are best suited for fine
cabinetwork.

C-Select or Custom. This lumber may have fine knots
and some minor imperfections—usually only on one side.

D-Select. This is the lowest of the so-called finishing
grades. Any knots and other blemishes can be easily covered
with putty or made into an asset with the use of a knotty pine
finish.

Number 1 Common. This is the first of the board
grades. This grade is almost as good as D-Select, and we have
found it most economical to use. The grade may have some
small imperfections, but it will take finishes well.

The other grades of wood, with the possible exception of
number 2 common, are not suited for the work discussed in
this book.

Nominal and Actual Sizes

When lumber people give you 2×4s, 1×8s, or 2×12s,
you won't be handed lumber that measures 2×4 inches, 1×8
inches or 2×12 inches. A piece of lumber that was called a
2×4 may actually measure 1½×3½ inches. A 1×8 board may
measure ¾ inch by 7¼ inches.

The quoted numbers—your 2×4s and 1×8s—refer to
the *nominal* or rough cut sizes. The lumber pieces were 2×4s
and 1×8s when first hewn from a log. In the milling and drying
processes the lumber pieces went through before they
reached you, the actual dimensions shrunk to the aforementioned 1½×3½ inches or ¾×7½ inches. See Fig. 3-1.

PLYWOOD

Plywood is made of thin wood sheets bonded together
with glue under pressure. It is graded from A to D, with A
representing top quality and D bottom quality. The quality
standards in the plywood industry are constantly changing.

Grade A plywood   clean, smooth
Grade B plywood   smooth, minor flaws

Size to Order	Actual Size	Size to Order	Actual Size
1×3	¾×2½	2×3	1½×2½
1×4	¾×3½	2×4	1½×3½
1×6	¾×5½	2×6	1½×5½
1×8	¾×7¼	2×8	1½×7¼
1×10	¾×9¼	2×10	1½×9¼
1×12	¾×11¼	2×12	1½×11¼

3″ & 4″ THICKNESSES = RESPECTIVE WIDTH ON TABLE ABOVE

Fig. 3-1. Standard dimensions of lumber.

Grade C plywood	more obvious flaws
Grade D plywood	rough, with splits and knotholes

Plywood is made from multiple veneered layers. The face and the back of a certain panel of plywood will each bear a specific grade which does not of necessity match. You will be able to find A-B, B-C, A-D, C-D, A-C, or B-D as well as A-A, B-B, C-C, or D-D. There are *interior, exterior,* and *marine* plywood. Plywood comes in many thicknesses.

Plywood resists warping and cracking. Furthermore, it comes in handy large panels.

The most common panel size for plywood is 4×8 feet, though you might find a 4×9-foot or even a 4×10-foot panel if you really need one. Your regular or common sizes tend to be a lot less expensive and much easier to obtain. We have based all our material calculations on a 4×8-foot panel. Often the people at the lumberyard will sell you half a panel if that is what you need. If you want the people at the lumberyard to do your cutting for you, present them with a sketch with the sizes of each piece clearly and accurately indicated.

An easy way to make a layout that you can move about is to cut out your pieces—if you use graph paper you won't even have to measure, just count—and then draw an 8×4 foot proxy in the same scale. You can move the pieces around on the background to get the best and most economical fit (Figs. 3-2 through Fig. 3-5).

If you want the grain of your plywood to run in the same direction on the finished piece, allow for it in the layout (Figs. 3-6 and 3-7). All pieces have to be turned to face in the same direction.

Handle plywood carefully because the top veneer is quite thin. Use sharp tools, particularly your saw, and keep the "good" side of the plywood up to prevent slivering.

Exposed edges of plywood can present a problem. This can be easily solved, though, by using thin strips of veneer or narrow molding glued to the exposed edges.

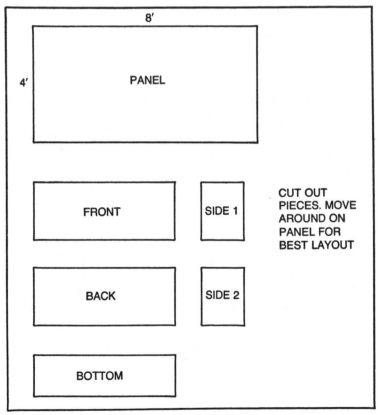

Fig. 3-2. Layout for planter box on plywood panel.

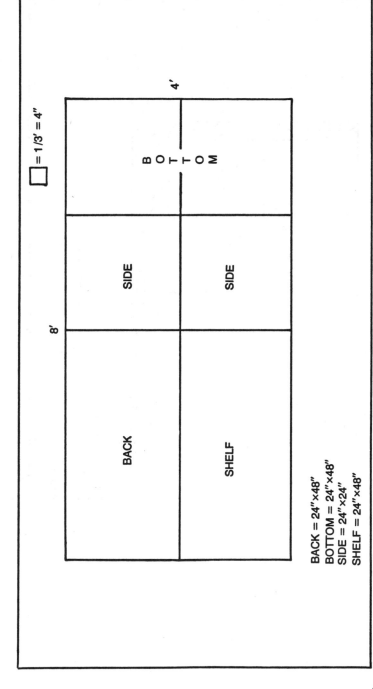

☐ = 1/3' = 4"

4'

8'

B
O
T
T
O
M

SIDE

SIDE

BACK

SHELF

BACK = 24"×48"
BOTTOM = 24"×48"
SIDE = 24"×24"
SHELF = 24"×48"

Fig. 3-3. Layout for bookcase on 8×4-foot plywood panel.

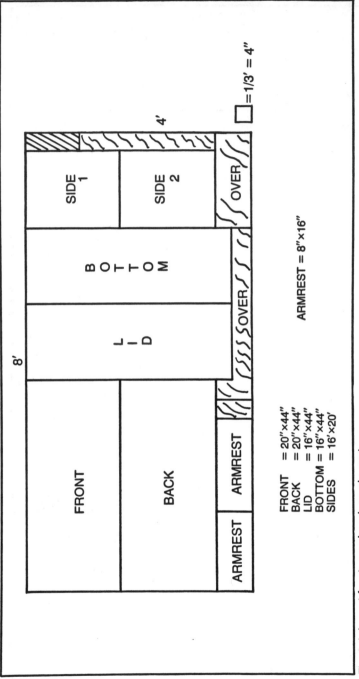

Fig. 3-4. Layout for storage bench on plywood.

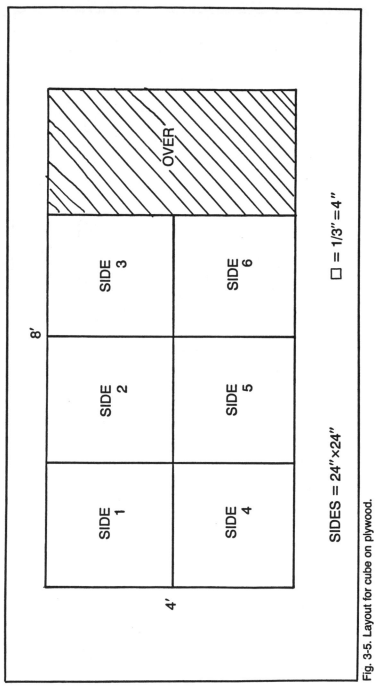

Fig. 3-5. Layout for cube on plywood.

61

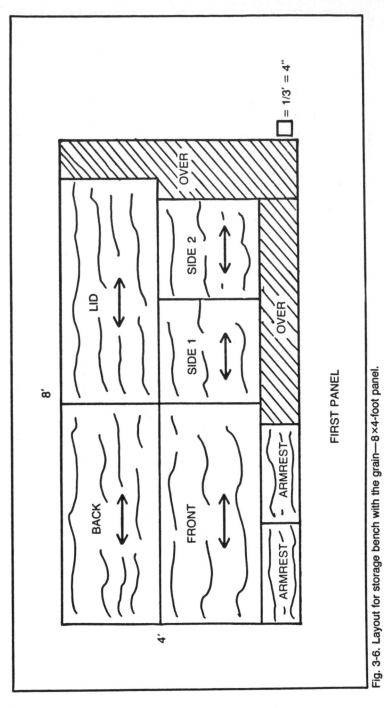

□ = 1/3' = 4"

FIRST PANEL

Fig. 3-6. Layout for storage bench with the grain—8×4-foot panel.

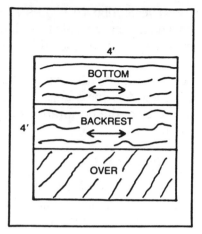

Fig. 3-7. Layout for storage bench on 4×4-foot panel.

HARDBOARD

Hardboard is made from wood chips reduced to the basic wood fibers and then reunited under heat and pressure to form panels. Hardwood is grainless, dense, durable, and can be used for many things. There are no imperfections or knots. It can be worked with the same tools you use for regular lumber, but you need to sharpen tools more often as hardboard is very abrasive.

Hardboard is graded as follows:

Tempered hardboard	hardest, stiffest, strongest, and most resistant to moisture
Standard hardboard	the regular kind
S1S	hardboard with one smooth side
S2S	hardboard with two smooth sides
Embossed hardboard	embossing on one side
Grooved hardboard	grooves on one side
Perforated hardboard	commonly called pegboard (with holes)

The hardboard comes in various thicknesses just like plywood. You can get it as thin as ⅛ inch and as thick as ¾ inch. The most common thicknesses are ⅛, 3/16, and ¼ inch.

Pegboard comes in different thicknesses, too. The thickness also affects the size of the perforations, so your thicker pegboard will have bigger holes than your thinner one. The diameter of the perforations corresponds to the thickness of the panel.

PARTICLE BOARD

Particle board is made by mixing wood chips with sawdust, adding adhesive, and then pressing the materials into panels under intense heat and pressure. Particle board is grainless and quite stable. Particle board is heavy and inexpensive.

Particle board comes in boards of various widths from 4×8 feet on up. We don't recommend a size larger than 4×8 feet, because it is impossible to store and is very heavy. The thickness runs from ¼ to ⅞ inch.

MOLDINGS AND PREFORMED LEGS

Moldings are thin strips of wood from ⅜ inch to 2½ inches wide. The molding can be flat, rounded, and quarter or half-rounded, or it can be embossed with a design. You can buy molding or trim by the foot. Glue or nail it to any raw edges of work that you would like to look more finished. Simply regard the trim as part of the piece and paint or finish it in the same manner.

You might like to use preformed legs that you can attach to form tables, chairs, beds, and couches. These legs come in many styles and sizes. There are tapered, rounded legs, four-sided legs, turned legs, and others. Sizes range from 2-inch-long legs to 26 and 28-inch-long ones that will make ideal legs for a desk or dining table. These legs will accept any finish.

Other small wood items that you might use are pieces of turned wood that fasten together, usually with threads that screw together, but sometimes with poles or rods that connect them on the inside. There are knobs, too, that finish off the rods on the top or bottom. Decorative brackets, wooden or otherwise, are also available.

PLASTIC PIPE

Polyvinyl chloride (PVC) pipe, *chlorinated polyvinyl chloride* (CPVC) pipe, *polybutylene* pipe, and *polyethylene* pipe can be worked with a saw, a knife, and some sandpaper. The material comes in 5 and 10-foot lengths and in diameters from ¼ to 4 inches. All types of couplings and fittings are available. Some are self-locking and require no tools or cement to fit them together permanently. Solvent cement is available from any plumbing or hardware store if you need it.

You can make lamps, tables, chairs, couches, and beds by fitting the pipes and couplings together. You can shorten the pipe by sawing it off, and you can lengthen it to any desired measurement by attaching another piece to the first via fittings or couplings.

Polyvinyl chloride pipe does not require finishing. It will fit in with most settings and colors.

ADHESIVE-BACKED VINYL

Adhesive-backed vinyl adds strength to a project. Even though the plastic is paper-thin, the resultant "skin" will give the object greater impact strength and protect it from dents and nicks. The plastic provides a smooth, easy-to-clean surface that is quite durable.

The material is inexpensive and comes in a multitude of colors and designs. You can get plastic covering in wallpaper stores, though it is not really adhesive-backed vinyl. Rather, it is vinyl that has adhesive on the backing. This adhesive has to be activated by putting the vinyl into a water bath. The vinyl will adhere quite well to smooth surfaces. It is usually quite tough and can be washed with soap and water. The vinyl often has a textured surface that makes it not very desirable for counter or tabletops.

When working with vinyl, watch for stretching and wrinkling. Stretching can happen easily if you hang on tightly to one side of the strip and smooth it in place while the other one hangs free. As you smooth, particularly around curves, you may tend to bear down, which will easily stretch the thin vinyl. The wrinkles on the surface seem to appear spontaneously and are tough to get out. Here are some considerations when working with vinyl.

● To begin with, measure your vinyl accurately and the thing you intend to cover as well. If the surface to be covered has a lot of irregularities or is composed of different curves, make a paper pattern first. Cut out the paper pattern and put it on the piece for a trial fit. Adjust your paper pattern by adding the necessary bits in the gaps with more paper fastened on with cellophane tape. Give it another try on the form to make sure

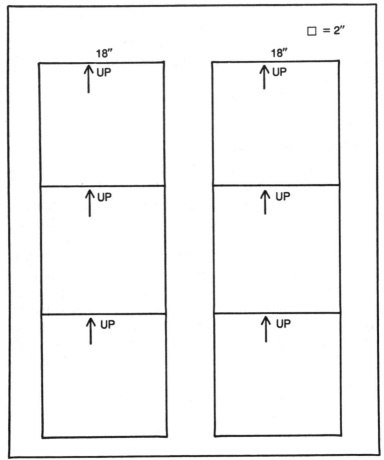

Fig. 3-8. Layout for adhesive vinyl cover for 18-inch cube.

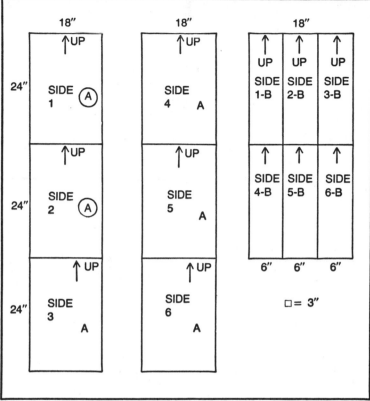

Fig. 3-9. Layout for adhesive vinyl cover for 24-inch cube.

it is perfect; then cut your vinyl to conform to the pattern (Figs. 3-8 through 3-11).

● Consider the matter of overlap. Be as sparing as possible with overlap. The vinyl does not stick to itself too well and tends to pull off the surface from the extra weight. You want to make sure, though, that the underlying surface does not peek through the joint. A ¼-inch overlap insures that the vinyl will cover the surface and stay put.

● Be sure to use a ruler or a straightedge to mark your cuts (unless you're dealing with curves) and make those cuts at right angles to the long edges of the vinyl sheet (Fig. 3-12). You will have no trouble lining up your top edges and side edges when you cover straight-sided pieces. Here are the steps involved in applying the vinyl.

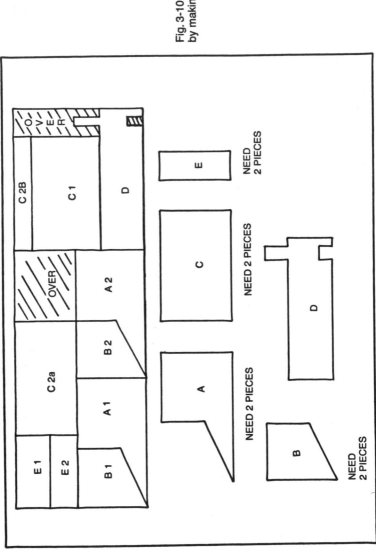

Fig. 3-10. Layout for irregular pieces by making paper patterns.

68

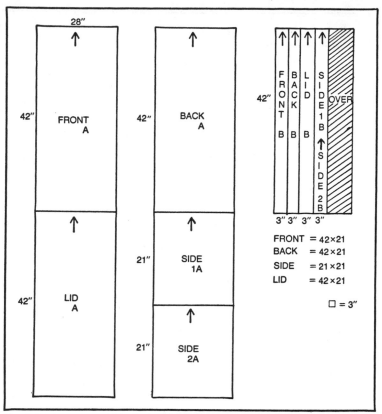

Fig. 3-11. Layout on 18-inch vinyl for covering a storage box.

Step 1. First, peel off about 2 or 3 inches of the backing all across the vinyl. This is usually best done by starting in the middle, because on most adhesive-backed vinyls the backing is in two separate strips that meet in the center. If your vinyl has a solid backing, fold the vinyl down the center for about 1 inch, crease, and split the paper backing. If you tear the vinyl by mistake, it won't show.

Step 2. Line up the vinyl, with the bare back to the surface, on the top and down about 3 inches along the sides. Smooth in place.

Step 3. Flip the vinyl up at right angles to the surface. Pull down the backing just past the halfway mark and gently let it settle in place on the piece.

Step 4. Repeat the flipping and removal of the backing

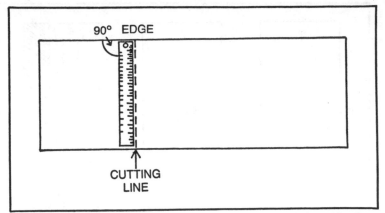

Fig. 3-12. Use a ruler at a right angle to the side edge to mark the cutting line.

(take off the rest this time). Let the vinyl fall in place.

Step 5. If there was wrinkling after your first try (step 3), smooth the backing back in place and remove the vinyl from the object. Handle carefully and do not stretch. Line it up once more and try again.

Step 6. If there is still wrinkling, pull it off again and line it up along the side only. Disregard the top. Fit the vinyl from side to side. Proceed as in steps 3 and 4.

Step 7. When the covering is on, smooth it down tightly with a sponge or a small paint roller or *brayer*.

Step 8. If you still find a bubble or wrinkle, work it out toward the bottom. Lift up the bottom edge if necessary. If the bubble is near one side, you can work it out in the same way toward the nearest edge and lift the side edge a bit.

Step 9. If the bubble is centered and relatively small, prick it with a pin and then smooth the area with your finger.

FOAM

There are basically three manifestations of *foam:* foam blocks or slabs, foam chips, and fiberfill. The blocks or slabs come in many sizes and thicknesses. Cushion forms are available in large department stores and specialty shops.

Pads are available in sizes starting with a 24-inch width and going up to a full double bed 54-inch width. Thicknesses range from 1 inch up to 4 and even 5 inches. The length of these pads varies from 5 feet up to 6 feet in proportion to the increase in width, though you can get a 26-inch pad that is 72 inches long fairly easily.

Foam chips and fiberfill come in sacks by the pound. Shredded foam is also available.

Filling a Cushion with Foam

Here is how to fill a cushion with foam:

● Construct the fabric cover for the foam. This should be an inner cover made out of sheeting or muslin that can be sewn up tightly. Then you can take off the outer cover and wash or clean it without going through the filling procedure again. Construct two covers for each pillow that is going to be filled with shredded foam—an inner one and an outer one.

● Set your plastic bag of shredded foam on the floor—on one of its shorter ends (Fig. 3-13). Open the top.

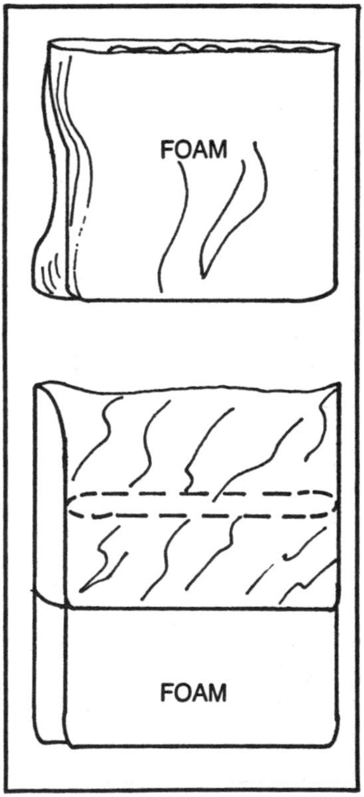

Fig. 3-13. Set an open foam-filled bag on the floor. Then pull the cover over the bag.

- Slip your cover over the plastic bag and turn the whole thing upside down (Fig. 3-14).
- Slit the plastic bag across the bottom.
- With a clean, dry sponge mop or wax applicator, push down the foam into the cover as tightly as you can. You may also use a paint roller if you don't have a sponge mop or wax applicator.
- If that is enough foam for you, remove the plastic bag. Be careful not to spill any foam. You can, alternately, slit the plastic along one side and leave it in the cover.
- Sew the top of the pillow shut by hand. Use small stitches and place them close together. If the pillow is not stuffed tightly, you may run over the seam with the sewing machine.
- If your pillow requires a second bag, have a friend hold open the cover as before. Lower the unopened plastic bag into the cover as far as it will go. With your hands inside the cover, open the bag and let the foam flow into the cover.
- Pull out your hands and push the foam down through the top of the plastic as much as possible. Remove the plastic bag

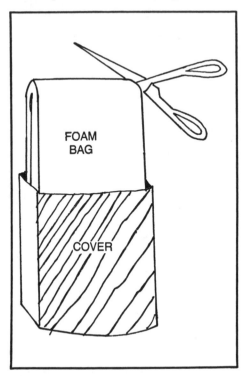

FOAM
BAG

COVER

Fig. 3-14. Invert the cover and plastic bag.Slit the top of the plastic bag.

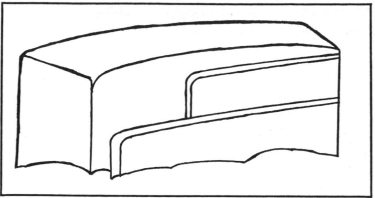
Fig. 3-15. Layering a cut or how not to cut foam.

gently while your partner hangs on to the cover. Sew the top while your helper keeps it upright.

● If you are using only a half bag or other fraction, wait until the required amount has come out of the plastic bag. With your hands inside the cover, close the opening of the plastic bag and gently bring it out of the cover. Tie immediately. Then proceed as you did in the previous step. You will use the same technique for filling a pillow with foam chips or fiberfill.

Foam Don'ts

● Don't try to cut a pad of foam thicker than 1 inch with anything but an electric knife.

● Don't cut into the foam until you have marked the cut with a straightedge or, if it is a curve, with a French curve. You must have a clean cutting line.

● Don't force the knife down into the foam. Cut along the entire line to the depth of about ½ inch. Go back to the beginning and cut another ½ inch, and so on. Be careful not to layer the foam as in Fig. 3-15. Instead, put your knife in the cut each time and work straight down.

Foam and Adhesives

You may want to fuse two pieces of foam together. This can be done fairly easily. You have a wide selection of adhesives for *polystyrene*. Nonflammable contact cement and Elmer's glue are ideal.

If you are working with *polyurethane* foam, you can use a spray adhesive called "Kingo." It bonds fabric and other materials, too.

Masking tape and aluminum tape can be used to affix foam pieces. Apply the tape in short strips across a corner joint (Fig. 3-16). If you are putting pieces flush to one another, you can use the strapping technique shown in Fig. 3-17. Curved or irregular edges may be taped in the same manner as straight ones (Figs. 3-18 and 3-19).

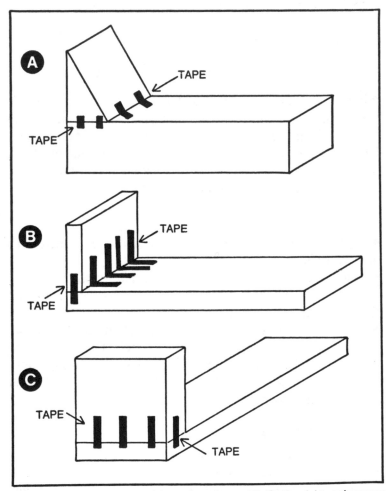

Fig. 3-16. (A) Taping a corner joint on foam forms. (B). Taping right angle corner joints. (C) Back view.

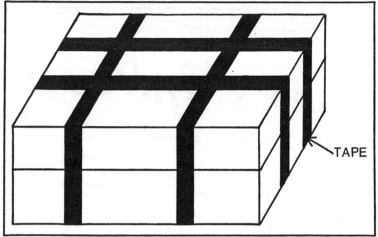

Fig. 3-17. Using strapping technique on foam blocks.

TYPES OF FABRICS

Fabrics are either woven or knitted. When woven fabrics are of medium weight and tightly woven so they won't ravel, they make great covers for cushions and pads. Their surfaces are generally smooth and will stay that way in spite of rather heavy use. These materials also will wash well (if they are of cotton or a combination of cotton and a synthetic) and keep their shape nicely. Such fabrics include denim, poplin, and most upholstery fabrics sold for slipcovers. Corduroy is another good fabric.

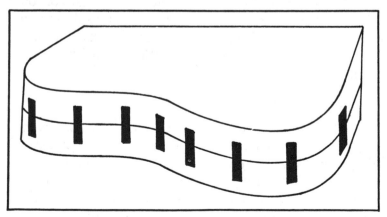

Fig. 3-18. Taping curved edges on foam.

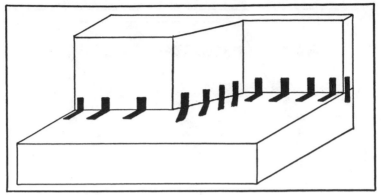
Fig. 3-19. Taping irregular foam shapes.

These fabrics have very little give to them. The real trouble comes when you have to follow curves or irregularities. When curves and irregularities are used, knitted materials will be specified.

Double knits have advantages for pillow and pad covers. The material will accommodate to movement and then snap back in shape—at least for a while. Washing will restore the elasticity and the original shape of the garment or cover. For anything requiring exacting work in fitting curves and irregularities, knitted fabrics are best. If you simply approximate the general pattern of the piece, the obliging knit will cling to those curves or irregularities as if you had spent many hours of fitting it just right.

Unfortunately, knits tend to catch on any sharp or rough object that comes in contact with them. This results in a snag or pulled thread. If there is a lot of rubbing or handling of the cover, many knits tend to develop little fiber knots above the surface.

UPHOLSTERY PLASTIC

There are many plastics available that simulate leather. A plastic covering can be used over padding, particularly if you tack it down directly to the wood or particle board that you are covering. Regular upholstery plastic goes on over springs or spring cushions. A variety of plastics come quilted to a backing. They are rather stiff but attractive.

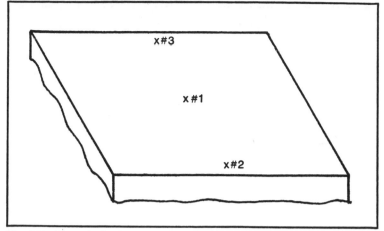

Fig. 3-20. To tack plastic, begin in the center of each piece.

Get the right kind of plastic for the project. Plastic stretches, so handle it with care.

When you tack plastic to a piece of plywood or particle board, first tack it in the middle of each piece (Fig. 3-20). Work outward evenly to each side (Figs. 3-21 and 3-22). When you sew plastic, support it on both sides of the needle. Have a table or chair behind your machine, so the plastic doesn't sag under its own weight.

Don't mar the surface when you pin plastic. Use pieces of basting tape. If you have to rip a seam, be careful as thread, when pulled, tends to cut through the plastic. If the needle is not the wedge-pointed kind, you might have a row of tiny holes that you can't get out. Avoid ripping as much as possible.

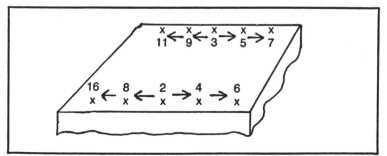

Fig. 3-21. Tacking plastic on long sides alternately.

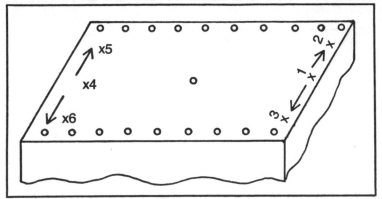

Fig. 3-22. Tacking short sides one at a time.

When making plastic covers, cut them a bit smaller than the foam. They will stretch a bit, and covers that are too tight look better than sagging covers.

JOINING FABRICS

The most common way to join fabric is to sew it either by hand or machine. The stitch length should be adjusted to fit the fabric. Small stitches are used with lightweight fabric, and longer stitches are ideal for heavy coarse fabrics. A longer stitch is usually best for plastic. You won't have as many perforations, and they will be spaced farther apart and less likely to tear out.

Straight stitching will be fine even on knits. You may, substitute a zigzag if your machine has one for the knits. When you are joining pieces, work as much as possible with flat pieces—that is, close those seams that will give the piece its

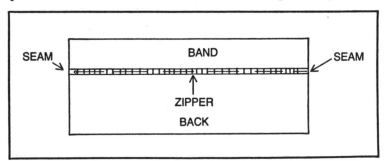

Fig. 3-23. Start by inserting zipper in the seam between band and back.

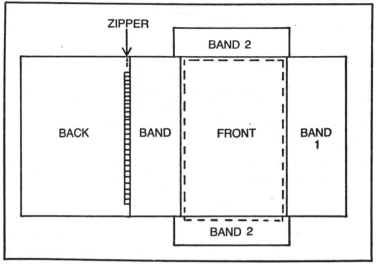

Fig. 3-24. Sewing cover for pad.

final form last (Figs. 3-23 through Fig. 3-25). Zippers and other fastenings should be inserted while the pieces are still flat.

Fusing is another method of joining fabrics together permanently. *Stitch Witchery,* the trade name used by the USM Chemical Company for their product (thin strips of special material), can be used. Generally speaking, the *polyamide* iron-on bonding net bonds with two layers of material to form a solid sandwich along the seam or joint line (Fig. 3-26).

You will need a good flatiron for fusing fabrics. When you use the iron for fusing or bonding, you will be using a different technique than is used in pressing clothes. Instead of sliding your iron back and forth, put the iron over the surface to be

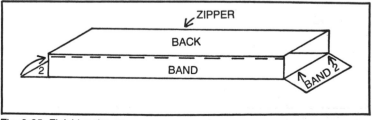

Fig. 3-25. Finishing the cover.

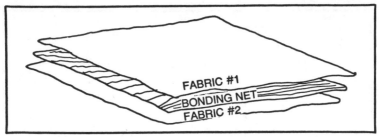

Fig. 3-26. A bonding net sandwich.

fused and press. Hold the iron perfectly still for 10 seconds on each side of the material to be joined. As in soldering, the heat comes up from underneath.

To do a perfect job of fusing, carefully put your bonding net between the two layers of fabric, with edges even as in Fig. 3-27. Pin the sandwich together with straight pins woven through at right angles to the length of the joint or seam. Put it onto your ironing board or on a padded table or counter top. Cover with a press cloth if you are using a dry iron. Steam irons may be used without a press cloth if the setting on the dial is "wool." Press for about 10 seconds after removing any pins that are in that particular section. Continue in the same

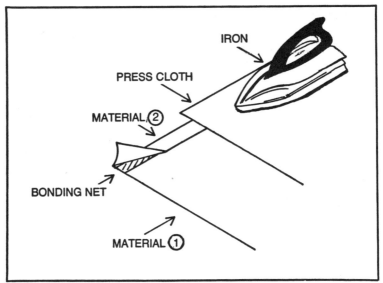

Fig. 3-27. Fusing materials with bonding net and iron.

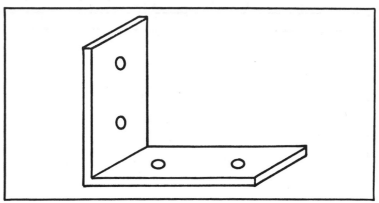

Fig. 3-28. A corner brace.

way. Turn the whole thing over and go through the same routine, except you won't have to remove any pins on this run. The seam will get heat and pressure from both sides. The polyamide will disappear completely into the fabric and fuse the two pieces together.

HARDWARE

Here are a few definitions of various types of hardware. A *corner brace* is a piece of metal that reinforces a corner from the inside of the piece (Fig. 3-28). A *corner iron* also reinforces corners but on the outside, along the edges of the piece (Fig. 3-29). A *T-plate* is used to join vertical and horizontal members of a structure (Fig. 3-30).

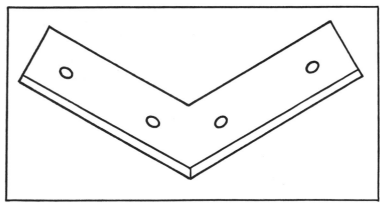

Fig. 3-29. The corner iron.

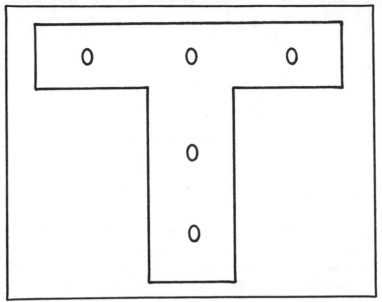

Fig. 3-30. The neat T-plate.

A *mending plate* is used for joining pieces of wood end to end (Fig. 3-31). These are usually used in pairs—one on one side of the piece and the other on the opposite surface.

Hinges make it possible to open and shut doors or lids. Butt hinges are the easiest to use (Fig. 3-32).

Nails

Nails are generally available in sizes that range from 1 to 6 inches long. As nails get longer, their circumference gets bigger.

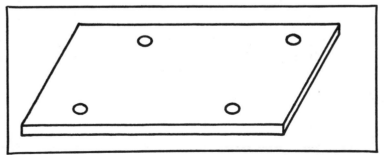

Fig. 3-31. The mending plate.

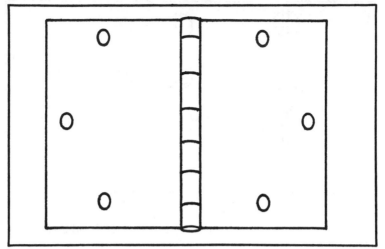

Fig. 3-32. The butt hinge.

Common nails have large heads. *Finishing* nails have small ones. Tacks have short shanks and relatively wide heads (Fig. 3-33). They range from sizes 1 to 24 and in actual dimensions from 3/16 inch to 1⅛ inches.

Screws

Screws are stronger than nails. They can be taken out easily if you want to disassemble a project. They are usually

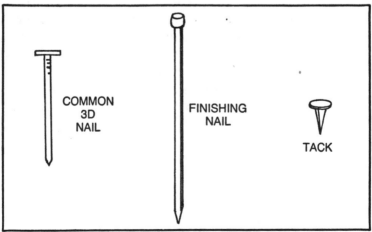

COMMON
3D
NAIL

FINISHING
NAIL

TACK

Fig. 3-33. Nails and tack.

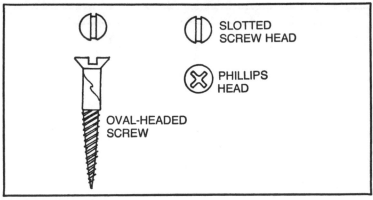

Fig. 3-34. Types of screws.

categorized according to the shape of the head and the slots in the head.

The straight slot screw goes with the straight slot screwdriver. The Phillips screw is used with the Phillips screwdriver (Fig. 3-34).

Flathead screws are used when you want the screwhead to be flush with or recessed into the surface. Roundhead screws are meant to have their heads exposed. While they are tightened more easily than any other screw, they have the disadvantage of that exposed head. Oval-head screws are partially recessed and usually have brass or chrome-plated finish that makes their heads quite decorative.

Screws range in size up to 4 inches. A screw should be ¼ to ½ inch shorter than the total thickness of the material it will hold together. Screws are classified according to the diameter or gauge, which usually ranges from number 5 to number 14. The gauge refers to the diameter under the head. Because the screw tapers, the gauge gets smaller as the screw gets thinner. Screws of the same gauge are also available in different lengths.

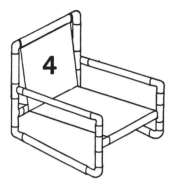

Customizing Projects

When you enter the do-it-yourself world you are over-whelmed with a multitude of choices. When you follow the instructions for the projects in this book, you still have a number of options open to you that will make your project distinctly different from that of another reader.

These choices will not affect the design itself; nor will they alter any significant construction detail. They will be mainly concerned with size, choice of material, and finish techniques. The choices will not make the work harder for you. They will simply allow you to get exactly what you want.

ADJUSTING PROJECT SIZE TO AN EXISTING SPACE

Probably the most common customizing effort is to adjust the size of a project to an existing space. Perhaps you want to make a planter in Chapter 6 that has the given dimensions of 14 inches by 42 feet by 10 inches. As you visualize that planter under your window, you may feel that there will be some extra space on either side that will look awful.

Carefully measure the place where you plan to put the project. On a piece of newspaper, draw the rough outline of the project according to the dimensions given. Put that rough pattern in place. This applies to the width, length, and height of an object.

Suppose the planter will leave about 3 inches on each side under that window. Maybe the planter might look better if it isn't exactly centered but put to one side and balanced with a big pot (Fig. 4-1). You might prefer to balance it on each side with a small pot (Fig. 4-2).

Fig. 4-1. Informal balance.

Fig. 4-2. Formal balance.

You may want a planter that completely covers the space underneath your window.

Simply measure the space you want covered—in this case the length of the window. Deduct the length of the planter as given which, according to our calculation, should leave 6 inches or ½ foot. Add these 6 inches to each length measurement.

For this planter you will need three long boards: one board for the bottom or floor of the planter and two boards of equal length to each other and the floor. The measurements are two boards 10×42 and 1 board 14×42. Add 6 inches to the

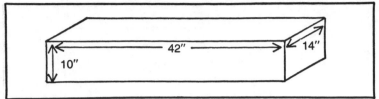

Fig. 4-3. Planter box.

long sides. New measurements are two boards 10×48 inches and 14×48 inches for one board. The height (10 inches) and the width, which require separate boards anyway (the 10×14-inch variety), remain constant. See Figs. 4-3 through 4-6 for further clarification.

Let's take another case. This time the length works fine, but you are worried about the height. It seems a bit low for

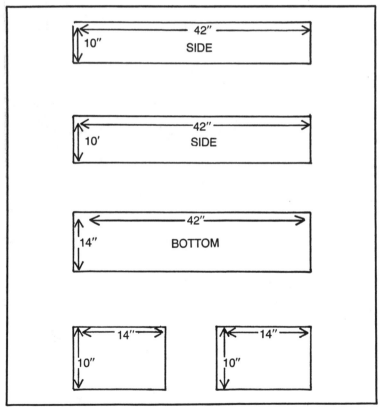

Fig. 4-4. Planter box pieces.

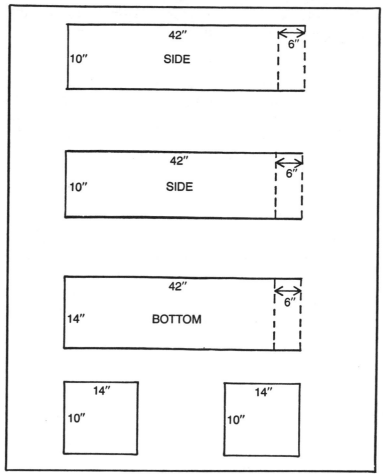

Fig. 4-5. Lengthening the planter.

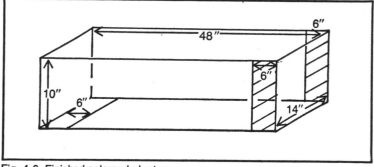

Fig. 4-6. Finished enlarged planter.

your big pots. So you hang up your newspaper pattern on the wall and set your pots in front of it. Your intuition was right. We specified that the planter be 10 inches high. Your pots, plus the 2-inch pebble layer, add up to nearly 14 inches. You need to add 4 inches to all height dimensions. This means all boards except the bottom board, as it is lying flat and has no height other than its thickness (Fig. 4-7A). You need two boards 14×42 inches for the long sides and two boards 14×14 inches for the short sides (Fig. 4-7B).

Let's pretend that your pots are of the low and wide variety, and you can't squeeze them into that 14-inch-wide planter. You need a planter 16 inches wide. In this case you are only going to deal with the two short end pieces, the ones that according to our project plans are specified to be 14×10 inches (14 inches being the width and 10 inches the height) and the bottom board that is 42×14 feet. For a 16-inch-wide planter, add 2 inches to the width dimension. Make the two short pieces 16×10 inches. Make the bottom 42×16 inches (Fig. 4-8).

If the proposed piece is to stand against a wall or be hung from a wall, you will have to determine if the added depth will give you enough room to walk by or maneuver around it. If the space requirement checks out positive, you need to consider how something protruding that far from the wall will look. Instead of a piece of paper as a pattern, use a box of the same dimensions. A piece of cardboard attached to the box should give you an idea (Fig. 4-9). As far as width is concerned, 4 inches will be the maximum.

In all likelihood, more height would refer to additional shelves in a shelving unit or longer legs on a table or bench. As far as the shelves are concerned, you can usually add another tier at the top without any trouble—even two will do nicely. The problem of keeping them from looking top-heavy will come in arranging whatever it is you plan to put on them. Put the larger pieces and the greater spaces between shelves at the bottom. Use smaller, more delicate pieces on top. Also, do not crowd items on your top shelves—even books. Always allow some space between—either by arranging other pieces among your books or by placing a book here so that the cover,

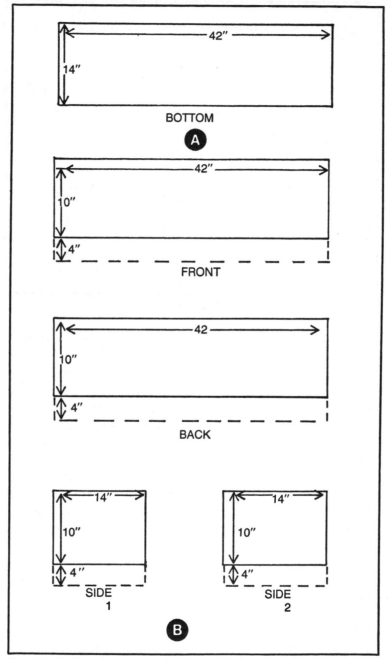

Fig. 4-7. (A) Changing height on the planter. The bottom remains the same. (B) Front, back, and side panels change in height.

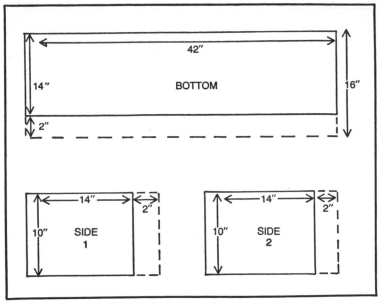

Fig. 4-8. Adding to the width of the planter box.

instead of the spine, faces to the front. You can stack a couple of books horizontally.

Benches and couches are also more comfortable if they fit the owner. Find a chair or bench which fits you. You should be able to sit with both feet flat on the floor—back against the backrest and your thighs parallel to the floor. Measure your chair as shown in Fig. 4-10, and use the measurement in adjusting benches and other seating pieces.

If you want to shorten a piece of furniture, you can take off 6 inches in length. While the piece will appear taller, it will retain pleasing proportions in most cases. To test your new design, resort to a mock-up—one that includes length and height.

If it does appear a bit tall, you can still use it and find other means to disguise the overgrown look. Let's go back to the planter, which we used for an example earlier. We now require a planter that is only 36 inches long, which will make it look taller and wider. If we arrange plants in the planter that are bushy, vine down over the edge, and are of uniform height throughout, the planter will look well balanced and shorter

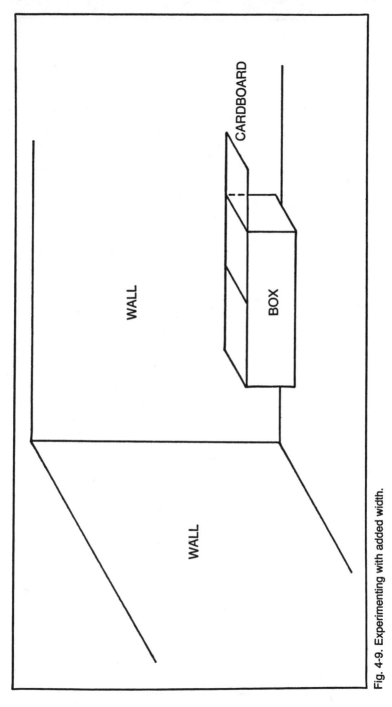

Fig. 4-9. Experimenting with added width.

93

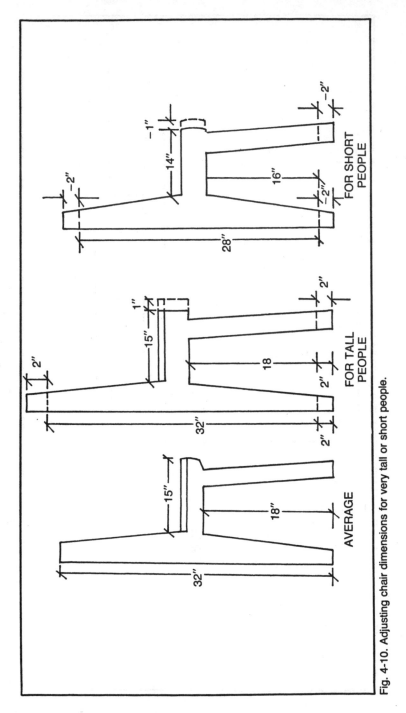

Fig. 4-10. Adjusting chair dimensions for very tall or short people.

than a longer one with stalky plants, even though the individual plants are not taller than the bushy ones. Color can make a difference, too. A light bright color will seem to reduce height. If you add a horizontal strip or other adornment, you will be amazed how much lower a piece can appear (Figs. 4-11 and 4-12).

Cutting the width by more than a couple of inches is usually not practical. You may, for instance, make shelves 2 inches narrower—say from 8 inches down to 6 inches. If you go from 8 inches to 4 inches, you would greatly limit what the shelves could hold.

SUBSTITUTING MATERIALS

It is possible to substitute one material for another and come up with a superior project. We will briefly review some materials and make you aware of some substitution possibilities.

Lumber

When it comes to boards, you really have little choice except to substitute one wood for another. It is mainly a matter of price. You will use the same grade of lumber, but you can use redwood instead of pine. Be careful of hardwoods, though, unless you only want to use them for shelves.

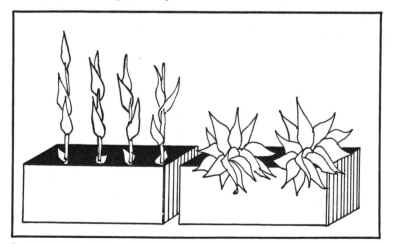

Fig. 4-11. Visual tricks, using plants, to make the planter appear lower.

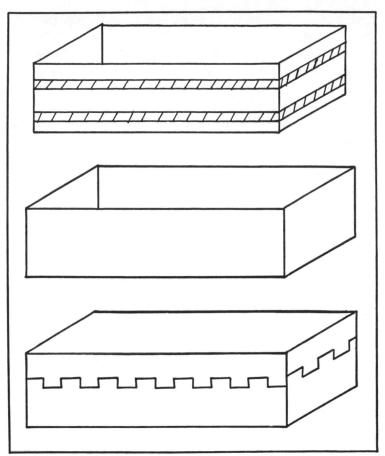

Fig. 4-12. Visual tricks to make the planter box look lower.

Hardwoods are much more time-consuming to work with than softwoods.

Particle board comes in all kinds of sizes and widths. It can be directly substituted if you remember to support your particle board shelves every 2 feet or so. Limit your finishing to paint, because only that looks good on particle board. Particle board is heavier than regular lumber, and supports need to be strong enough for the added weight.

When it comes to 2×4s, 1×2s, 2×3s, and 1×4s, you have no choice but to take the lumber. There simply is no substitute.

Trim or molding is interchangeable. You can substitute almost any design for another, provided it is the right width and conforms to the contour that you want. There is a vast difference between a flat piece, a beveled edge piece, a quarter-round piece, and a half-round piece. While most trims and moldings are made out of lumber, there are some plastic trims available. They should not be used unless there is other plastic—such as a plastic cover for the top of the piece.

Plywood

You can substitute particle board for plywood in most cases. Particle board is cheaper and heavier than plywood. It is equally strong. With platforms or other uses where appearance does not matter, use particle board. Do not substitute the same thickness.

Hardboard can also be used for plywood. Again, use a lesser thickness just as with particle board. Finishes are limited, though hardboard accepts paint better than particle board.

Fabric

A fabric can be substituted for any other of the same weight and durability. You can substitute plastic for fabric in upholstery jobs, but be sure that the plastic is sturdy enough to withstand the wear.

Fabric can be used as a covering or finish. We recommend that you either put a layer of clear plastic vinyl on top or finish it with a coat of polyurethane varnish, so you can clean the surface. Vinyl-coated papers may also be substituted if they are heavy enough.

COLOR

Light colors will generally make things appear larger; dark colors make items look smaller. Consider the rest of the room before deciding on a color for a particular piece. If you want it to blend in, use a color that is near the wall color and a matte or dull finish. If you want to use the piece as an accent, go to a bright contrasting color.

Don't use too many colors in the same room and beware of almost-matching shades. Blues tend to take on a different shade when seen under incandescent and fluorescent light.

If you use a pattern that matches other patterns in your room, the piece of furniture will blend in. If you use a pattern that contrasts sharply, the piece will stand out. As with color, or actually even more so, be sparing. It takes a very good eye to mix patterns.

DESIGN AND RHYTHM

Design is based on balance, proportion, form or shape, rhythm, and unity. Balance and proportion require two or more aspects of a piece available for comparison. Rhythm can only be applied to a finished sketch or mock-up of the project. Rhythm refers to the movement of an observer's eyes as they view various areas of a painting, sculpture, or piece of furniture.

When you look at a piece of sculpture or at a chair, you look first at the whole object in space. You follow its outlines with your eyes until some feature catches your interest. You concentrate on that feature until you are satisfied and continue on to the others.

Some items may have no particular feature of interest. You lose interest because your eyes have nothing to follow. Other pieces may have so many features that your eyes do not know which to follow first. You give up after a while and feel

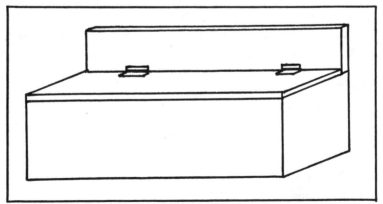

Fig. 4-13. Original bench design.

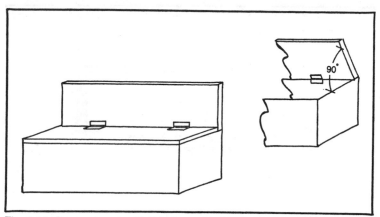

Fig. 4-14. Storage bench with 6 inches added to the backrest height.

vaguely irritated and confused. These are samples of pieces with no rhythm or unpleasant rhythm.

DESIGN AND UNITY

Unity means a oneness of design and blending of features into a single whole. Work with as few types of materials as possible. A completely wooden bench will have a unity of material that draws the plain seat, slatted back, and thick legs together. A cube has unity of form and can have its surfaces painted in two different colors.

ALTERING A STORAGE BENCH DESIGN

A basic idea is that one thing always leads to another, and everything is connected to everything else. A change you make will change both the area or feature you are working with and the entire project.

Here is an example. You are making a storage bench designed to look like Fig. 4-13. You decide to have a backrest that is 6 inches higher. The bench now looks like Fig. 4-14. Then you want a padded seat and back (Fig. 4-15). The bench definitely has taken on another look. Due to the protrusion of the backrest padding, the seat is now narrower and less comfortable. There is an even bigger problem. The storage function of the bench has been hampered as you need to remove the seat cushion or else you have only partial access

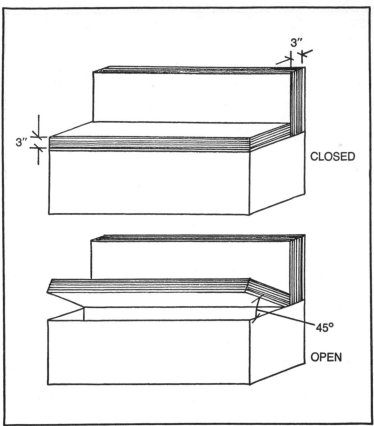

Fig. 4-15. Storage box with a 3-inch thick seat and backrest pads.

to the interior. Yet the bench's storage function was the main feature of the original design.

Form follows function. As you can see with the storage bench, changing some feature interfered with the function. If you decide to add decorative armrests, the bench's function will be hampered further (Figs. 4-16 and 4-17).

You may be able to attach those armrests at the sides of the storage bench, so they won't be in the way when you open the lid. If you change one thing, though, it will affect something else. You will have to measure the space where your storage bench is going to be. You have added ½ foot to its length dimension (Fig. 4-18). When you change the form of a piece, you will likely have to compensate somewhere else.

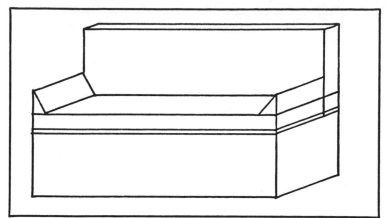

Fig. 4-16. Armrests interfere with opening the storage bench's lid.

FINISHING PROJECTS

The finish of a piece is important. Many finishes take a long time to apply. We will examine some finishing and materials that you may find appropriate.

Paint

Paint makes an ideal finish for lumber, plywood, hardboard, pegboard, or particle board. Painting is fairly quick to do. It leaves a nice surface that is easy to clean.

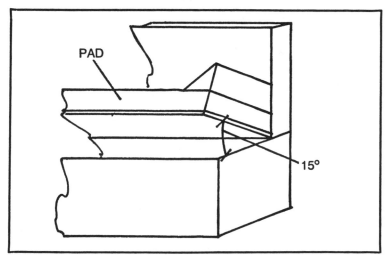

Fig. 4-17. Detail showing the interference.

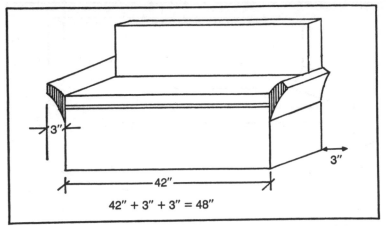

Fig. 4-18. Armrests added to the outside of the box so there won't be any interference with opening the lid. Six extra inches are thus added to the storage bench.

We recommend a good brand of semigloss latex paint for furniture projects. You can use latex enamel, which is harder to find. Acrylic enamels are also available.

If you paint a piece of furniture with acrylic enamel, do not scrub the furniture until the paint has cured. Curing time is about four weeks. Until the paint has cured, it tends to be quite soft and is easily scratched or marred. If the paint is scratched, it will tend to peel along the edges of the scratch. The acrylic enamel does give a nice glossy finish.

Latex semigloss paint dries almost as fast as acrylic enamel or semigloss. It requires only a couple of days for curing. After both paints are cured, latex is much harder than acrylic. Hardness means durability and a good look for your project.

If you want to use acrylic, go over the dried and cured acrylic enamel or semigloss with a coat of clear polyurethane varnish. The varnish will change the color very little. It will provide extra durability for the painted surface.

Surface Preparation

The most important part of any paint job is the preparation of the surface. A well-prepared surface for paint should be smooth, clean, and free of dust.

When you are working with lumber or plywood, light sanding will produce a smooth, clean surface. Wipe the surface with a damp cloth or sponge to remove dust.

Sealer

Sealer is a white or clear liquid that you brush or roll on a surface. Unlike paint it penetrates the wood and seals it permanently. Sealer is a must on particle board. Sealer does a fair smoothing job.

Hardboard and pegboard do not need sealer. The surface on both is hard and dense; there is nothing for the sealer to fill.

When you buy sealer, make sure it is compatible with your paint. Use oil-based sealer for oil-based paint and latex-based sealer for latex paint.

Apply sealer as carefully as you would paint. Runs or drips of sealer will show through. Let it dry thoroughly. If you can, let the sealer dry overnight. The overnight drying time is mandatory on damp days. Avoid painting on damp days if possible.

Brushes, Rollers, and Applicators

Brushes can be difficult to clean. Foam applicators leave no brush marks. They are easy to keep filled with just the right amount of paint, as there are no bristles. The applicators are easy to clean, inexpensive, and light weight.

You may like to use rollers, on larger projects such as shelves. Make sure the paint goes on smoothly.

The Painting Job

After your can of paint has been thoroughly shaken, pry off the lid. Set the can of paint into an aluminum foil pie plate or a plastic-coated paper plate. With a nail and hammer, make a row of holes all around the rim of the paint can. This will allow the paint to drip back down into the can and not run down the outside. Set out another paper plate or pie plate for your brush or applicator.

If you use a roller and pan, line the pan smoothly with some aluminum foil before pouring in the paint. Dampen the brush, applicator, or roller a bit before you dip them in paint.

The paint job can begin if you have prepared the surface as suggested earlier. Apply sealer in the same way as paint is applied.

Apply the paint to the surface as smoothly as you can. Keep your brush, applicator, or roller reasonably full but not dripping. Roll the roller toward you (Fig. 4-19). Dip your brush or applicator only halfway into the can (Fig. 4-20).

Work smoothly. Cover one surface at a time. Start with those surfaces that are hard to get to and finish with the more accessible ones. Do little surfaces such as legs first and finish with large ones. You will thus be less likely to smear paint on you and your surroundings or mar the paint that has already been applied.

On a table, for instance, you will start at the bottom. Turn it upside down. Do the legs and any part of the inside apron of the table that might show. Then turn the table right side up. Your work is now more or less protected by the tabletop. Finish the side or outside apron of the table if it has one. Finally, tackle the tabletop itself (Figs. 4-21 and 4-22). You use the same sequence whether you seal, paint, or varnish. When you use enamel paint, finish your paint job on any larger

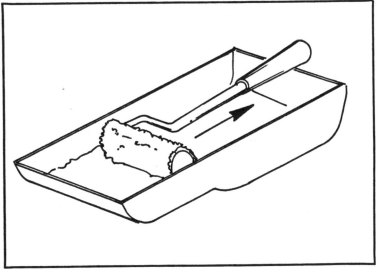

Fig. 4-19. Roll the paint roller toward you.

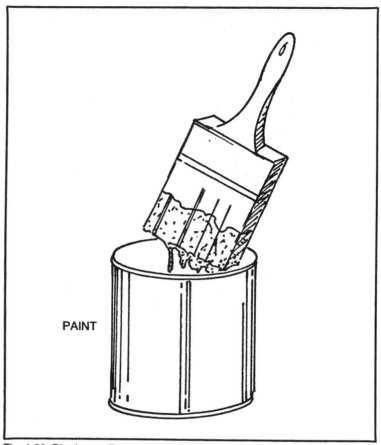

PAINT

Fig. 4-20. Dip the applicator only halfway into the paint.

surface by brushing or rolling the paint in one direction to avoid leaving brush or roller marks. Long strokes are needed.

Using a Drop Cloth

Using a drop cloth when painting is essential. Cover the painting area with your drop cloth. Then cover the drop cloth with two layers of newspaper. Put your project, paint, and applicators on the newspaper and proceed. If your project is small enough to be painted on a table, proceed as indicated earlier, but make your setup on the table instead of the floor.

Remove the top layer of newspaper at clean-up time. Leave the second layer in place for the second coat.

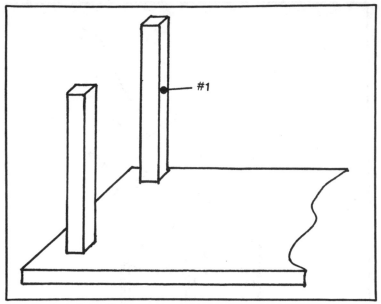
Fig. 4-21. Paint legs first.

If you are going to have three painting sessions—one for sealer, one for the main painting job, and a third for a light second coat and touch-up—you may put down three layers of newspaper. Remove a layer at each cleanup session. When your project is dry, roll up or fold your drop cloth and store it in a plastic garbage bag until your next painting job. Brushes and rollers can also be stored in plastic bags.

Varnishes

You can buy clear and colored varnishes. With varnish you can omit the sealing step, because the varnish acts as a sealer. Colored varnish can seal, color, and finish your surface all in one easy operation.

The colors on the color varnish chart and the result when you apply the varnish to your piece may or may not match. The thickness with which you apply your varnish—how full your brush is—has much to do with the resultant color. If your application is not absolutely even, you will have darker and lighter spots on your piece. These spots are particularly noticeable when you apply the varnish to horizontal and verti-

106

cal surfaces. The varnish tends to run down the vertical surface in a hurry and make the application thinner and the color lighter. A second coat usually will turn out darker than the top or horizontal surface that had one coat, which was darker than the single coat on the vertical surface.

Once your varnish is on, you can't get it off except with varnish remover. Even then the wood will retain a certain amount of stain. The same holds true if you go the stain/ varnish route. Apply your stain first, directly to the wood, and then go over it with clear varnish. You may have the problem of getting the stain on evenly all over. You have a little more control because you can wipe it off with a cloth to lighten it. The stain/varnish route gives you more control, but it does take longer.

Your varnish needs a long time to dry properly. It requires a dust-free and humidity-controlled environment.

The only way to apply varnish well is to dilute it with varnish thinner and build up a finish on your piece using several thin coats. It will take three or four. Don't worry about the bubbles that proliferate as you apply this thinned varnish. They will disappear as the piece dries.

Applying varnish over a nice coat of paint will give you a hard finish. The paint should be completely dry before you apply an even coat of varnish all over the surface. Don't miss a

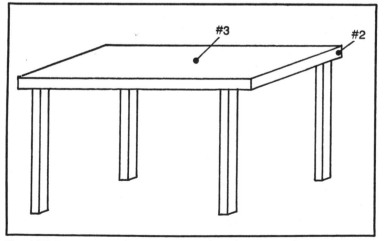

Fig. 4-22. Paint the apron second and the top third.

spot or crack, or the varnish might peel. Make sure to allow enough drying time for the varnish, too.

If your urge to varnish is really pressing, make sure you only try it on lumber. Particle board and hardboard will not accept varnish well.

Stenciling

Stenciling can be used successfully and quickly by anybody. It doesn't require any prior knowledge, skill, or aptitude. Stenciling involves dabbing paint through a cutout onto a surface.

You can buy stencils in arts and crafts shops, or you can make your own by cutting a shape out of some posterboard or stencil paper. When you want to decorate a piece of furniture, it is best to use a simple shape such as a triangle, circle, or square. Decide where the design would look best by moving the stencil around and studying the effect. Cut out shapes exactly like the stencil and move them around (Fig. 4-23). Now you are ready to stencil.

●Make sure that the paint on your table is dry and cured.

●Place your stencil where you want the design. Tape edges down with masking tape. Don't use cellophane tape, because it often sticks too well to the paint and doesn't come off very easily.

●Dip a small round brush into a contrasting shade of paint—of the same kind you are using.

●Dab the paint through the opening onto the table. Fill the entire opening with paint.

●Hold your brush upright at all times, so paint won't seep under the stencil.

●Leave the stencil on until paint is dry to the touch, so you won't smear it when you remove the stencil.

●If you want the same stencil in another location on the same piece, you can move the stencil while the paint is still wet. Remove the tape gently and then raise the stencil with both hands straight up.

●Use two or more stencils for different locations, so you won't have to go through this risky procedure.

●Finish with a thin coat of clear polyurethane varnish.

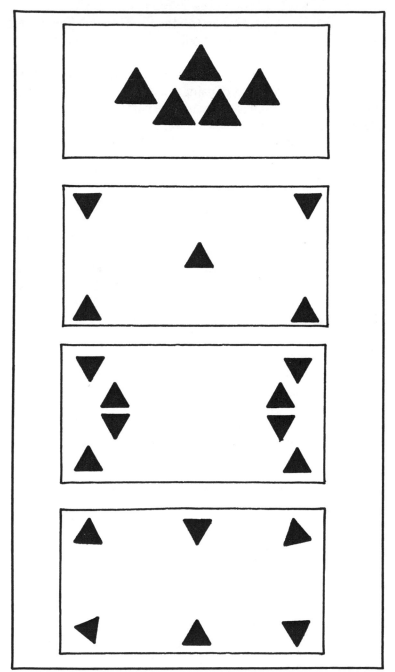

Fig. 4-23. Stencil options.

There is a simpler way to stencil. This will require an equal amount of two different colors of paint and some rubber cement. This method is based on the *resist method*. You paint on one color and dab on your rubber cement through your stencil. Put another coat of paint in a different color over your first one and the rubber cement. The paint won't stick where the rubber cement is. You will have a stencil effect after you remove the rubber cement when the top coat of paint is dry.

Paint Plus Cutouts

You may be familiar with the craft of *decoupage*. This is the space-age variation on the theme. Basically, you cut out shapes from paper or plastic, paste them on a painted surface, and cover with polyurethane (Fig. 4-24).

You can cut shapes from adhesive-backed vinyl and stick them directly on the painted surface without any coating. You might also use one of the other adhesive-backed materials like burlap or felt for an interesting textured effect.

Paint and Plastic Tape

All kinds of neat effects can be accomplished by decorating your painted project with plastic tape. The tape comes in many colors and widths. It has a sticky backing so you simply press it into place (Figs. 4-25 and 4-26).

Be sure, however, to first lay out your design on a piece of paper of the appropriate size. Draw the design lightly on your painted surface using a ruler and a very soft pencil. Then press down the tape (Fig. 4-27).

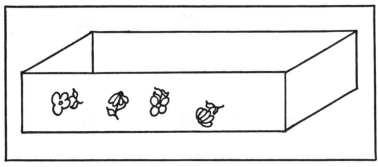

Fig. 4-24. Decorating with paint and cutouts.

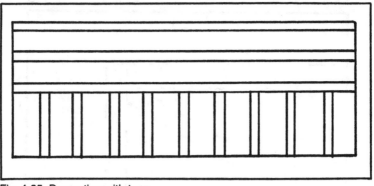

Fig. 4-25. Decorating with tape.

Paint and Pictures

Instead of applying a cutout, you will apply an entire picture to the painted background. You can use anything as long as the paper is not thick. You might use related pictures on different surfaces or use the same kind on all. In any case, pictures and paint are again covered with polyurethane.

The picture is pasted on a painted background and then sealed over with polyurethane. This particular application of the technique usually requires three or four coats of the clear varnish in order to bring the rest of the surface up to the height of the pictures.

Adhesive-Backed Vinyl

Adhesive-backed vinyl comes in all sorts of patterns. There are foil and color combinations that are quite striking.

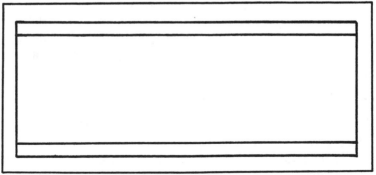

Fig. 4-26. Tape decoration variation.

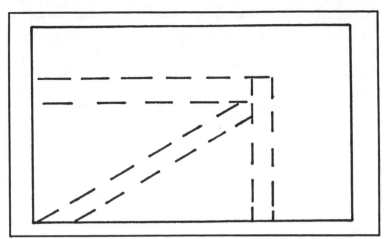

Fig. 4-27. Making soft pencil guidelines for taping.

The "wet look" patterns from a few seasons ago still look quite good, particularly in some of the striking black and whites. Furthermore, the adhesive vinyl can also be bought in a marble pattern. It can imitate brick, cork, various woods, and even tile.

The adhesive-backed vinyl can be bought by the roll—usually about 4 yards long and 18 inches wide. It is also available by the yard. Buy more adhesive-backed vinyl than you need, so you will be able to cover any mistake you may make in cutting. You will then have some extra in case someone punches a hole in the covering or scratches it.

Wallpaper

You can cover your projects with wallpaper. There are some vinyl wallpapers and others that have glued backings. The backing needs to be activated by submerging the paper in water and then smoothing it wet into place. Other kinds of wallpaper can be applied as coverings if you use white glue as an adhesive.

Think of wallpapering a project as "wrapping the project in wallpaper." That will keep you from cutting many small pieces. Wrap tightly and smoothly and cut only when needed. Miter corners and avoid bulk. You can use clear polyurethane. You might try the varnish on a scrap of the paper first, because

112

sometimes the polyurethane either distorts the color or makes it run. If you use vinyl-coated paper, you can forget the polyurethane. If the wallpaper is washable, the same applies.

Cloth and Plastic

Cloth, along with lightweight plastic, can be glued to the surface of projects for a finish. Again, white glue is a good adhesive. Fabric may be sprayed with scotch guard to keep it from spotting. Another way to protect fabric is the use of clear adhesive-backed vinyl. A coat of polyurethane is still another way to keep your cloth fresh and looking new. As with wallpaper, try the varnish on a scrap first to make sure you like the result. Some spray varnishes are available, but we are leary of these sprays and other sprays for several reasons:

● Spraying takes a certain skill. The larger the area sprayed, the greater the chance that you will come up with runs, streaks, bubbles, and other horrors.

● When you spray, hopefully most of the spray lands on the article to be sprayed. Usually some of the spray settles on unwanted places. The only way to use any kind of spray properly, be it varnish or paint, is in a spray booth.

● Spray should not be inhaled. The only way to use a spray is with adequate ventilation such as an exhaust fan.

Plastic is in many ways the ideal covering for projects. Plastic is usually attractive, easy to clean, and quite durable. It can be applied with glue and/or tacks and may even be stapled to the surface if the staples are concealed by some decorative tape (Fig. 4-28).

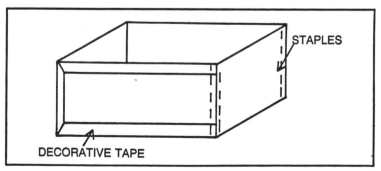

Fig. 4-28. Hiding staples under the tape.

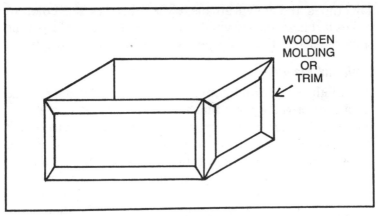

Fig. 4-29. Toy box finished with wooden trim.

Like cloth plastic can be cut according to a pattern and sewn to form a slipcover. This makes fitting a relatively easy matter. Plastic has an unfortunate tendency to stretch. Also, plastic tends to be bulky and, as an all-over covering, might make the project look clumsy.

If you just want to cover a top, mattress, cushions, or seat pads with plastic, go right ahead. There won't be any problem.

When you cover an entire project like a toy box with plastic, do not use the wrap method advised earlier. Instead, cut patterns of each side and apply the plastic to each side separately using glue and/or staples or tacks. Cover any raw

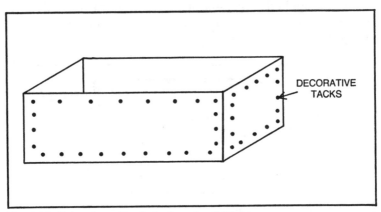

Fig. 4-30. Using decorative tacks for edge finishing.

edges either with a wood trim or some handsome tacks (Figs. 4-29 and 4-30).

Carpeting

While carpeting certainly can't be used for all projects, there are occasions when some carpet tiles can be applied to great advantage. These carpet squares are self-adhesive and make a nice cover for toy boxes and pet beds. They are easy to apply; peel off the backing and stick them in place. Press them down well.

Carpet squares can be cut with utility scissors. Be sure to measure accurately first. Mark the cut on the back of the piece with a soft pencil.

If you have some extra carpeting on hand that you would like to use to match your room, use double-faced tape to put it on. Reinforce with a strategically placed tack or glue. Beware of too thick a nap.

Edges

When covering a project, you often end up with edges that need covering—some simply for aesthetic reasons but most for protection and reinforcement. Usually the material used for the covering job is either too weak and thin or too bulky and clumsy to make an attractive finished edge. Don't despair. Manufacturers have arrived at solutions to these problems.

Wooden Edges. Wooden edges, particularly plywood edges, do not take finishes well and are best hidden from view. Simple molding strips painted a matching or contrasting color will solve this problem easily. Molding and trim comes in many widths, shapes, and patterns.

Vinyl Tape. Wooden edges can be covered with vinyl tapes. You will probably have to settle for contrast as far as color is concerned. We have had no luck in matching paint to vinyl tape or vice versa.

Serrated Tape. Serrated tape, actually designed for table edges, is usually gold or chrome-colored. It goes well with some simple designs and is an easy-to-use, inexpensive substitute for those chrome strips used so much some years ago.

Snap-on Strips. Snap-on plastic edge strips are very easy to apply. They simply snap in place after you have cut them to the exact proportions needed.

CUSTOMIZING RULES

Here are five customizing rules:

- Substitute only those materials that are recommended for substitution and in the way that they are recommended.
- If you make changes in dimensions, follow the guidelines in this chapter.
- Remember that everything is connected to everything else. Compensate for alterations in design.
- Consider the function of the piece and keep it intact.
- Most customizing can be done successfully through the use of different finishes and colors. Make sure that the finishes are appropriate for the materials and the intended use.

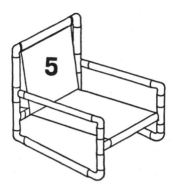

Projects for Pets

Like children, pets need special paraphernalia to be comfortable. Furnishings such as beds, feeding and grooming stations, pet box superstructures, and special setups for confined pets like hamsters and gerbils, are all easy and quick to make.

PET BEDS

While some dogs and cats happily curl up on the floor, most prefer to sleep on a chair, sofa, or bed. This isn't solely because pets want to imitate you, which they do. They also like to have a secure place away from big feet that might step on tender paws, drafts that come in under doors, and vacuum sweeper wands that invade happy hunting dreams.

By providing your pet with his own bed, you can keep him off your good furniture. Once the habit is established your pet will be delighted with his quarters. You can easily include some features that make life easier for you.

Basic Cat Bed

materials and tools

One piece of ½-inch plywood 8×16 inches, two pieces of ½-inch plywood 8×8 inches, two pieces of 1×4 16 inches long, two pieces of 1×4 6½-inches long, ½ yard of quilted upholstery plastic, one small sack of shredded foam, 2½ yards of braid or tape, four small glides, decorative tacks, 3d nails, white glue, 4d nails, ordinary tacks, hammer, tack hammer (optional), sharp large scissors, small scissors, ruler, measuring tape, needle and heavy thread or sewing machine, marking pencil.

shopping

1. Get your lumber cut at the lumberyard. You should be able to get a small leftover piece of plywood.

2. You can use the lowest grade of plywood on both sides, as none of it will show.

3. You will find the plastic on large rolls in the automotive departments of K-Mart stores.

preparation

1. Measure and mark a rectangle 17×18 inches on the back of your plastic.

2. Measure and mark two 9×17-inch rectangles on the plastic (Figs. 5-1 and 5-2).

3. Measure and mark two pieces 14×9 inches and two triangles 5×6×3 inches, which will make the bolsters.

4. Cut out those pieces.

assembly and finishing

1. Set out your 1×4s as shown in Fig. 5-3, with the 1-inch side up, to make a frame for the bed.

2. Nail the frame together with 3d nails.

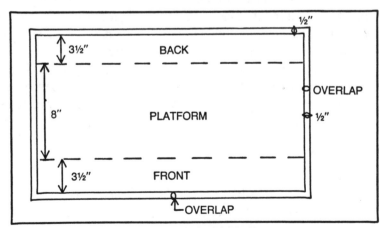

Fig. 5-1. Cutting pattern for the plastic for the platform.

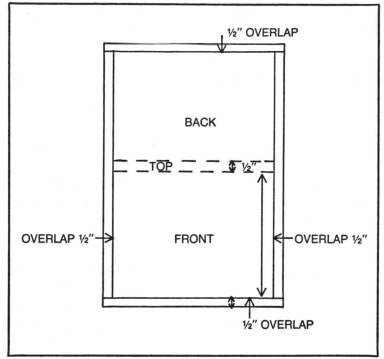

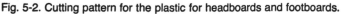

Fig. 5-2. Cutting pattern for the plastic for headboards and footboards.

3. Nail the 8×16 piece of plywood to the top of the frame (Fig. 5-4).

4. Cover the box with a 17×18-inch plastic rectangle. Tack the plastic to the bottom edges on the long sides and to the side of the box on the short edges (Fig. 5-5).

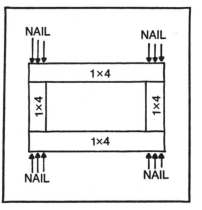

Fig. 5-3. Cat bed, frame detail, 1-inch side up.

119

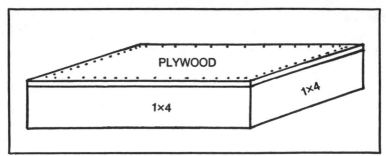

Fig. 5-4. Cat bed base.

5. Cover 8×8-inch plywood pieces with plastic as shown in Fig. 5-6. Tack the plastic at the bottom edge and use glue on the side edges.

6. Cover edges with tape and decorative tacks (Fig. 5-7).

7. Attach side pieces to platform with 4d nails (Fig. 5-6).

8. Cover nails with decorative tape and tacks.

9. Fold plastic for bolsters as shown in Fig. 5-8. Sew together around the triangle, leaving the 5-inch side open on one end.

10. Repeat with the other bolster pieces.

11. Stuff bolsters with shredded foam. Sew the open edges (Fig. 5-9).

12. Attach glides, one to each corner, at the bottom of the platform.

13. Put bolsters on the cat bed. The project is finished (Fig. 5-10).

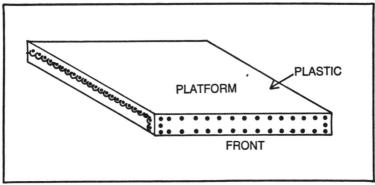

Fig. 5-5. Covering the base with plastic.

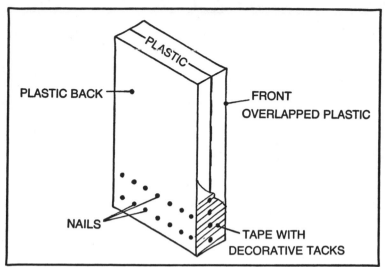

Fig. 5-6. Trimming edges with tape and decorative tacks.

Three-Sided Cat Bed

This variation of the basic cat bed boasts a backrest, which will protect your walls from ambitious claws. Carpeting is used for the cover.

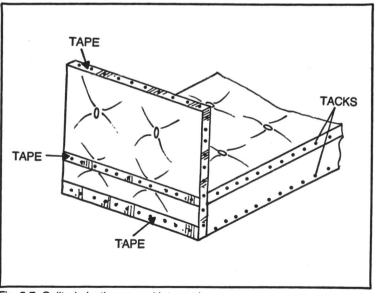

Fig. 5-7. Quilted plastic cover with tape trim.

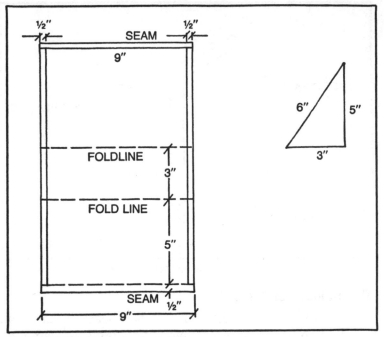

Fig. 5-8. Fabric pattern for the bolster.

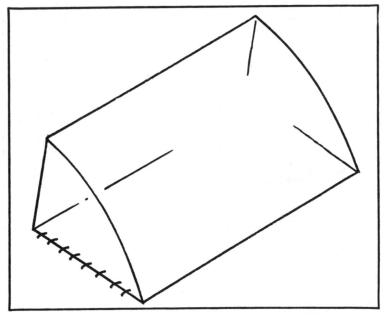

Fig. 5-9. Bolster for the cat bed.

122

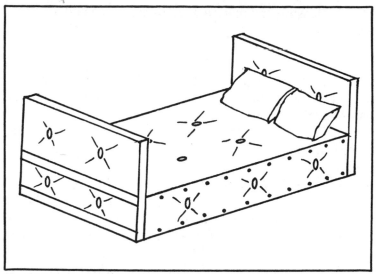

Fig. 5-10. Basic cat bed complete with bolsters.

materials and trim

Two pieces of plywood 16×8 inches, two pieces 8×8 inches, two pieces of 1×4 16 inches long, two pieces of 1×4 6½ inches long, two running feet of indoor/outdoor carpeting 6 feet wide, six ½-inch-long small corner braces and screws to match, 4d and 3d casing nails, latex-based adhesive, carpet tacks, hammer, tack hammer (optional), heavy-duty scissors, ruler, measuring tape, small brush for applying glue, marking pencil, drill.

shopping

1. Have lumber cut to specifications at a lumberyard. You can use a very low grade plywood, because the wood will be covered with the carpeting.

2. You can buy the carpeting off the roll or look for leftovers at a carpet shop. You can substitute other carpeting for the indoor/outdoor type, but make sure that the nails are long enough to go through the carpeting (twice) plus the plywood and the 1×4.

3. Buy the rug adhesive at the carpet store.

preparation

1. On the carpet backing, measure two rectangles 17×9 inches. Mark out with a ruler.

2. Measure and mark a 17×16-inch piece and a 17×18-inch piece.

3. Cut pieces with your utility scissors.

4. On the 8×8 plywood pieces, using your corner braces for a guide, mark the position for the screw holes. Do this with the center of the brace set in ½ inch from the edge of the plywood (Fig. 5-11).

5. On one of your 16×8-inch pieces, mark the corner braces with the center of the brace even with the short edge (Fig. 5-12).

assembly and finishing

1. Lay out your 1×4 as in Fig. 5-3, with the 1-inch side up, and nail together with 3d casing nails.

2. Nail one of the 16×8-inch pieces, the one without markings on top of the 1×4 framing, as in Fig. 5-4.

3. Drill starter holes for screws as marked in the corner braces.

4. Nail sides to the back as in Fig. 5-13.

5. Reinforce joints with corner braces as in Fig. 5-14.

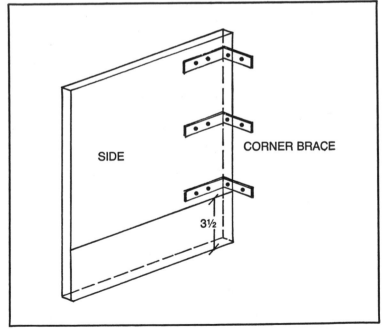

Fig. 5-11. Beginning to mark for corner braces.

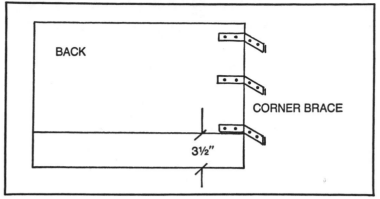
Fig. 5-12. Marking for corner braces.

6. Cover the platform with carpeting, using glue on the surface and tacks on the edges as in Fig. 5-5. Omit the tacks along the front and back edges and tack underneath to the 1×4 frame on the 1-inch edge.

7. Cover the back panel of the back/side framing with carpeting, using glue on the flat surfaces and tacking underneath.

8. On side panels, mark and cut carpeting (Fig. 5-15). Be sure to have both panels facing down as you mark and cut.

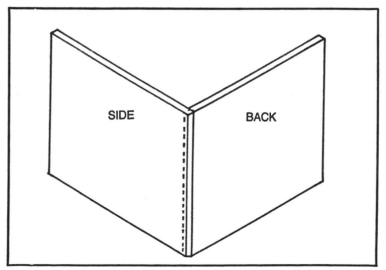
Fig. 5-13. Attaching the back to the sides with nails.

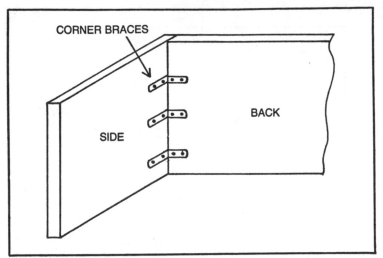

Fig. 5-14. Attaching the back panel to the sides with corner braces.

You will be needing a right and a left panel, which will be mirror images of each other.

9. Glue carpeting to the side panels with the cutouts on the inside of the frame and adjoining the back panel.

10. In the back of the frame, wrap the carpet extension around the exposed edge of the side piece. Glue and reinforce with a few tacks.

11. In front, wrap the carpeting around the front edge. Glue and tack in place.

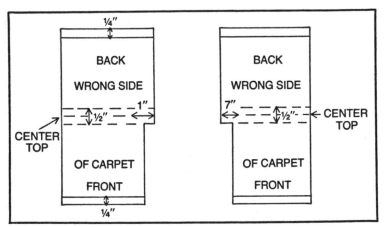

Fig. 5-15. Pattern for cutting carpet for the sides.

12. Nail the side and back frame to the platform with 4d casing nails as shown in Fig. 5-16. Attach glides to the corners of the platform.

13. Invite your cat to try out the new snuggling place (Fig. 5-17).

Canopy Bed

The canopy is a variation on the basic cat bed theme. It is somewhat more ambitious in terms of work and time investment.

materials and tools

One piece of ½-inch plywood 16×8 inches, one piece of ½-inch plywood 17½×9½, two pieces of 1×4 16 inches long, two pieces of 1×4 6½ inches long, four pieces of 1×1 12 inches long, 1 1/3 yards of smooth-surfaced sturdy fabric, one middle-sized sack of shredded foam or a 16×8-inch foam pad 2 inches thick, 3 yards of narrow Velcro fastening tape, 3d and 4d casing nails, four small glides, small can of paint, sandpaper, ribbon or cord, four decorative tacks, hammer, ruler, marking pencil, measuring tape, crayon or dress-

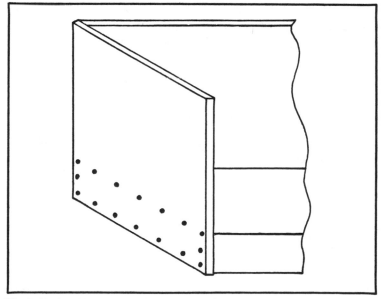

Fig. 5-16. Attaching the back and sides to the platform.

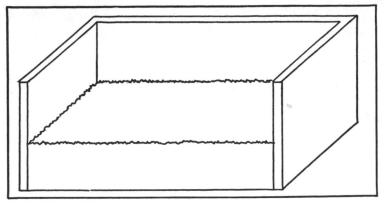
Fig. 5-17. The three-sided carpet-covered cat bed.

dressmaker's pencil, scissors, needle and thread or sewing machine, small paint brush.

shopping

1. Have lumber precut at the lumberyard. If you happen to have some scrap of plywood that would be large enough for the canopy but thinner than ½ inch, use it.

2. When you buy your fabric, match it to your own bed cover and/or draperies. Make sure the fabric is firmly woven.

3. Instead of getting the Velcro fastening tape in one long band, you may get packages that have the short pieces. Use those at 1-inch intervals all around the top.

preparation

1. Lay out the fabric as shown in Figs. 5-18 and 5-19 and cut pieces.

CANOPY 16×24		COVER 16×24			□ = 4" D = DRAPERY
9×9 D	9×9 D	9×9 D	9×9 D		1¼" YD
INNER PAD COVER 20 × 20		PAD COVER 20 × 20			

Fig. 5-18. Fabric layout.

128

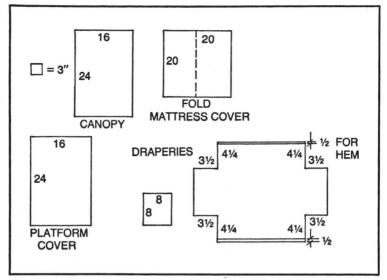

Fig. 5-19. Patterns for cutting draperies, canopy, mattress cover, and platform cover and details for the platform cover.

2. Mark on the back to indicate the pieces. Use a light-colored crayon or your dressmaker's marking pencil. Make sure that the crayon, if that is what you are using, doesn't show through to the right side. Try it on a scrap first.

3. Cut out pieces. No marking on the lumber is necessary.

assembly

1. Set out your 1×4s as shown in Fig. 5-3 with the 1-inch side up to form the bed frame.

2. Nail the framing together with 3d nails.

3. Nail your 8×16 piece of plywood on top of your frame, again using your 3d nails (Fig. 5-4).

4. Attach one of your 1×1s, upright, at each corner of your platform as shown in Fig. 5-20. Use 4d casing nails.

5. Nail the remaining plywood piece to the top of the 1×1s.

6. Cut your 16×24-inch fabric piece in at the corners.

7. Turn up the edges and narrowly hem all the way around the piece. Reinforce the corners by stitching across them twice if you are sewing by machine (Fig. 5-21) or whipping over them if you sew by hand (Fig. 5-21).

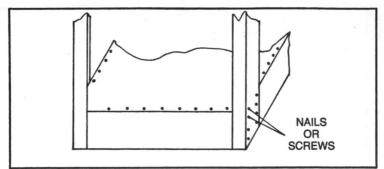

Fig. 5-20. Fastening 1×1s to the platform.

8. Hem narrowly all around the other large piece—your canopy.

9. Narrowly hem all edges of your drapery pieces.

10. Fold one of your 20×20-inch pieces in half, wrong side out, and sew it along one long side and one short side (Fig. 5-22).

11. Repeat with the other piece.

12. Insert shredded foam or foam pad. Sew closed as in Fig. 5-22B.

13. Sew a strip of Velcro fastening tape to the open edge of the outer cover or, if you are using the packages, sew several pieces of Velcro fastening tape to the edge (Fig. 5-22C).

14. Put the outer cover over the pad and fasten the open edge.

finishing

1. Lightly sand the entire wooden structure.

2. Paint the 1×1s and the underneath surface of the canopy. Use two coats of latex paint. If you like, paint the rest of the structure, too. Let it dry well.

3. Attach glides, one to each corner, to the bottom of the bed.

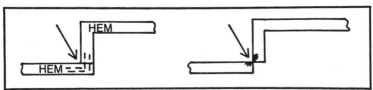

Fig. 5-21. Construction details for the canopy.

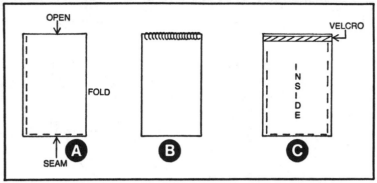

Fig. 5-22. Mattress construction details.

4. Glue a strip of Velcro fastening tape along the top front and back edges and the platform front and back edges, so the strips are even with the front edge.

5. Drape your canopy piece over the top and center it. Mark with pins where the canopy covers the Velcro fastening tape.

6. Repeat the procedure with the platform cover and platform.

7. Attach an 8-inch strip of Velcro fastening tape 4 inches on each side of the corner on top along the ½-inch edge of the plywood (Fig. 5-23).

8. Sew or glue Velcro fastening tape to the top end of each drapery piece on the wrong side of the fabric.

9. Sew and/or glue Velcro fastening tape to the pin-

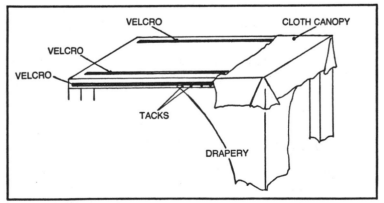

Fig. 5-23. Canopy and drapery fastening.

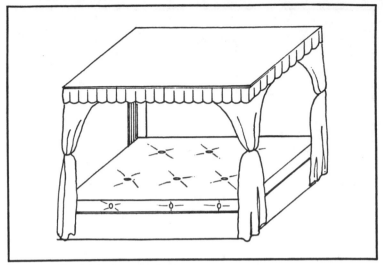

Fig. 5-24. The finished canopy bed.

marked line along the long edges of the canopy and platform covers.

10. Cut the cord into four equal parts.

11. Put the platform cover on. Press down on the Velcro fastening tape so it will seal.

12. Put the cover over the canopy. Press down on the Velcro fastening tape.

13. Fold back the canopy and attach draperies to edges. Press the Velcro fastening tape down.

14. Loop the cord around the drapery and fasten it to a 1×1 with a decorative tack. Repeat on all four sides.

15. Put a mattress on the bed and invite your pet to relax (Fig. 5-24).

We will interrupt our discussion of cat furnishings to show you how to adapt the aforementioned bed designs to fit dogs ranging from Pekingeses to Dobermans. A Pekingese dog can curl up in a regular cat bed.

Three-Walled Bed for Small Dogs

materials and tools

One piece of ½-inch-thick plywood 18×16 inches, one piece of plywood 18×10 inches, two pieces of plywood 16×10 inches, two pieces of 1×4 18 inches long, two pieces of 1×4 14½ inches long, 1 2/3 yards of 60-inch-wide plastic (quilted or not), small corner braces, 3d and 4d nails, glue, braid, decorative tacks, small tacks, small screws to fit corner braces, medium glides, hammer, tack hammer (optional), drill (optional), marking pencil, ruler, measuring tape, heavy scissors, straightedge, screwdriver.

shopping

1. Follow the instructions given for the three-sided cat bed. Make allowances for the larger dimensions when you order the lumber cut. You can use low-grade plywood, because it will be covered with plastic.

2. Use upholstery weight plastic for the covering. You will find it on large rolls in the upholstery departments of discount stores. The quilted kind is available in the automotive departments of discount stores.

preparation

1. On the back of the plastic, mark off the pieces with your marking pencil and straightedge. Follow the layout given in Fig. 5-25. Mark each piece on the backing, so you can easily identify it later.

2. Cut out the pieces with heavy scissors.

3. On your 16×10-inch pieces, mark the position for the screwholes for the corner braces, using the corner brace for a guide. Be sure to have the center of the brace set in ½ inch from the edge of the plywood (Fig. 5-11).

4. On your 10×18-inch piece, make the corner brace screws. Hold the center of the brace even with the short edge (Fig. 5-12).

assembly and finishing

1. Lay out your 1×4s as in Fig. 5-3, with the 1-inch side up, and nail them together using 3d nails. If your dog is quite heavy and/or bouncy, you might want to reinforce the corner with corner braces. Simply mark the position for the screws by holding your corner brace in position in the corner. Drill a starting hole and fasten the screws.

2. Nail an 18×16-inch piece of plywood on top of the frame to form the box.

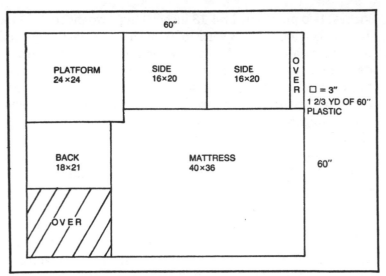

Fig. 5-25. Layout for plastic.

3. Make starter holes for screws on the back and side pieces as marked.

4. Nail pieces together, sides to back, as shown in Fig. 5-13.

5. Reinforce the joints with your corner braces (Fig. 5-14).

6. Cover the platform with plastic, starting at the bottom edge of one long side. Tack in place with carpet tacks. Center the plastic.

7. Glue plastic to the platform front, top, and back surfaces. Leave the sides open for the moment.

8. Pull taut and tack again underneath the rear 1×4 as you did in the front.

9. Miter the corners. This can be done by cutting into the corner diagonally and folding the front edge around the corner. Trim, glue, and reinforce with one tack. Trim the side edge and tack down with decorative tacks after you have glued the side pieces. Repeat for all corners.

10. To cover the back panel, glue plastic to the back. Wrap it around smoothly and tack it at the bottom.

11. For the sides, you will have to mark and cut the plastic. Make allowances only for the size of the piece—that

is you will be trimming the same amount. Only your piece will be longer.

12. Make sure that both of your pieces face right side down when you cut, because you will be needing mirror images.

13. Glue and tack pieces in place.

14. Using glue and decorative tacks, put braid in the inner corners of back framing, along the outer corners of back framing, and along the front edges of the framing.

15. Attach the frame to the platform using 4d nails.

16. Cover the nails with braid and decorative tacks.

17. For the mattress, fold the plastic piece in half and sew as shown in Fig. 5-22, using shredded foam for a filler. Remember to make an inner liner for the foam. You can use a plastic garbage bag.

18. Gather up your pet's toys and invite him in (Fig. 5-26).

Three-Walled Bed for Medium-Sized Dogs
materials and tools
One piece of ½-inch-thick plywood 22×16 inches, one piece of plywood 22×10 inches, two pieces of plywood 10×16 inches, two pieces of 1×4 22 inches long, three pieces of 1×4 14½ inches long, 2 yards of plastic, one medium sack of shredded foam, corner braces, 3d and 4d nails, glue, braid, decorative and small tacks, small screws to fit the corner braces, medium glides. Tools are the same as for the three-walled bed for small dogs.

shopping
Same as for smaller dog bed.

preparation
1. Mark your 1×4s for corner braces. Hold your corner of the corner brace ¾-inch in from the short edge on the long pieces. Hold the corner flush with the edge on the short pieces.

2. Measure and mark the center point on both long pieces of 1×4. Draw a line at the points perpendicular to the long edges. Draw lines on both sides of these lines ⅜ inch away from the center line and parallel with it.

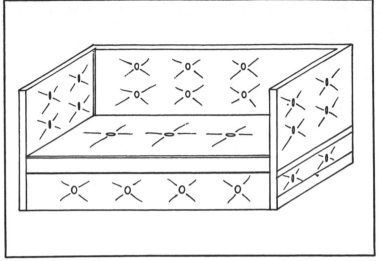

Fig. 5-26. Three-walled dog bed.

3. Lay the center of your corner brace on the outer line, ½ inch from the top mark for screws. Repeat on the other outer line, but set the brace 1 inch lower. Repeat on the other 1×4.

4. On your remaining short 1×4, use the short end as a corner mark for screws ½ inch down from the top on each end of the 1×4.

5. On the other side of the 1×4 (4-inch face), again using the short edge for a guide as a corner, mark 1½ inches down from the top edge for screws.

6. Follow other preparation instructions as given for the small three-walled dog bed.

assembly

1. Lay out your 1×4s as in Fig. 5-3, with the 1-inch side up, and be careful to get the markings for the corner braces lined up. Put the third 1×4 in the center between the lines. Nail in place.

2. Reinforce corners with corner braces all around the frame. Anchor the center 1×4 with four corner braces (Fig. 5-27).

3. Proceed through the remaining steps as for the small dog bed.

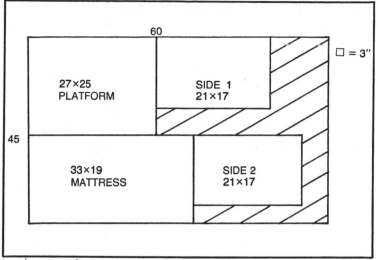

Fig. 5-27. Layout for plastic of the basic dog bed for small breeds.

Three-Walled Bed for Larger Dogs

materials and tools

One piece of ½-inch-thick plywood 25×16 inches, one piece of plywood 25×10 inches, two pieces of plywood 16×10 inches, two pieces of 1×4 25 inches long, four pieces of 1×4 14½ inches long, 2 1/3 yards of 60-inch plastic, one large sack of shredded foam, corner braces, 3d and 4d nails, glue, braid, decorative and small tacks, small screws to fit the corner braces, medium glides. Tools are the same as for the three-walled bed for small dogs.

shopping

Same as for small and medium-size dog beds.

preparation

1. Mark the fourth short 1×4 in the same manner as the third.

2. Mark long 1×4s 8 inches in from each end. Mark for corner braces.

assembly

1. Follow step 1 under assembly for the medium-size dog bed. Set in your two extra 1×4s at the 8-inch markings. Nail together and reinforce all joints with corner braces.

2. Other steps are the same as for the small dog bed.

Variations on the Three-Walled Dog Bed

1. Instead of using plastic coverings, substitute indoor/outdoor carpeting. Because carpeting can be bought in 6-foot widths, you can use the same yardage requirements as given for the plastic. You can omit the braid and the decorative tacks or use only decorative tacks.

2. Instead of using the shredded foam for a mattress, you may substitute a foam pad, 1 or 2 inches thick, in the required sizes—17×15 inches, 21×15 inches, or 24×15 inches.

3. Use a small washable rug or cushion instead of the mattress.

Basic Dog Bed

This is an adaptation of the basic cat bed. The difference in construction is the reinforcement of the frame. We have accompanied the text with a layout for each size in which the adjustments and allowances for overlap are already included.

You can decide between making a separate mattress or bolsters. Another decision is whether to use shredded foam in the mattress or go with a 1 or 2-inch foam pad cut ½ inch smaller all around than the platform. If your platform is 18×16 inches, your pad would be 17×15 inches or 17½×15½ inches at most. For your 16×22-inch platform, the pad would measure 15×21 inches.

Another alternative for stuffing a mattress is a folded quilt or several thick bath towels. You can open up the cover, take out the quilt or towels and wash them, turn the cover inside out to air it, and then put the mattress back together. You can air the foam pad (don't put it in direct sunlight), but washing is taboo. You can also replace the shredded foam with a new bag.

Basic Dog Bed for Tiny Breeds

Follow directions for the basic cat bed.

Basic Dog Bed for Small Breeds
materials and tools

One piece of ½-inch-thick plywood 18×16 inches, two pieces of plywood 10×16 inches, two pieces of 1×4 18 inches long, two pieces of 1×4 14½ inches long, 1 2/3 yards of 60-inch-wide plastic (quilted or not), small corner braces, 3d and 4d nails, glue, braid, decorative and small tacks, small screws to fit corner braces, four medium glides. Tools are the same as for the cat bed.

shopping

Same as for the cat bed.

preparation

Same as for the cat bed. Follow Fig. 5-23 for cover layout.

assembly and finishing

Same as for the basic cat bed.

Basic Dog Bed for Medium Breeds

materials and tools

One piece of ½-inch-thick plywood 22×16 inches, two pieces of plywood 10×16 inches, two pieces of 1×4 22 inches long, three pieces of 1×4 14½ inches long, 1 2/3 yards plastic 60 inches wide or 6-foot-wide carpeting, corner braces, 3d and 4d nails, glue, braid, decorative and carpet tacks, small screws to fit corner braces, medium glides. Tools are the same as for the basic cat bed.

shopping

Same as for the basic cat bed.

preparation

1. Measure and mark plastic or carpeting following the layout given in Fig. 5-28.

2. Mark pieces on the back to identify and cut out.

3. Mark your 1×4s for corner braces: on the long ones draw a line ¾ inch from the short edge on each end. Line up your corner brace on the line, so the corner of the brace is even with the line. Mark the holes on the wood. For the short ones, line up the corner of the corner brace even with the edge and mark the holes. The brace should be ½ inch down from the top edge.

4. Measure the center on your long 1×4s and mark with a perpendicular line. Mark again ⅜ inch to either side of that line and draw two more lines. Repeat for the other long 1×4.

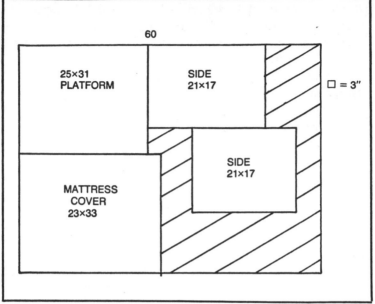

Fig. 5-28 Layout for plastic of the basic dog bed for medium breeds.

5. Line up the center of the corner brace with a line on the right of center. Mark for holes, holding the brace ½ inch from the top of the 1×4.

6. Line up the brace with a line to the left of center, but hold the brace down 1½ inches from the top of the 1×4. Repeat on the other 1×4.

7. Mark the remaining short 1×4 with a corner brace. Hold the corner flush with the edge. Mark on the side of the 1×4 on each end ½ inch from the top and the other on both ends 1½ inches from the top (Fig. 5-29).

assembly

1. Lay out your 1×4s as shown in Fig. 5-30 with the 1-inch side up. Line up the markings of the corner braces.

2. Put the third short 1×4 in the center at markings. Line up all the screw hole marks on the short and long pieces.

3. Nail in place.

4. Reinforce all corners with the corner braces. Make starter holes in markings if you haven't done so during preparation. Then attach the corner braces where marked (Fig. 5-29).

140

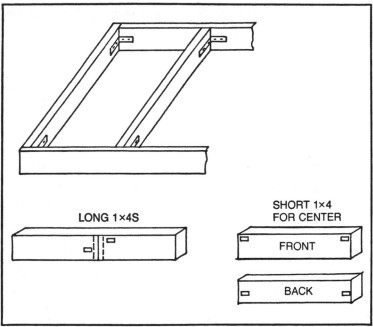

Fig. 5-29. Platform frame—modification details.

Proceed through the remaining assembly steps as given for the basic cat bed.

Basic Dog Bed for Larger Breeds
materials and tools

One piece of ½-inch-thick plywood 25×16 inches, two pieces of ¼-inch-thick plywood 16×10 inches, two pieces of 1×4 25 inches long, four pieces of 1×4 14½ inches long, 2 1/3 yards of 60-inch plastic or 6-foot carpeting, corner braces, 3d and 4d nails, glue, braid and decorative tacks (optional if you use carpeting), carpet tacks, small screws for corner braces,

Fig. 5-30. Layout for 1×4s for frame modifications.

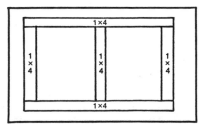

four medium large glides. Tools are the same as for the basic cat bed—plus a drill.

shopping

Same as for the basic cat bed.

preparation

1. Mark the ends of your 1×4 for corner braces. Hold the corner of your corner brace ¾ inch in from the short edge on the long pieces. Mark this with a line before you do the actual marking for holes.

2. Mark the short pieces, all four of them, at each end. Place the corner of your corner brace flush with the edge— the short one. Place all markings ½ inch from the top edge.

3. On two of your 1×4s (the short ones), mark the other side of each end. Place the markings 1 inch lower than the ones on the reverse side.

4. Mark your long 1×4s 8 inches in from each edge. Draw a perpendicular line and draw a parallel perpendicular one ¾ inch toward the center.

5. Using lines as corners, mark for the screws for corner braces. Place the outer ones ½ inch down from the upper edge and the inner ones 1½ inches.

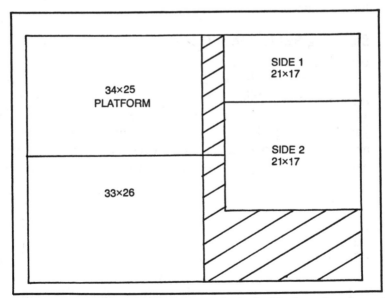

Fig. 5-31. Layout of the covering for the basic dog bed for larger breeds.

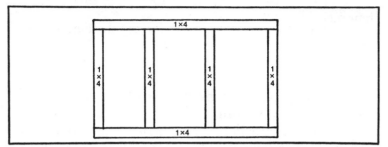
Fig. 5-32. Layout of 1×4s for the framing of the basic dog bed for larger breeds.

6. Lay out your plastic as in Fig. 5-31. Mark on the reverse side to identify pieces and cut.

7. Follow other preparation directions as given for the basic cat bed.

assembly and finishing

1. Lay out your 1×4 as in Fig. 5-31, 1-inch edge up, using the short 1×4s that are marked only on one side. Be careful to line up the markings for your corner braces.

2. Set in your other 1×4s at the markings, again being careful to get the markings to match (Fig. 5-32).

3. Nail framing together starting with the two center 1×4s and following up with the outer two 1×4s.

4. Reinforce each joint with a corner brace placed at the marked places.

5. Follow directions for the basic cat bed.

6. Attach medium-large glides—one to each corner.

Basic Dog Bed for Super Breeds

materials and tools

One piece of ¾-inch-thick plywood 28×18 inches, two pieces of ¾-inch-thick plywood 18×12 inches, two pieces of 2×4 28 inches long, 3 pieces of 2×4 16½ inches long, 2 2/3 yards of 60-inch plastic or 6-foot-wide carpeting medium-sized corner braces with matching screws, ¾-inch-wide decorative braid (optional for carpeting), decorative and plain carpet tacks, glue, four large glides, 4d and 5d nails. Tools are the same as for the basic cat bed, but the drill is required.

shopping

Same as for the basic cat bed.

preparation

1. Follow instructions given for the medium dog bed. Substitute 2×4s for 1×4s in steps 1 through 7.

2. Follow the layout for marking plastic and carpeting (Fig. 5-33).

3. Follow directions given for the basic cat bed.

assembly and finishing

1. Follow instructions for assembling the platform of the medium dog bed. Substitute 2×4s for 1×4s in steps 1 through 5.

2. Follow instructions for assembling and finishing the basic cat bed. Attach large glides to the corners of the platform.

Super Dog Corner Bed

materials and tools

One piece of ¾-inch-thick plywood 28×28 inches, two pieces of ¾-inch-thick plywood 28×14 inches, two pieces of 2×4 28 inches long, three pieces of 2×4 26½ inches long, medium-sized corner braces, 4d nails, screws, medium and fine sandpaper, glides, sealer, small can of paint, polyurethane varnish, ¾-inch trim 23 feet long, ¾ yard of 60-inch plastic or carpeting, 27×27 2-inch foam pad, 2d finishing nails, hammer, screwdriver, straightedge, ruler, marking pencil, drill for starter holes, paintbrushes (foam), miter box (optional).

shopping

1. Buy plywood with a good face on one side, perhaps B/D as you are not going to cover it.

2. Select the trim you like best. It can be flat, rounded, or have a carved pattern.

3. You can have the trim cut to size at the lumberyard along with your plywood, but it really isn't necessary.

4. Buy deck paint if it is available. If not, use a good grade of latex semigloss or enamel.

5. The polyurethane varnish needs to be clear, so the color of your paint will remain the same.

preparation

1. Mark your 2×4s for corner braces in the same manner

144

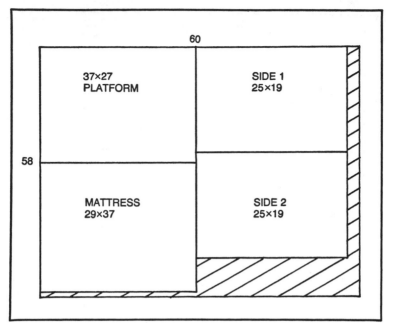

Fig. 5-33. Cutting layout for plastic or carpet.

as for the medium basic dog bed. Follow steps 3 through 7 for preparation. Substitute 2×4s for 1×4s.

2. Mark and cut plastic for the mattress.

3. Measure your trim into eight 28-foot-long pieces and three pieces 14 inches long. Do not cut yet.

assembly

1. Follow steps 1-5 in the assembly of the medium dog bed to construct a platform.

2. Nail your 14×28-inch pieces to two sides of the platform (Fig. 5-34).

3. Cut some of your 28-inch trim pieces. Nail them along the edges as shown in Fig. 5-34 using finishing nails.

4. Fit other trim pieces to the remaining raw edges. Cut and nail in place with the small finishing nails.

finishing

1. Sand the entire structure. Attach glides—one to each corner.

2. Seal the entire structure and let it dry.

3. Paint the structure and let it dry. Two coats are best.

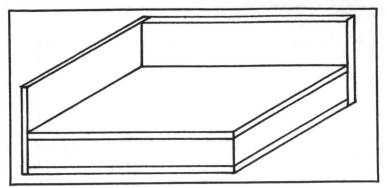

Fig. 5-34. Super dog corner bed.

4. Seal with polyurethane varnish. Let it dry at least 24 hours.

5. Sew mattress pieces together, leaving one side open.

6. Insert the pad.

7. Sew it closed. The bed is finished (Fig. 5-34).

Super Dog Snuggery

materials and tools

One piece of ¾-inch-thick plywood 30×25 inches, one piece ¾-inch-thick plywood 30×15 inches, two pieces ¾-inch-thick plywood 25×15 inches, two pieces of ¾-inch-thick plywood 15×8 inches, two pieces of 2×4 30 inches long, three pieces of 2×4 23½ inches long, corner braces, 4d nails and 2d finishing nails, screws for corner braces, 12 feet of flat trim ¾ inch wide, 3 feet of outside corner trim ¾ inch wide, 2-inch-thick foam pad 24×29, four large glides, glue, 2 2/3 yards of plastic or carpet, masking tape, decorative and carpet tacks, paint, polyurethane varnish, sealer, sandpaper, hammer, drill, screwdriver, ruler, marking pencil, measuring tape, scissors, saw, paintbrushes.

shopping

1. Get plywood with one good side—as in B/D.

2. Have the man at the lumberyard cut the pieces for you.

3. Cut the trim yourself. It will be more exact.

preparation

1. Measure and mark plastic following the layout in Fig. 5-35.

146

2. Identify pieces by marking on the back; cut them.

3. Mark your 2×4s for corner braces following the preparation instructions (steps 3 through 7) given for the medium dog bed. Substitute 2×4s for 1×4s.

4. Measure your trim into two 25-inch-long pieces, two 8-inch-long pieces, 1 30-inch-long piece, one 14-inch-long piece, and two 15-inch long pieces. Don't cut them yet.

assembly and finishing

1. Assemble 2×4 framing following steps 1 through 5 given for the medium dog bed frame. Substitute 2×4s for 1×4s.

2. Cover platform with the 39×27-inch piece of plastic. Tack the front edge to the underneath side. Glue on flat surfaces. Secure with small tacks along the remaining edges. Clip corners.

3. Cover the pieces for the back, sides, and front with plastic or carpeting. Start on the underneath edge and tack that edge in place. Glue the plastic along one surface, bringing it over the top and ½ inch down on the other side. Hold with a few tacks on top. Cover the side edges also. See Figs. 5-36 through 5-38.

4. Attach the 30×15-inch piece to the 25×15-inch pieces along the short edges. Nail in place.

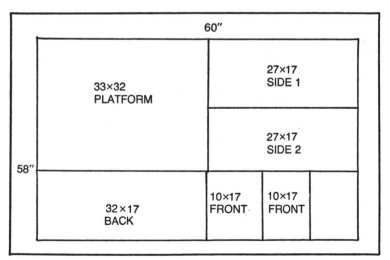

Fig. 5-35. Layout for plastic for super dog snuggery.

147

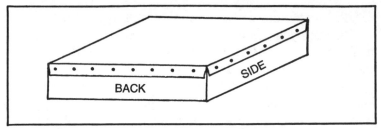

Fig. 5-36. Covering platform detail—side and back.

5. Attach the remaining two short pieces to the sides. Nail in place (Fig. 5-39).

6. Attach the entire frame to the platform. Nail along the lines indicated in Fig. 5-39.

7. Cut trim to fit. Miter corners if desired.

8. Attach trim along the top edges of the sides and back and along the front edges as shown in Fig. 5-39.

9. Cut corner trim to fit and nail to outside of corners.

10. If desired, reinforce and decorate top edges and inside corners with decorative tacks.

11. Cover top edges with masking tape. Sand the structure.

12. Paint the outside of the structure including trim. Let it dry and repeat with a second coat.

13. If desired, cover with a coat of clear polyurethane varnish.

14. For the mattress, fold plastic or carpeting in half lengthwise. Sew one short side and the long side closed. You can use your machine if the carpeting isn't too thick. If you have trouble with your machine, sew it by hand, overcasting the edge from the inside. Turn it right side out.

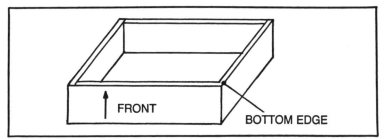

Fig. 5-37. Covering platform detail—front.

148

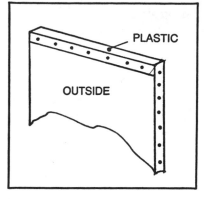

Fig. 5-38. Covering the back, sides, and front pieces with plastic.

PLASTIC

OUTSIDE

15. Insert the mattress pad and sew the open edge closed.

REST AND RECREATION PROJECTS FOR CATS

Here are some designs for rest and recreation furnishings for cats. Hopefully your cats will enjoy these projects.

Triangular Lair

This can be used by small dogs and cats.

materials and tools

Three pieces of ½-inch plywood 12×18 inches, two pieces of short napped carpeting 37×18 inches, wide aluminum tape, tacks, carpet adhesive or double-faced tape, ruler, scissors, small hammer.

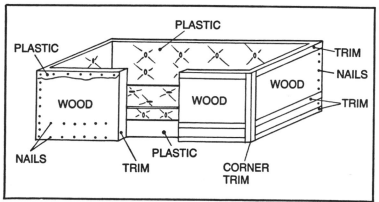

Fig. 5-39. Super dog snuggery.

shopping

1. Have the man at the lumberyard cut the plywood to size; C/D or D/D will do.

2. Have the man at the carpet shop cut the carpeting if possible.

3. You can use a different color for the inside.

assembly and finishing

1. Lay out your plywood panels side by side (Fig. 5-40).

2. Cut a 4-inch strip of the aluminum tape and tape across joints at 2-inch intervals. Then cover the joints with two long strips of aluminum tape (Fig. 5-40).

3. Glue one of the pieces of carpeting over the plywood and tape (Fig. 5-41).

4. Form a three-sided pyramid out of your carpet-covered plywood, with the carpeting on the inside. Tape the joint together with aluminum tape as before.

5. Starting in the center of one of the panels, glue the carpeting to the structure, ending in the center again. Reinforce the seam with tacks. This face is the bottom of your structure (Fig. 5-42).

6. Using your decorative tacks, reinforce the open edges of your structure.

Cat Cube with Separate Scratching Post

This is a particular favorite of kittens who are kept inside.

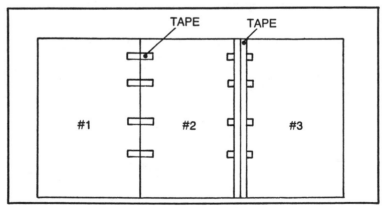

Fig. 5-40. Triangular bed detail—taping sides.

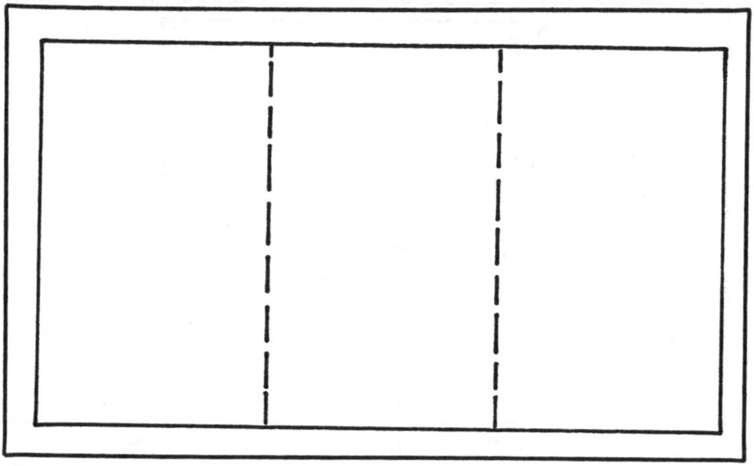

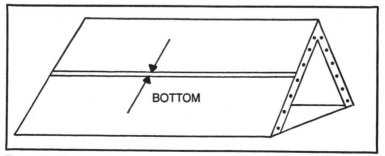

Fig. 5-41. Gluing carpet to the inside of the three panels.

materials and tools

Four pieces of ½-inch-thick plywood 12×12 inches, one piece 12½×12½ inches, one piece of 1×1 6 inches tall, one piece of plywood 4×4 inches, one piece of indoor/outdoor carpeting or low nap carpeting 12×12 inches, one piece of same or similar carpeting 3×6 inches, 2d nails, glue, small piece of fabric about 4×4 inches, string, a bit of catnip, a large-headed tack, sandpaper, paint, pencil, ruler, scissors, needle and thread, hammer, keyhole saw, drill, paintbrush.

shopping

1. Have the man at the lumberyard cut your plywood and 1×1s.

2. If you can, have someone cut out the holes in three of the 12×12-inch pieces.

Fig. 5-42. Triangular bed—wrapping carpet around outside.

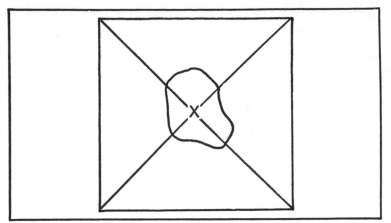

Fig. 5-43. Establishing the center and drawing a free-form opening.

preparation

1. If you haven't been able to get someone to do it for you, mark three of your plywood pieces as shown in Fig. 5-43.

assembly and finishing

1. Cut out the openings in marked pieces by first drilling a hole at the center mark (Fig. 5-44). Then saw along the broken line to the hole markings and follow the hole markings around.

2. Sand openings smooth.

3. Set out your four 12×12-inch pieces (Fig. 5-45).

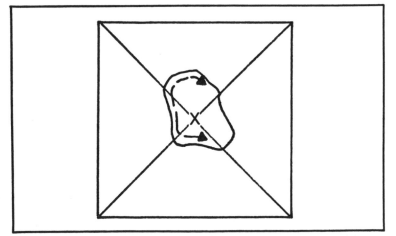

Fig. 5-44. Cutting an opening starting at the center. Follow the contours.

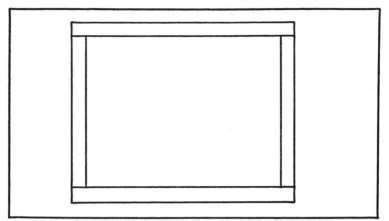

Fig. 5-45. Cube construction detail—layout of cube sides.

4. Glue and nail together along the edges (Fig. 5-46).

5. Nail and glue a 12½ × 12½-inch piece to the structure forming an open cube.

6. Sand the structure inside and out.

7. Put glue on all the long sides of your 1×1 and one of the short ends.

8. Wrap carpeting around the 1×1. Tack along the seam.

9. Cover one face of your 4×4-inch piece of plywood with glue. Glue on the carpeting.

10. From underneath, nail plywood to the 1×1.

11. Fold your fabric as shown in Fig. 5-47 and hem. Fold in half and sew up. Put a drawstring through the hem. Fill with catnip.

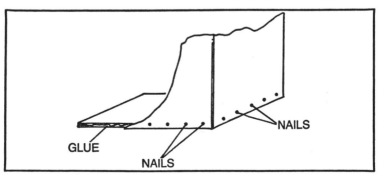

Fig. 5-46. Cat cube construction detail—gluing and nailing walls.

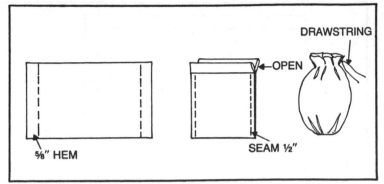

Fig. 5-47. Making a catnip bag.

12. Using your large-headed tack, attach a catnip bag to the post (Fig. 5-48).

13. Paint the cube inside and out with two coats of latex paint. Allow ample drying time between coats.

14. Glue carpeting to the bottom of the cube. Set the scratching post in place (Fig. 5-49).

Elegant Cat Perch

materials and tools

Four pieces of ½-inch plywood 18×12 inches, two pieces 12×12×12 triangles, two pieces 6×8 inches, one piece of 4×4 5 feet long, 4 running feet of 6-foot-wide carpeting, four medium-sized corner braces, 3d nails, screws for the corner braces, rug adhesive, two decorative brackets about 4 inches long with screws (be sure screws are long enough to go

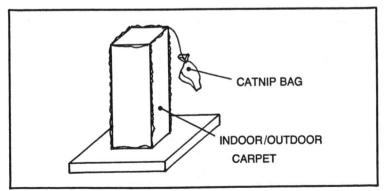

Fig. 5-48. Scratching post.

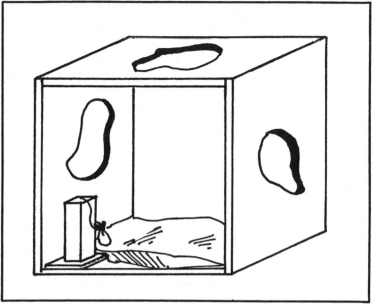

Fig. 5-49. Cat cube.

through carpeting), catnip, small piece of material and string, tacks, hammer, ruler, marking pencil, drill, saw, screwdriver, compass.

shopping

1. Have lumber cut to size at the lumberyard.

2. If possible, have a 6-inch-diameter hole cut into the center of one of the 12×18 pieces.

3. Buy indoor/outdoor or other low-napped carpeting, so you can cut it easily.

preparation

1. Locate the center in one of the 12×18-inch plywood pieces by laying in the diagonals from all corners using your marking pencil and ruler.

2. Using your center point, draw a 6-inch-diameter circle with your compass.

3. Mark your triangles along one side for two corner braces each. Hold the corner of the brace flush with the edge.

4. Mark one of the 18×12-inch pieces along the short edges, ½ inch in from the edge with your corner braces, and two to a side to match the triangular pieces.

5. Flip this board over and again find the center by using the diagonals. From the center, measure 1¾ inches in all four directions. Make a square connecting the marks.

6. Holding your larger corner braces even with this line, mark for a brace on each side. Use the line to line up your corner brace.

7. On one of the remaining 12×18-inch pieces, again find the center and draw a square as in step 5.

8. Mark the carpeting on the backside according to the layout in Fig. 5-50. Note the half-triangles pieced down the center. If you don't like to piece, simply buy 4½ feet of the carpeting instead of the 4 feet.

assembly and finishing

1. Attach one of the triangles to each short edge of the 18×12 piece you have marked for the corner braces by nailing to the base along one short edge (Fig. 5-51).

2. Reinforce joint with corner braces (Fig. 5-51).

3. Repeat with the other triangle.

4. Drill a starter hole in the center of the circle.

5. With your saw, cut from the center to the circumference of the circle and then follow the circle's contour. Sand smooth.

6. Lay the 18×12 piece with the hole in the middle next to another 18×12 piece, with long edges together. Spread glue or other rug adhesive over the entire surface (Fig. 5-52).

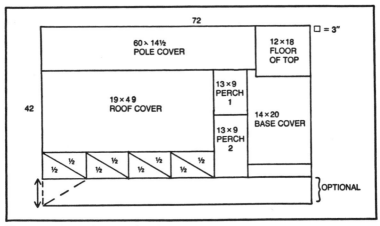

Fig. 5-50. Layout for carpeting.

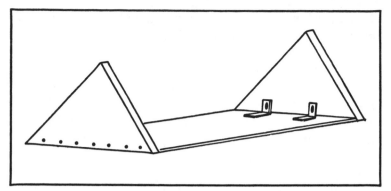

Fig. 5-51. Cat perch detail—using corner braces to reinforce framing.

7. Cover with the roof cover piece, flip wood, and cover the reverse side with adhesive.

8. Fold remaining carpeting over the wood. Secure edges with a few small tacks.

9. Carefully cut out carpeting on both sides along the circle line using your circle cutout as a guide. Secure edges with a little extra adhesive and a few tiny tacks.

10. Lay the rug piece marked "pole cover" on the floor and spread with adhesive.

11. Put a 4×4 on top of the pole cover. Line up edges and roll carpet over a 4×4. Be sure to keep edges straight and carpeting smooth. Put in a few tacks along the first long edge close to the corners to hold the carpeting in place as you work.

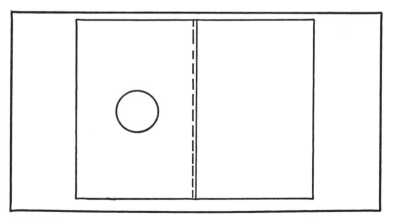

Fig. 5-52. Attaching roof sides to each other by covering them with carpeting on both sides.

12. As you wrap the carpeting, put some more tacks along the edges as you come to them.

13. Overlap your carpeting a tiny bit at the seam. Secure with extra tacks (Fig. 5-53).

14. Cover your two 6×8-inch pieces with the appropriate sized carpeting pieces, the ones marked "perch 1" and "perch 2". Spread adhesive on the carpet backing, wrap the wood in the carpeting, and secure the edges with tacks.

15. Glue your base cover to the last of your 12×18-inch pieces.

16. Glue the piece marked "floor cover" to the underneath side of the piece with the triangles on them.

17. Cover triangles with carpeting inside and out.

18. If desired, cover the floor on the inside between the triangles with leftover carpeting.

19. Using your larger corner brackets, attach the top, the piece with the triangles, to one short end of the 4×4 (Fig. 5-54).

20. Attach the floor piece to 4×4s, nailing from below as shown in Fig. 5-55.

21. Measure up one side of the 4×4 and mark at 2½ feet.

22. Mark the opposite face of the 4×4 at 3½ feet.

23. Mark for holes for decorative brackets at those places.

24. Drill starter holes and attach one side of the brackets with screws.

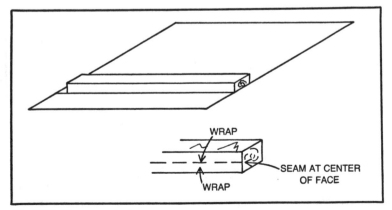

Fig. 5-53. Wrapping 4×4s.

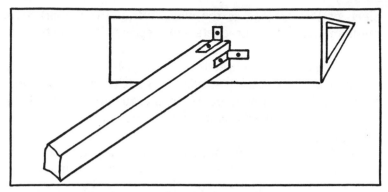

Fig. 5-54. Attaching the post to the top with corner braces.

25. Drill starter holes in perch pieces and attach to brackets with screws.

26. Make two little catnip bags following the assembly and finishing instructions (step 11) given in the cat cube with separate scratching post project.

27. Set the whole thing upright and tie your catnip bags to the decorative brackets. Put the roof section on top of the structure.

28. For added comfort, you can fold a towel and put it inside the top structure. This provides your cat with added comfort and can easily be removed for washing (Fig. 5-56).

Version A of the Economy Cat Perch
materials and tools

One piece of plywood 12×18 inches, two pieces of plywood 18×6 inches, two pieces of plywood 11×6 inches, one

Fig. 5-55. Nailing the base from underneath.

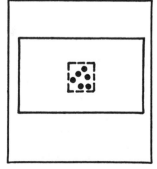

piece of 1×4 as long as the window frame (optional), two medium decorative brackets with screws to match, two pieces of firmly woven material or heavy plastic 19×25 inches, one small sack of shredded foam or a 1-inch 18×12 foam piece, sandpaper, 2d nails, paint to match your woodwork, hammer, drill, screwdriver, ruler, measuring tape, marking pencil, scissors, needle and thread or sewing machine.

shopping

1. Obtain sturdy, decorative brackets. If your woodwork is white or light, get white brackets. If you can't find appropriate white or light ones, consider painting the brackets to match the woodwork and the perch.

preparation

1. Locate the window that you want for your cat perch.

2. If the wood framing around or below your window is wide enough to attach your brackets onto, you can either center your perch or attach it toward one side.

3. If not, measure the width of the window and buy a piece of 1×4 to match the measurement.

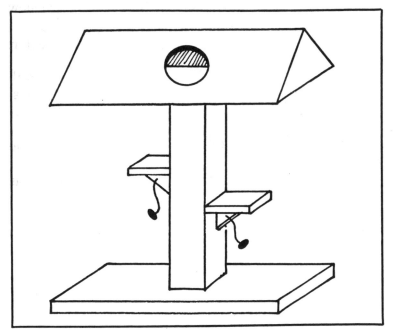

Fig. 5-56. Elegant cat perch.

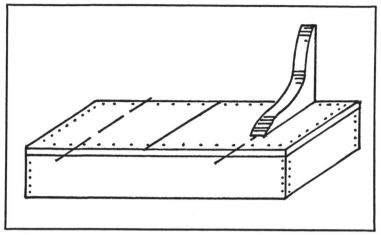

Fig. 5-57. Version A—economy cat perch details.

4. Find the center for the window if you want to center your perch. Measure 6 inches to each side from center. Draw a line and mark for screw holes for brackets.

5. If you are using the 1×4, mark it in the same manner.

6. If you use the 1×4, mark every 16 inches from window edge to window edge.

7. One side of your 12×18-inch board, mark the center, then a line 6 inches to each side of center.

8. Line up your bracket so that the corner is even with one long edge of your board and even with one of the lines. Mark for screw holes. Repeat on the other line (Fig. 5-57).

assembly

1. Nail your two short 6-inch-wide pieces between the two longer pieces to form a frame (Fig. 5-58).

2. Nail the 12×18 piece marked side up to the framing as shown in Fig. 5-57.

3. Sand the entire box.

4. Drill starter holes for brackets in marked places.

5. Drill starter holes on the window framing.

6. Attach brackets to the window framing. If you need the extra 1×4, proceed as follows.

5A. Nail the 1×4 to the wall directly under the window facing. Line up edges. Nail directly under the outside framing and on each 16-inch marking (your studs) using 4d nails.

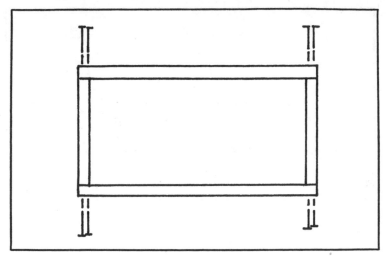

Fig. 5-58. Form the frame as shown.

6A. Drill starter holes for brackets as marked (lined up with the ones on the window facing above).

7. Sand 1×4 and paint to match the window.

finishing

1. Paint the entire box. Let it dry. Apply the second coat. Paint should match woodwork.

2. Fold material in half to form a 12½×19-inch rectangle. Sew along one short side and the long side.

3. Stuff with shredded foam or put in a pad.

4. Sew shut.

5. Repeat the sewing bit with the second piece, but leave the top open and put in two strips of Velcro fastening tape if you like.

6. If you prefer, you can whip the edges together loosely after inserting the filled mattress cushion.

7. Attach the box to brackets. Put in the mattress and invite the cat to try the perch (Fig. 5-59).

Version B of the Economy Cat Perch

materials and tools

One 12×18 board, 1×4 as long as the window frame (optional), one piece of carpeting 19×25 inches, two medium-sized decorative brackets and screws, glue or carpet

162

adhesive, decorative tacks, hammer, screwdriver, drill (optional), ruler, marking pencil.

shopping

Nothing special.

preparation

1. Follow instructions for preparation in version A from steps 1 through 7.

assembly and finishing

1. Drill starter holes for screws in marked places on your board.

2. Drill starter holes on the window frame.

3. Attach brackets to the window frame. If you need to use an extra 1×4, follow steps 5A-7 for version A.

4. Spread glue or adhesive on the board.

5. Transfer markings to carpeting.

6. Wrap the board in carpeting.

7. Secure edges with decorative tacks.

8. Attach the board to the top of the brackets (Fig. 5-60).

CAT BOX SUPERSTRUCTURES

Cat box *superstructures* keep odor down and litter inside the box. The one problem is to match the superstructure to the cat box. Any plastic container will do for a cat box. Make sure, though, that it is at least 4 inches deep. Plywood or cardboard can be used for the superstructure.

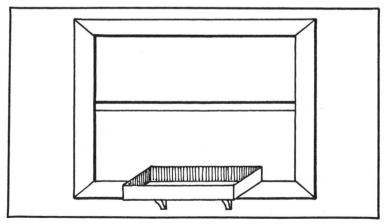

Fig. 5-59. Economy cat perch—version A.

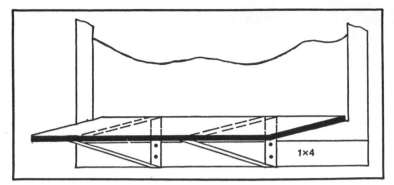

Fig. 5-60. Economy cat perch—version B.

Plywood A-Frame Cat Box Superstructure

We will go with a 19×15-inch size. You can fit your own box by measuring the size and adjusting the measurements for the plywood accordingly.

materials and tools

Two pieces of plywood or particle board cut into triangles with a 16-inch base, a height of 16 inches, and sides of 18 inches, two pieces of plywood 18×20 inches, sandpaper, markers or paint for details, paint or adhesive-backed vinyl (4 yards), 2d nails, glue, hammer, saw, scissors (optional), ruler and marking pencil, and paintbrush.

shopping

1. You can buy the cheapest grade of plywood if you use the ⅜-inch-thick vinyl, or you might use particle board.

2. While you can paint the structure, we prefer to use the vinyl inside and out because it can be wiped clean so easily. You can achieve that smoothness with a lot of sanding if you paint, but who wants to spend all that time?

3. Buy your litter box first. Make sure that each side of the structure is 1 inch longer than the box itself.

4. Have the man at the lumberyard cut your pieces. You will probably have to cut out the door yourself.

preparation

1. On one of your triangles, mark a line from the apex down to the center point of your base.

2. Mark up 4 inches from the base. Measure 3½ inches to each side of the center line.

3. From the 4-inch mark, measure up 5 inches. Measure 3½ inches to each side.

4. Connect the dots into a rectangle.

5. If your box is higher than 4 inches, make the initial mark at the same height as the top edge of the box. Go on from there.

5A. If that makes the upper corners of the door fall too close to the edge of the triangle, measure only 3 inches on each side.

assembly and finishing

1. Cut out the door and sand for an opening.

2. Nail one of the 18×20 pieces to one of the triangles matching 18-inch sides. Repeat on the other side.

3. Repeat the whole operation with the other piece (Fig. 5-61).

4. Nail together on the top.

finishing

1. Sand the whole thing inside and out.

2. If you want to paint it, use two coats of latex paint. Add a coat of polyurethane varnish for extra protection.

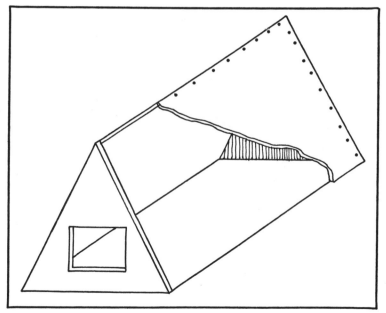

Fig. 5-61. Construction details for the A-frame.

3. Decorate with extra windows or whatever suits your fancy (Fig. 5-62).

or

2A. Cut two pieces of adhesive-backed vinyl in a wood-grain pattern or another design if you prefer (18×40).

3A. Cut four pieces into triangles just like your wooden ones.

4. Cover wood with vinyl—first the inside, then the outside.

5. At the opening, clip the vinyl. Then cut out allowing ¼ inch extra on each side to cover the opening edge.

6. Again, mark extra features with felt pens or paste them on.

7. Set the structure over the box.

Cat Castle

materials and tools

Three pieces of plywood 20×16, two pieces of plywood 16×16, fancy carved molding about 6 feet long and as wide as you like, 3½ yards of adhesive-backed vinyl (optional),

Fig. 5-62. Finishing details for the A-frame.

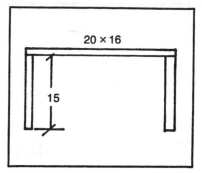

Fig. 5-63. More construction details for the A-frame.

sandpaper, glue, 2d nails, paint, markers or paint for details, hammer, saw, scissors, ruler, paintbrush, marking pencil.

shopping

See shopping instructions for A-Frame.

preparation

1. Mark your door opening—a 5×7 rectangle about 4 inches above the bottom and in the center of your 16×16 piece.

2. If you want, you can have the opening in the long piece, either in the center or off to one side. Just make sure that the bottom is above the upper rim of the litter box.

assembly

1. Cut out the door opening. Sand.

2. Nail and glue your 20×16-inch pieces to your 16×15 pieces (Fig. 5-63).

3. Nail the remaining 20×16 piece on top to form an open box.

4. Cut trim to fit the upper edges of the box—that is, two pieces 20 inches long and two 15 inches long. Nail and glue in place, so the trim projects up from the top for at least ½ inch.

finishing

1. Sand the structure.

2. Paint with two coats of latex paint inside and out.

3. Add details such as shown in Fig. 5-64 either with paint or by gluing on cutouts.

or

2A. Cover structure inside and out with vinyl except for molding.

2B. Add details as discussed earlier.

Fig. 5-64. Finishing details for the cat castle.

Cat Hacienda

materials and tools

Two pieces of plywood 20×16, two pieces of plywood 15×16, one piece of plywood 20×20, four pieces of ½-inch dowel 3 inches long, sandpaper, 2d nails, glue, hard finished string, black paint, white paint, two or more small Mexican pottery bowls, tiny cacti, hammer, saw, paintbrush, small pointed paintbrush for glue, marking pencil, ruler.

shopping

Follow instructions for the A-frame.

preparation

1. On your 20×20 piece, mark down 4 inches from the edge and draw a line.

2. Mark at 4-inch intervals along the same edge.

3. Draw a perpendicular to your long line at each of the 4-inch marks. Mark at 3 inches from the top (Fig. 5-65).

4. Mark the center of the base of the board. Draw a line across the face of the board. Mark for the door opening (Fig. 5-65).

assembly

1. Cut out the door opening. Make sure the base of the opening is higher than the rim of the box.

2. Nail two 15×16-inch pieces to one of the 20×16 pieces, forming a U-shaped structure (Fig. 5-66).

3. Nail another 20×16-inch piece on top (Fig. 5-66).

4. On your 20×20-inch piece, make slits at the 4-inch marks. Saw down 3 inches from the top and make the slits about ½ inch wide each.

5. Nail the 20×20-inch piece to the rest of the structure. Line up sides and the line on the board with the top of the box.

finishing

1. Sand the entire structure inside and out.

2. Paint the entire structure with white paint inside and out. Two coats of enamel would be best.

3. Draw details such as windows and grills on the structure (Fig. 5-67).

4. Dip your cord in black paint, hang it up and let it dry.

5. Paint glue along the lines of your windows and doors with a paintbrush.

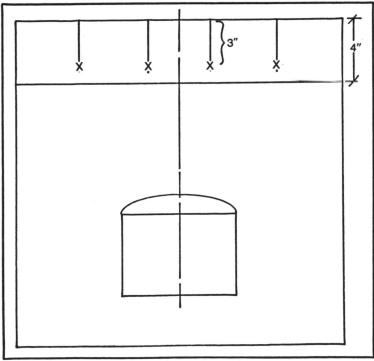

Fig. 5-65. Construction details for the cat hacienda.

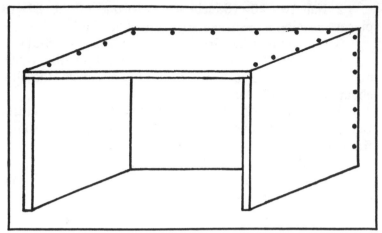

Fig. 5-66. More construction details for the cat hacienda.

6. Put black dyed cord on the glue and press down. Reinforce with black map pins or tiny tacks if desired.

7. Paint dowels black or dark brown. Allow for drying.

8. Glue dowels in place under the slits.

9. Set Mexican pots with succulents on the roof at corners (Fig. 5-68).

Cardboard Cat Castle

1. Instead of using molding, you can cut a strip of 4-inch-wide cardboard as long as the molding strip(s).

2. Measure an inch and draw a line parallel to the long edges.

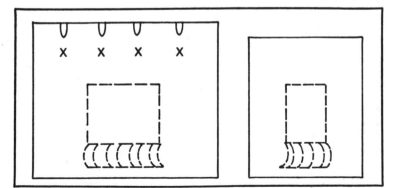

Fig. 5-67. Finishing details for the cat hacienda.

Fig. 5-68. The cat hacienda.

3. Measure and mark the other long edges at 2-inch intervals.

4. Mark another line 2 inches down from the top. Mark likewise at 2-inch intervals. Connect to form a pattern as shown in Fig. 5-69.

5. Cut along the line with heavy scissors.

6. On the other side of the strip, score along the line with a straightedge and knife. Bend the cardboard along the score line.

7. Glue or staple cardboard trim to the top of the structure along the bent part of the strip.

8. Staple or tape at the corners.

finishing

Use adhesive-backed vinyl or paint.

Cat Hacienda

1. Follow steps 1 and 2 for the cat castle.

2. Measure every 4 inches along the other edge.

3. Make 2½-inch cuts at each of the marks—about ½ inch wide.

4. Follow steps 6 and 7 for the cat castle.

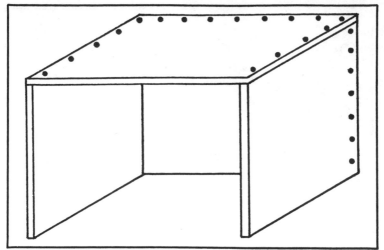

Fig. 5-69. Construction details for the outhouse.

finishing

Follow directions for finishing the wooden hacienda.

Outhouse

This is a slightly different version of the superstructures. It requires an almost square litter pan.

materials and tools

One piece of plywood 15×40 inches, one piece of ½-inch-thick plywood 15×15 inches, two pieces of ½-inch-thick plywood 14×40 inches, one piece of ½-inch-thick plywood 15×42 inches,, 2d nails, paint or adhesive-backed vinyl (5 yards), sandpaper, paint, felt pens or cutouts to decorate if you like, hammer, saw, scissors (optional), paintbrushes, ruler, marking pencil.

shopping

Same as for other superstructures.

preparation

1. On the 15×42 panel, mark a line 2 inches down from one short end.

2. Mark the center of the panel and draw a line vertically.

3. Measure up 4 inches or however high your cat box is and mark on the line. Mark 3½ inches to the right and 3½ inches to the left.

172

4. Measure up 5 inches and repeat. Connect dots with lines.

assembly

1. Cut out for the door on markings (rectangle).

2. Nail the 14×40 panels to the 15×40 panel as in Fig. 5-69.

3. Nail the 15×15-inch piece on top.

4. Nail the 15×42-inch panel across the front, with the top extending 2 inches above the roof panel.

finishing

1. Sand the structure inside and out.

2. Paint with two coats of latex paint inside and out. Let it dry or cover the structure inside and out with adhesive-backed vinyl.

3. Decorate the front in the traditional outhouse manner with a half-moon.

4. You can attach the cutout piece from the door with a couple of tiny hinges and let it sag open (Fig. 5-70).

Cat Tower

materials and tools

Same as for the outhouse.

shopping

Same as for the outhouse.

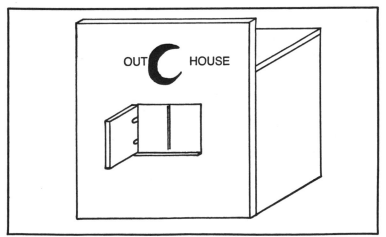

Fig. 5-70. The outhouse.

preparation

1. Follow steps 1-4 for measuring and marking the outhouse.

2. Mark the top edge for battlements in this manner—1 inch in from the long edge, then every 2 inches until the other end, which will be a 1-inch segment. Mark the same along the 2-inch line.

3. Connect the dots as shown in Fig. 5-71.

assembly

1. Cut out battlements by following Fig. 5-71.

2. Follow steps 1-4 for outhouse assembly.

finishing

1. Sand the inside and outside thoroughly.

2. Paint or cover with adhesive-backed vinyl.

3. Draw barred windows on the front to resemble the tower. Paint in or use cutouts.

4. You can go the string/paint/glue route for the windows and bars as in the hacienda project.

PET GROOMING STATIONS

It is nice to have all the things needed for a grooming session in one place. Here are some simple solutions that you can hang on the inside of a closet door or cupboard door.

Pegboard Grooming Station

materials and tools

One piece of pegboard 16×18 inches, two pieces of 1×1 18 inches long, two pieces of 1×1 14½ inches long, 2d nails, pegboard hangers, cord, two plastic spice baskets (about 10 inches long and 3 inches deep), paint, two medium screw eyes, hammer, saw (if you are going to cut your 1×1s yourself), ruler, marking pencil.

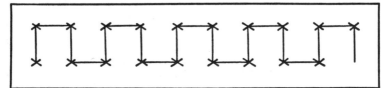

Fig. 5-71. Construction details for cat tower battlements.

shopping

1. When you get the hanger, make sure it will hold a leash, collar, and whatever else you want to hang up—including the trays.

preparation

1. Measure your 1×1 as specified. Mark the center on an 18-inch one.

assembly

1. Nail your 18-inch 1×1s along the long edges of your pegboard. The top edge of the 1×1 should be even with the top edge of the pegboard.

2. Nail the remaining 1×1s in between along the shorter edges, again matching edges.

3. On the 1×1 that has the center marked, measure 4 inches to each side and mark.

4. Put in the screw eyes.

finishing

1. Paint the entire board with two coats on both sides. Let it dry.

2. Tie the cord (14 inches of it) to the screw eyes for hanging. Lengthen or shorten the cord if you need it in your particular setup.

3. Fasten a nail or screw to the cupboard door or to a wall with the 1×1s against the wall.

4. Attach hangers and trays (Fig. 5-72).

Compact Pet Grooming Station

materials and tools

One piece of plywood 16×6 inches, two pieces of plywood 16×4 inches, two pieces of plywood 5×4 inches, 2d nails, large cup hooks and shoulder hooks, adhesive-backed vinyl, (optional) or paint, two small screw eyes, sandpaper, cord, hammer, drill for starting holes (optional), ruler, marking pencil, paintbrush, scissors (optional).

shopping

1. Get the large cup and shoulder hooks. They are usually brass-finished.

preparation

None.

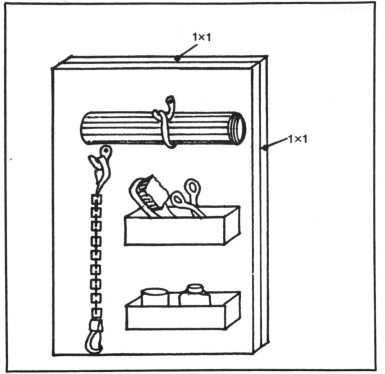

Fig. 5-72. Pet grooming station.

assembly and finishing

1. Attach your short pieces of plywood to the 15×4 pieces with nails. Put the short pieces between the long pieces.

2. Nail the remaining piece of plywood to the framing to form an open box.

3. Sand thoroughly inside and out.

4. Cover with adhesive-backed vinyl or two coats of paint.

5. Attach cup hooks and shoulder hooks to the underneath side of the box.

6. Put two small screw eyes on the back of the box. Tie cord or wire to them for hanging the grooming station (Fig. 5-73).

A nice accessory for the grooming stations is a grooming mat. It is particularly useful for long-haired dogs or cats.

176

Grooming Mat for Cats
materials and tools
One piece of quilted plastic 24×12 inches, 3¼ yards of strong cotton tape in a matching color, measuring tape, ruler, pencil, scissors, needle and thread or sewing machine.
shopping
1. If you hate to sew, you may be able to find plastic adhesive-backed tape wide enough to bind the edges of the pad. You will need 2 yards at least 1½ inches wide. If desperate, you might use aluminum tape.

2. About 40 inches of cotton tape is needed. It will have to be sewn on.
preparation
1. Cut your cotton tape into two 20-inch lengths.

2. If you are using plastic tape, cut it into two 24-inch pieces and two 12-inch pieces.
assembling and finishing
1. Bind the quilted plastic with tape all around. If you use cotton tape, sew by hand or machine. Miter the corners as shown in Fig. 5-74.

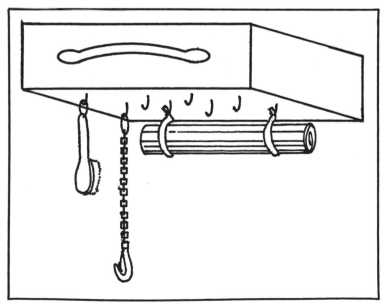

Fig. 5-73. Back view of the compact grooming station.

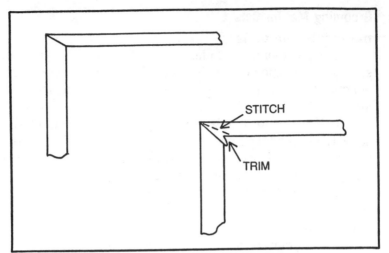

Fig. 5-74. Mitering corners for grooming mat with cotton tape.

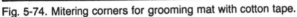

2. If you use self-adhesive plastic tape, apply the long edges first, then the short ones. Cut the short ends at the corners to miter as in Fig. 5-75.

3. Fold cotton tape in half and sew through the halfway mark to one corner of the pad. Sew the other tape to the same long side at the other corner.

Grooming Mat for Dogs

To arrive at the proper size of grooming mat for your dog, you need to measure your pet from stem to stern and add 3 or 4 inches at each end. If your dog measures 25 inches from the tip of the nose to the tail, you will want a mat that is 31 to 33 inches long. If it is a full 36 inches, that is fine, too. Width can be 20 inches for small to small/medium breeds, 24 inches for medium breeds, and 30 inches for large breeds. These measurements are arbitrary and can be adjusted to fit your needs.

materials and tools

Same as for cat grooming mats. Allow extra for larger sizes.

shopping

1. You will need more tape as well as more plastic. Forty inches of tape are required for ties.

178

preparation
Same.
assembly and finishing
Same.

PET BUFFETS

One of the annoying things about pets is the way they tend to spill food and water around their dishes. Here are ideas for spillproof eating areas.

Pet Buffet Number One

materials and tools
One piece of plywood 14×7 inches, two pieces of plywood 14×5 inches, two strips of felt ¾ inch wide and 14 inches long, two pieces of plywood 6×5 inches, two pieces of 1×1 14 inches long, glue, 2d nails, 1 yard of adhesive-backed vinyl, sandpaper, two medium suction cups, hammer, saw, ruler, scissors.

shopping
1. You might have trouble finding suction cups, unless you have old crib toys, baby cups, and other items around the house. Suction cups attached to the arrows of cheap target sets will work quite well.

preparation
1. Cut your adhesive-backed vinyl into the following pieces: one piece 14×14, two pieces 14×10, and two pieces 6×10.

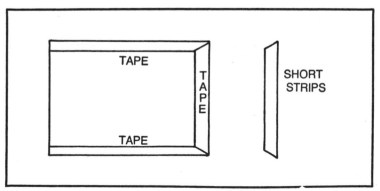

Fig. 5-75. Mitering plastic tape.

assembly and finishing

1. Cover your plywood pieces with the appropriate adhesive-backed vinyl pieces. Wrap the plywood into the vinyl and cover both sides of the wood.

2. Nail your two 6×5 pieces between your 14×5 pieces to form a frame.

3. Nail your 14×7 piece over the top.

4. Nail one of your 1×1 pieces along each long edge. Set these 1×1s in 1½ inches from the edges (Fig. 5-76).

5. Glue a felt strip to the lower faces of the 1×1s.

6. Turn over and set your feeding dishes into the box. Use 6-inch-diameter dishes. Mark where the dishes sit.

7. In that space attach one or more suction cups to the box with glue.

Pet Buffet Number Two

This is mainly for large dogs.

materials and tools

One piece of board 24×12 inches, two pieces of board 24×8 inches, two pieces of board 11×8 inches, two pieces of 1×1 24 inches long, 3½ yards of adhesive-backed vinyl, 2d nails, two 2-inch safety gate hooks and eyes, two felt strips ¾ inch wide and 24 inches long, glue, two suction cups for each dish, hammer, drill, marking pencil, scissors.

shopping

Try to find larger suction cups. If you can't, simply use two or more cups for a dish.

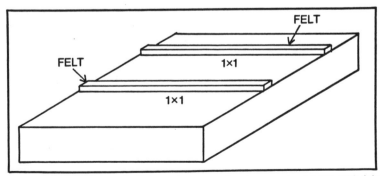

Fig. 5-76. Bottom of pet buffet number one, showing recessed 1×1s with felt strips.

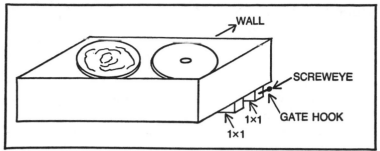

Fig. 5-77. Pet buffet number two detail—fastening gate hooks to the wall.

preparation

Same as for pet buffet number one using the measurements given earlier.

assembly and finishing

1. Follow steps 1-5 for pet buffet number one.

2. Mark for your dishes, centering them as much as possible. You will notice extra space around them, and that is intentional to keep the spillage inside the box. Attach two or more small suction cups or a larger one for each feeding dish.

3. Attach your gate hooks to one of your 1×1s, one to each short end. Predrill holes.

4. Measure on your wall against which the pet buffet is going to sit. Mark the places opposite your gate hooks and attach screw eyes.

5. Fasten gate hooks to screw eyes (Fig. 5-77)

AQUARIUM STANDS

A basic aquarium stand can be built without too much difficulty

Basic Aquarium Stand

materials and tools

Two pieces of 49×13-inch plywood ¾-inch-thick (top and bottom of stand), two pieces of 13×30-inch plywood ¾ inch thick (sides), one piece of 49×31½-inch plywood ¾ inch thick (back), one piece 47½×13-inch plywood ¾ inch thick (shelf), two pieces of 1×2 13 inches long, 27 feet of ¾-inch trim, 3d nails, sandpaper, paint, small finishing nails for trim, glue, saw, hammer, ruler, marking pencil, paintbrush.

shopping

1. Have all lumber cut to size except trim.

2. Use plywood with one fair surface, so the finish will look good.

preparation

1. Measure each board and mark on the back what it is, so you won't get confused because of the small variance in size.

2. Measure halfway up your side pieces (15 inches) and draw a line.

assembly

1. Nail your 1×2s to your side pieces with the top of the 1×2 even with the line and the 2-inch side face against the side piece.

2. Nail your side pieces between your top and bottom pieces, with the 1×2 facing in as in Fig. 5-78.

3. Nail the shelf to the tops of the 1×2 supports.

4. Nail the back in place.

5. Measure and cut trim to fit edges, starting with the long edge (top and bottom), the shelf edge, the upright edges, and the short side edges.

6. Nail and glue trim in place.

finishing

1. Sand the entire structure inside and out.

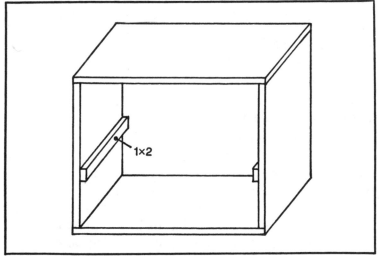

Fig. 5-78. Construction detail showing shelf supports.

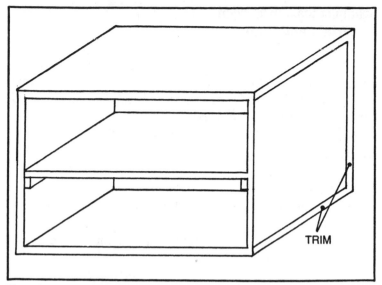

Fig. 5-79. Aquarium stand.

2. Paint the entire structure with two coats of paint. You may want to apply sealer before painting (Fig. 5-79).

Smaller Aquarium Stand

materials and tools

Two pieces of ¾-inch-thick plywood 24×13 inches (top) and bottom), two pieces of ¾-inch-thick plywood 13×30 inches (sides), one piece of ¾-inch-thick plywood 24×31½ inches (back), one piece of ¾-inch-thick plywood 22½×13 inches (shelf), two pieces of 1×2 13 inches long, 20½ feet of ¾-inch trim, 3d nails, sandpaper, small finishing nails for trim, glue, paint sealer (optional). Tools are the same as for the large aquarium stand.

shopping

Same as above.

preparation

Same as above.

assembly

Same as above.

finishing

Same as above.

Aquarium Stand with Light
materials and tools

Follow the materials list for either the large or smaller stand plus two pieces of 1×4 6 feet high and one 1×4 50½ inches long for the big stand or 25½ inches long for the small stand. You need one fluorescent fixture, 15 feet of cord, hardware, and insulated staples. Tools include those mentioned earlier plus the drill and screwdriver.

shopping

1. Use a light stick to get the light you want.
2. Consult Chapter 8 if you want something else.
3. Follow instructions given for the aquarium stand.

preparation

1. Follow preparation steps 1 and 2 for the aquarium stand.
2. Mark your side pieces with a vertical line down the center as well as with the horizontal line on the other side of the wood.

assembly

1. Follow steps 1-4 for the basic aquarium stand.
2. Nail the short 1×4 to the top of the two long 1×4s to form a U-frame.
3. Center the 1×4s on the lines on your side pieces and nail in place.
4. Follow steps 5-6 given for the basic aquarium stand.

finishing

1. Follow steps 1 and 2 for the basic aquarium stand (Fig. 5-80).
2. Install a light stick or other fixture on the top 1×4 following directions given in Chapter 8.

HAMSTER/GERBIL SETUPS

There is such a variety in sizes and shapes of cages for gerbils and hamsters that it is hard to come up with some good designs for stands that will fit a particular setup. Units by Habitrail can be assembled in many ways.

Habitrail Base
materials and tools

Two pieces of ½-inch-thick plywood 26×14½ inches

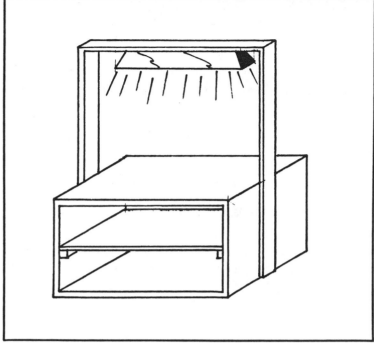

Fig. 5-80. Aquarium stand with light.

(top and bottom), two pieces of plywood 14½×25 inches (sides), one piece of plywood 26×26½ (back), one piece of plywood 25×14½ (shelf), two pieces of 1×2 14½ inches long, 7 feet of 1×1, 21 feet of ½ or ¾-inch trim, 2d nails, sandpaper, small finishing nails for trim, glue, paint, sealer (optional). Tools are the same as for the small aquarium stand.

shopping

Same as for the small aquarium stand.

preparation

Same as for the small aquarium stand.

assembly

Same as for the small aquarium stand. Cut 1×1 into 26-inch-long pieces and two 13-inch pieces. Nail 1×1s to the top of the structure to form a railing (Fig. 5-81).

finishing

Follow instructions for finishing the small aquarium stand.

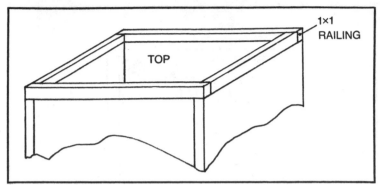

Fig. 5-81. Construction details for the 1×1 railing on top.

Habitrail Base—Alternate Version
materials and tools
Two pieces of ½-inch-thick plywood 26×26 inches (top and bottom), two pieces of ½-inch-thick plywood 26×26 (sides), one piece of ½-inch-thick plywood 26×27½ (back), one piece of ½-inch-thick plywood 24½×26 (shelf), two pieces of ½-inch-thick plywood 12×26 inches (drop leaves), 17 feet of 1×1, 20 feet of ½ or ¾-inch trim, 2d nails, sandpaper, small finishing nails for trim, glue, paint sealer (optional), four table leaf braces, hardware for table leaf braces, four medium glides. Tools are the same as for the aquarium stand plus a screwdriver.

shopping
Same as for the aquarium stand.

preparation
Same as for the aquarium stand.

assembly
1. Follow steps 1-4 for aquarium assembly.

2. Measure and cut trim to fit edges. Cut enough to trim all front edges, the side bottom edges, and the side back edges.

3. Cut 1×1 into four 12-inch pieces and six 26-inch pieces.

4. Edge your 12×26-inch boards with the 1×1, leaving one 26-inch edge open.

5. Edge the structure itself with a 26-inch 1×1 front and back.

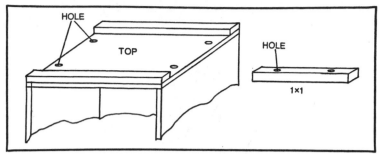

Fig. 5-82. Drilling holes for the toggle bolts.

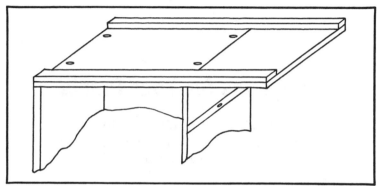

Fig. 5-83. Construction details for the drop leaf and brace.

6. Drill two holes through each of the remaining 26-inch 1×1s, one on each end about 2 inches in.

7. Drill two holes to match ½ inch in from the edge of the structure and 2 inches in from each end at each top side edge (Fig. 5-82).

8. Fasten table leaf braces, with one at each end of the 26-inch edge of the 12×26 piece of plywood, on the opposite side from the 1×1s (Fig. 5-83).

9. Fasten the other end of the table leaf braces to the stand (Fig. 5-83).

10. Apply trim along edges.

11. Attach glides to the bottom—one at each corner.

finishing

1. Follow instructions for finishing the aquarium stand. Paint the extra two pieces of 1×1 as well.

2. Attach the extra 1×1s to the stand with short toggle bolts.

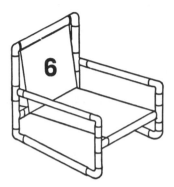

Projects for Your Plants

Plants should have "furniture" designed to make them comfortable and help them grow. Take a look around your house or apartment and see if you would like to build a few things for your plants.

TRAYS

While plants are not mobile in the sense that we are mobile, they do manage to move into places where the light, water, and air conditions are most favorable. Kept as house plants, however, they have little choice about their growing places, and that is the best reason for making them portable.

Roll-Around Trays
materials and tools

One 60×36-inch piece of ¾-inch marine plywood, two cedar 1×6s 60 inches long, two cedar 1×6s 34½ inches long, four plate-type metal ball casters with mounting screws, marine sealer, paint or stain, 4d casing nails, two dozen 1¼-inch 5-gauge flathead wood screws, white glue, hammer, drill, screwdriver, glue brush, paintbrush.

shopping

1. Get plywood and cedar lumber cut to exact size.

preparation

1. Mark ends of 60-inch 1×6s with a line ⅜ inch in from ends as a guideline for driving casing nails.

2. Mark a line ⅜ inch in from the edge of plywood around all four sides as a guideline for drilling starter holes for screws.

assembly

1. Nail the four sides together to make a box frame after spreading glue on edges (Fig. 6-1).

2. Secure plywood to the frame with wood screws and glue.

3. Fasten casters to the underside of the plywood bottom about 1-inch in from each corner.

finishing

1. Waterproof the bottom by painting with marine sealer.

2. Paint or stain the frame to suit your decor.

Trays for Self-Contained Plant Environment

The structure in Fig. 6-2 is made from two trays like the one just described (sans casters) earlier. The top tray is turned upside down and supported by 2×4 posts. It is fitted with two lights to bring "sunshine" to your plants and an ion

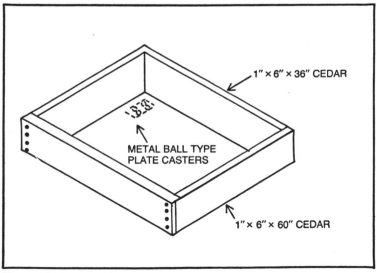

Fig. 6-1. Roll-around plant tray.

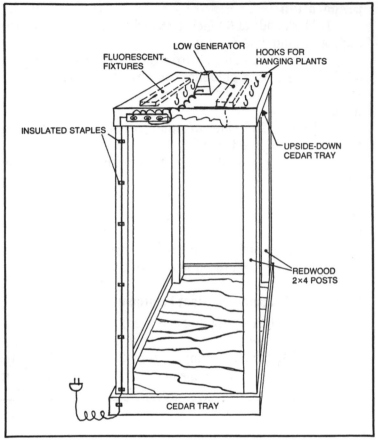

Fig. 6-2. Self-contained plant environment.

generator to bring fresh "mountain" air to both you and your plants.

materials and tools

Two 60×36-inch pieces of ¾-inch marine plywood, four cedar 1×6s 60 inches long, four cedar 1×6s 34½ inches long, four redwood 2×4s 72 inches long, two fluorescent light fixtures with 40-watt bulbs and power cord, one ion generator with near zero ozone output, one 15-foot extension cord with power plug on one end and three power outlets on the other end, marine sealer, paint or stain, white glue, 4d casing nails, 48 1¼-inch 5-gauge flathead wood screws and 32 1&¾-inch

10-gauge flathead wood screws, one dozen insulated staples, marble chips, about 6 screw hooks, hammer, drill, screwdriver, stapler, glue brush, paintbrush.

shopping

1. Get plywood, cedar, and redwood lumber cut to exact size.

preparation

1. Mark ends of 60-inch 1×6s with a line ⅜ inch in from the ends as a guideline for driving casing nails.

2. Mark a line ⅜ inch in from the edge of the plywood around all four sides as a guideline for drilling starter holes for screws.

assembly

1. Nail the four sides together for each box frame after spreading glue on the edges.

2. Secure plywood to frames with glue and 5-gauge screws.

3. Install screw hooks in the "bottom" of one of the trays that is to become the top of the structure. Allow proper spacing for hanging light fixtures and a few pots.

4. Place a 2×4 in each corner of the bottom tray and fasten it in place with four 10-gauge screws.

5. Invert the tray with screw hooks over the tops of 2×4s. Secure with four 10-gauge screws at each corner (Fig. 6-2).

6. Waterproof the bottom of the bottom tray with marine sealer.

finishing

1. Paint or stain the entire structure to suit your room decor.

2. Staple an extension cord to the back of one post with power outlets at the back of the top (Fig. 6-2).

3. Hang fluorescent fixtures and plug them into outlets.

4. Place an ion generator on top of the structure and plug it into an outlet.

5. Fill the bottom tray with marble chips and set in a collection of potted leafy foliage plants. Hang a couple of "aerial" plants from the spare hooks.

Copper Gutter Plant Tray System

This wall-hung planter system can be quickly assembled on a 3½ ×8-foot wall space to take dozens of potted plants. The gutter will hold excess water to prevent spillage when you water your plants. It will provide a watering feature when you must leave your plants for an extended period of time. Just fill the gutter with water and let the plants drink it up through the hole in the bottom of the pots.

materials and tools

One 13-foot length of 5-inch copper guttering, one dozen 10-gauge 3-inch roundhead screws, screwdriver, drill and metal bits.

shopping

1. Purchase the copper guttering. Have it cut into two 5-foot pieces and one 3-foot piece . Solder end caps on all the open ends.

preparation

1. Screw your copper tray units directly into the studs in your wall. This calls for careful measuring and marking. Studs will be 16 inches apart on centers along the wall, so start your first tray approximately 16 inches in from one corner of the wall.

2. To find the first stud, measure along the wall 14½ inches from the corner. Drive a tiny 4d finishing nail into the wall. If the stud is there, the nail will go into solid wood after it penetrates about ½ inch of wallboard. If the nail does not go in, move it a bit to the left or right until you locate the stud. The tiny holes made by the nail can easily be filled once you have located the stud.

3. Measure and mark the location of each stud by measuring exactly 16 inches from the first wall stud. You should have the center of each wall stud marked.

4. Place your copper guttering trays following the locations suggested in Fig. 6-3. Mark spots on the trays where you will drill holes for the screws to go through. These holes will all be 16 inches apart.

5. Mark places on the wall where starter holes are to be drilled for screws.

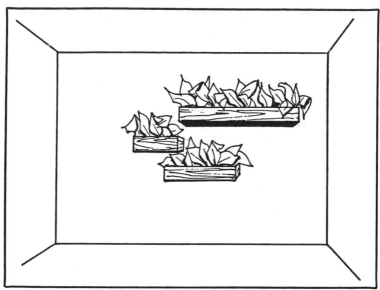

Fig. 6-3. Copper gutter plant tray system.

assembly

1. Drill holes into copper trays with a metal bit where marked.

2. Drill starter holes into the wall. Double-check your marks by holding the drilled tray up in place on the wall and remarking if necessary.

3. Screw trays to the wall.

finishing

1. Place the potted plants in trays.

King-Sized Tray/Room Divider

This freestanding plant tray is easy to build and accommodates many plants. It makes an excellent room divider.

materials and tools

Two 2×4s×96 inches, two 2×4s×72 inches, four 2×4s×24 inches, two 2×4s×21 inches, two 2×4s×18 inches, one ⅜-inch plywood 89×21 inches, 36 10-gauge 3-inch-long flathead wood screws, gravel, 4d common nails with threaded shanks, marine sealer, paint or stain, small can of wood putty, screwdriver, drill, three bits: slightly larger than screwhead for countersink, same size as screw shank for clearance hole,

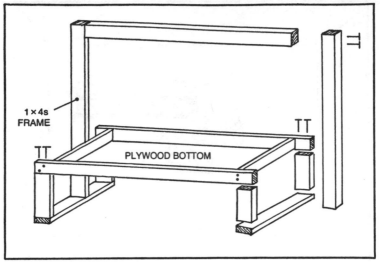

Fig. 6-4. Room divider tray.

and slightly smaller than screw shank for pilot hole. For 10-gauge screws, use ⅜, 3/16, and ⅛-size drill bits.

shopping

1. Shop for a good grade of fir lumber for the frame. Buy marine grade plywood for the tray bottom.

2. Have all wood cut to exact size.

preparation

Study Fig. 6-4 carefully and mark all screw holes.

assembly

1. Study Fig. 6-5.

2. With the largest bit in the drill, drill all countersink holes.

3. With a middle-sized bit, drill the rest of the way through the 2×4.

4. With the smallest bit, drill a pilot hole in the adjoining 2×4.

5. Drive all screws to assemble the frame, except for the hanger bar.

6. Turn the tray frame upside down and nail on the plywood bottom with threaded nails.

7. Drive all screws to complete the assembly with hanger bar in place.

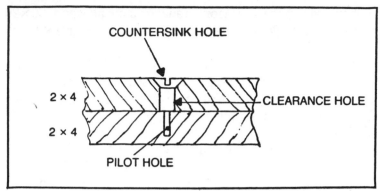

Fig. 6-5. Three holes for countersinking.

finishing

1. Waterproof the plywood bottom with marine sealer.

2. Fill in all countersink screw holes with wood putty and sand lightly when hardened.

3. Paint or stain.

4. Place gravel on the bottom of the tray and set in potted plants. Hang your hanging plants from the crossbar.

BOXES

Boxes may serve as containers for potted plants. If boxes are to be planted, they must be treated on the inside with liquid fiberglass to protect the wood. You must also use a couple inches of gravel in the bottom of the box for drainage, because the fiberglass will also waterproof the box. Use exterior grade ¾-inch plywood for sides and bottom. Put the sides together (frame) with glue and 4d casing nails. Fasten on the bottom with screws or common nails with threaded shanks. Large boxes should have their bottoms screwed on, while smaller boxes can be built with threaded shank nails. Glue should also be used on the bottom.

Music Box for Planting

This box is easy and quick to make. Chimes are made from a fishing pole and line.

materials and tools

Two pieces exterior grade ¾-inch plywood 20×12 inches, two pieces exterior grade ¾-inch plywood 18½×12 inches, one piece exterior grade ¾-inch plywood 20×20 inches, four 1×2-inch boards 22 inches long, four 1×2-inch boards 20 inches long, one cane fishing pole at least 15 feet long, approximately 72 inches of fishing cord, staples, 1 quart liquid fiberglass, stain or exterior house paint, 4d casing nails, glue, hammer, stapler, drill, glue and paintbrush, brush for fiberglass, small handsaw.

shopping

1. Get plywood and lumber cut to size.

preparation

1. Measure the fishing pole off into chime lengths as follows: six 7-inch lengths; eight each of 6, 5 and 4-inch lengths, and six 3-inch lengths.

2. Measure ⅜ inch in from the edges of plywood pieces (along 12-inch edge) and draw a line to serve as a nail guide. Draw a rectangle ⅜ inch in from all four sides on the bottom piece.

assembly

1. Nail and glue the box frame together.

2. Nail and glue the bottom on the frame.

3. Nail and glue 1×2 boards to the top and bottom sides of the box, so they project 1 inch out from the box (Fig. 6-6).

4. Cut the cane fishing pole into segments 3 to 7 inches long as marked with a saw.

5. Drill one small hole through each of the pieces.

6. Tie short lengths of fishing line to each cane piece through a hole and staple the other end to the 1×2 at the top of the box with the spacing and patterns shown in Fig. 6-7. Alternate the patterns on every other box side.

finishing

1. Paint the interior of the box with liquid fiberglass.

2. Turn the box upside down so chimes fall away from the sides. Paint or stain the box to look attractive in its surroundings.

Box with a Rustic Look

Long, low boxes planted with petunias are ideal for bordering decks and patios. This one will take you no time at all to build, but it is rugged enough to last for years (Fig. 6-8).

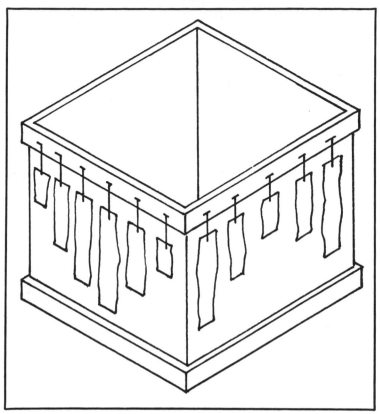

Fig. 6-6. Music box planter.

materials and tools

10 2×4s×96 inches long, 48 corrugated fasteners, 14 corner braces, eight corner irons, coarse gravel or crushed pottery, stain if desired, 96 roundhead 10-gauge, 1-inch-long wood screws, hammer, small handsaw, drill.

shopping

1. Shop for pressure-treated Douglas fir lumber.

2. Buy regular 8-foot lengths of 2×4. No cutting will be necessary at the lumberyard, unless you want one of the 2×4s cut into 13½-inch lengths. These are the end pieces—you need six.

assembly

1. Lay three 2×4s out on a flat, hard surface side by side. Drive corrugated fasteners into adjoining boards at each end

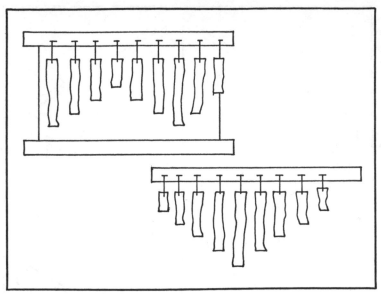

Fig. 6-7. Chime patterns.

and at 2-foot intervals, making one side of the box.

2. Lay three more 2×4s out in similar fashion and cleat together with the corrugated fasteners to make the other long side of the box.

3. Lay out a third set of three 2×4s and cleat together to make the bottom of the box.

4. Cut the marked 2×4 into six pieces with a handsaw.

5. Make two ends for the box by cleating together three of the 13½-inch 2×4s for each of the two ends.

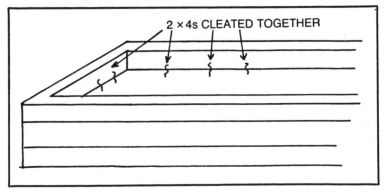

2 × 4s CLEATED TOGETHER

Fig. 6-8. Box with a rustic look.

6. Fasten the bottom of the box to the sides with corner braces about every 2 feet along each side.

7. Fasten ends to the box by placing a corner iron on each corner—top and bottom.

8. For additional rigidity, add a corner brace in each of the four corners on the inside of the box midway between top and bottom. Use screws to fasten corner irons and braces in place.

finishing

1. If you have used pressure-treated Douglas fir, no finishing work is necessary on the wood. You may stain it if you wish.

2. Be sure to put this box into its finished position before you fill it with planting soil mixture.

3. Put a layer of coarse gravel or crushed pottery in the bottom under the potting soil to assist drainage.

4. Plant and enjoy.

Window Box with a Lattice Face

This window box is designed to go under a 36-inch single window. You can easily make it twice as long for a double window.

materials and tools

Two 12×36-inch pieces of ½-inch exterior plywood, two 12×8-inch pieces of ½-inch exterior plywood, one 9×36-inch piece of ½-inch exterior plywood, two 9½-inch-long pieces of 1-inch molding, two 9½-inch-long pieces of ½-inch molding, two 10½-inch-long pieces of ½-inch molding, one 12½-inch piece of 1-inch molding, one 12½-inch-long piece of 1-inch molding, one 12½-inch-long piece of ½-inch molding, two 10½-inch-long pieces of corner molding, two panels stock lattice 10½×8 inches, one panel stock lattice 10½×35 inches, three utility brackets and 12 14-gauge, 1-inch-long screws, 2d finishing nails, 4d casing nails, 4d common nails with threaded shanks, glue, exterior house paint, hammer, drill, screwdriver, glue brushes, paintbrush.

shopping

1. Have all lumber, molding, and lattice cut to exact size.

preparation

1. Measure and mark nail guidelines ¼ inch in from the

edges of plywood pieces to be used for the frame and around the entire periphery of the piece for the box bottom (36×9-inch piece).

assembly

1. Nail and glue the box frame together using casing nails.

2. Glue and nail the bottom on the box using common threaded nails.

3. Using 2d finishing nails, nail on all molding as shown in Fig. 6-9.

4. Nail the stock lattice panels into place with 2d finishing nails.

5. Put the finished box in place with utility brackets.

Found Boxes

If you look around in unlikely places like brickyards and sewer tile factories, you are likely to find some unusual flower boxes and planter boxes. Figure 6-10 illustrates what you can do with large cement blocks, flue tiles, etc. Make a border of old bricks around a gravel bed and place your found boxes in the gravel. These boxes needn't have bottoms—just four sides deep enough to take your pots or potting soil. Make your brick-bordered gravel bed just a few inches wider and longer than your row of found boxes. Space the boxes a few inches apart.

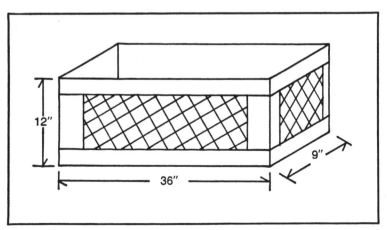

Fig. 6-9. Window box.

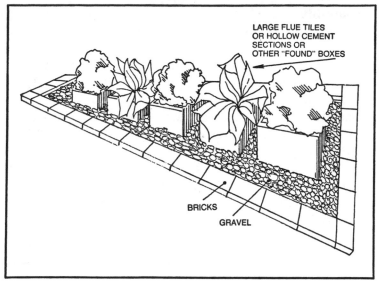

Fig. 6-10. Flue tile planter.

SKYSCRAPER GARDEN RACK

Racks are ideal when you want lots of plants in a very small space. You can have a very sizable vegetable garden using this rack-type planter. It is the old skyscraper principle.

Figure 6-11 illustrates what your finished garden rack will look like. It can be nailed together quickly when all the pieces are cut to size. Figure 6-12 will guide you in cutting pieces. Use nails with threaded shanks.

materials and tools

One 48×96-inch sheet of ½-inch exterior plywood, one 48×30-inch sheet of ½-inch exterior plywood, 2 pounds of 4d common nails with threaded shanks, 1 quart of polyurethane liquid plastic, paint or stain, hammer, brushes, saw.

shopping

1. Shop for a good grade of plywood—A/B grade at least—as almost all of the rack will be visible sometimes. If you have your plywood precut, get it cut to the exact dimensions shown in Fig. 6-12.

preparation

1. Measure and mark your plywood for cutting exactly as shown in Fig. 6-12.

assembly

1. Like all skyscrapers this one is built from the ground up. Put your end panels (E1 and E2 in Fig. 6-12), wide side down, on each end of the widest bottom piece you have (B1). Place some ¾-inch scraps of plywood under board B1, so it will be spaced ¾ inch off the ground or floor. With one end against a wall or other solid "stop," drive three nails to secure the tray bottom. Turn around and nail the other end of the bottom in place.

2. Nail both side pieces. Use at least three nails into each end piece and eight nails into the bottom piece.

3. Proceed with each of the next three trays on the rack exactly as discussed. Nail the bottom piece in first, securing it to the end pieces, and then nail on the side pieces.

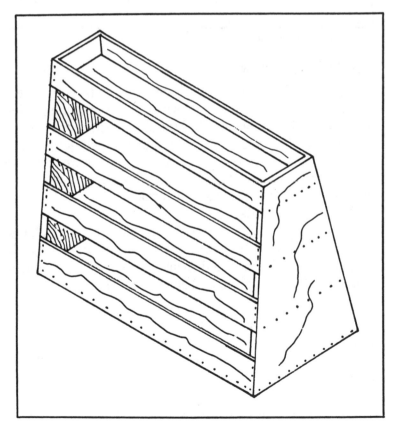

Fig. 6-11. Skyscraper garden rack.

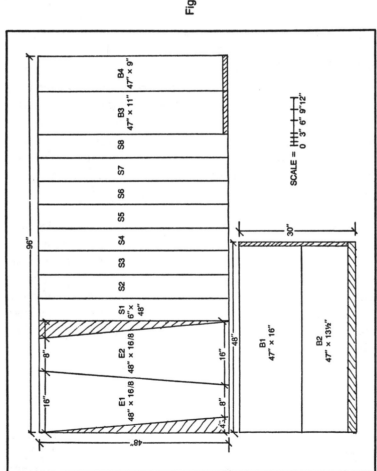

Fig. 6-12. Layout for skyscraper garden rack.

finishing

    1. Coat the entire inside of your skyscraper garden rack with polyurethane, sides, end pieces, and bottoms.

    2. Paint or stain it.

    3. For good drainage, put some small gravel on the tray bottoms before putting in your potting soil.

PLANT STANDS

    This pair of stands is designed to go under a window or a pair of windows. If our dimensions don't suit your space, vary the length. The stands can be placed side by side or one in front of the other. Both are 15 inches deep. One stand is 15 inches high; the other is 10 inches high.

Coffee Table Plant Stands

    The legs of these plant stands are glued together from spruce 2×2 for that popular butcher-block look. The ones for the large stand are 18 inches high, while the smaller one is 12 inches high. They can be finished with varnish. A 1×2 added to the edge of the plywood tops gives it that thick look, and a plastic laminate top makes a durable surface. Tops and ends are fastened together with lag screws (Fig. 6-13).

materials and tools

    Twenty spruce 2×2s 18 inches long, 20 spruce 2×2s 12 inches long, two pieces of interior plywood 13½×40-inches, four 1×2s 40 inches long, two pieces of plastic laminate 13½×40 inches, 12 ¼-inch, 3-inch-long lag screws, wood glue, laminate glue, 4d casing nails, your choice of wood varnish, hammer, drill with ¼-inch and 3/16-inch bits, adjustable wrench, large C-clamps, brushes for glues and varnish.

shopping

    1. Get all wood and the plastic laminate cut to size.

assembly

    1. Glue 10 2×2s together, side by side, on a flat surface so they are aligned perfectly.

    2. Carefully clamp in a large C-clamp. Make sure both surfaces are smooth and all ends are aligned perfectly. Wipe off excess glue and let dry. Repeat steps 1 and 2 until you have

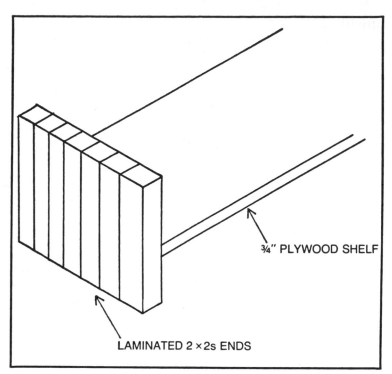

¾" PLYWOOD SHELF

LAMINATED 2 ×2s ENDS

Fig. 6-13. Coffee table plant stand.

all four legs. The gluing of each leg will take you about 10 minutes.

3. Drill ¼-inch shank clearance holes in legs 2⅝ inches from the top. Drill three of these holes spaced 3¾ inches apart (Fig. 6-14A and 6-14B). Repeat step 3 on all four legs.

4. Line up the ends of the top with each leg that will be attached to it. Carefully mark the position of pilot holes. Drill 3/16-inch pilot holes in the exact center of top ends (Fig. 6-14C). Repeat until all 12 pilot holes are drilled in both tops.

5. Insert lag screws into shank holes and turn by hand into the pilot hole to start. Tighten each screw with an adjustable wrench. Tighten firmly but not so tight as to mar the wood underneath the screwhead.

6. Spread laminate glue over both tops and press laminate firmly in place.

7. Add 1×2 pieces to both edges of each tabletop and secure with glue and casing nails.

finishing

1. Varnish the four butcher-block legs.

Plant Stand for Ferns

materials and tools

Two 1×3 oak boards 16 inches long, two 1×3 oak boards 8 inches long, four 1×2 oak boards 33 inches long, 3d casing nails, white glue, stain and varnish of your choice, putty stick or wood putty for filling nail holes, wood filler, hammer, nail set or heavy spike for countersinking nails, glue brush, brushes for varnish and stain, sandpaper, a coping saw if you are going to cut the notches yourself.

shopping

1. Have oak boards cut to the exact size when you buy them. If possible, get a lumber-yard worker to cut the 1-inch "U" out of the 8-inch boards and the ¾-inch square lap joint notch out of all four boards. You can do it yourself with a coping saw, but this will be more time-consuming (Figs. 6-15 and 6-16).

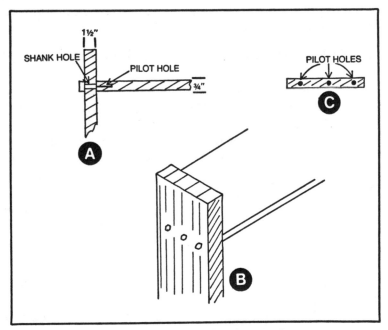

Fig. 6-14. Construction details of coffee table plant stand.

2. Buy a polyurethane varnish. You will get a tough, water-resistant finish that will have a great antique look.

preparation

1. Following the dimensions shown in Fig. 6-16, mark the top and bottom pieces for their cuts to the exact dimensions shown. Remember that your 3-inch lumber is actually only 2½ inches on one side and ¾ inch on the other—not a full 3×1 inches.

assembly

1. Cut out notches and pot holder with a coping saw if not precut. Go slow to not overheat or strain the saw blade cutting

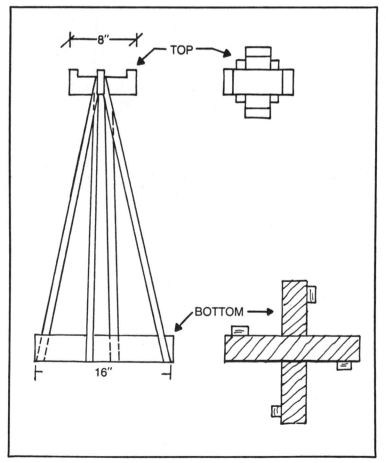

Fig. 6-15. Plant stand.

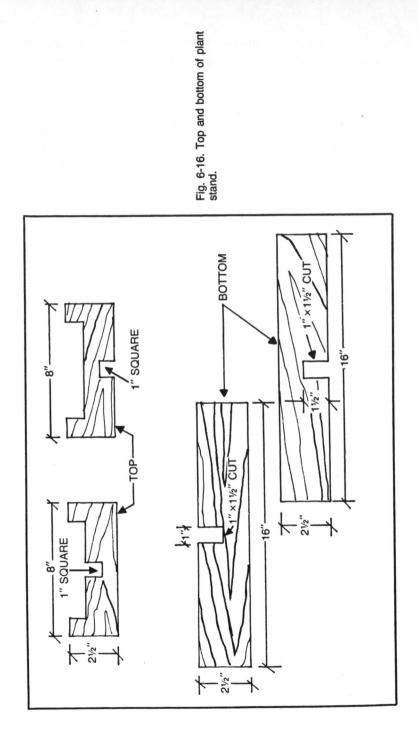

Fig. 6-16. Top and bottom of plant stand.

1" SQUARE

1" SQUARE

TOP

8"

8"

2½"

BOTTOM

1" × 1½" CUT

1" × 1½" CUT

16"

16"

2½"

2½"

1½"

1"

through the 3-inch lumber. Adjust the blade to go around corners.

2. Glue the bottom and top pieces together with a lap joint.

3. Nail and glue legs between the top and base.

4. Countersink all nails with a nail set and cover with wood putty from a stick. Sand lightly over the filled nail holes.

finishing

1. Use a wood filler.

2. Stain with a light or dark stain according to your preference and cover with a polyurethane varnish for the look of an expensive antique. If you want to make several of these flower pot stands, just change the dimensions of the four 1×2 legs. The one you have just built is 34 inches tall. Our other two stands are 13 inches and 21 inches tall, taking 12 and 20-inch legs.

Indoor Lattice Arbor

If you want to give your family room a June look during bleakest January, you will be immensely pleased with this traditional lattice arbor designed to frame a window and be filled with lush foliage plants. Lattice is an easy material to work with and gets you quick professional looking results.

materials and tools

Three 48×24-inch pieces of ¾-inch interior plywood, two 24×24-inch pieces of ¾-inch interior plywood, four 2×4s 84 inches long, two 84×24-inch pieces of lattice, one 48×12-inch piece of lattice, 528 inches of ½-inch molding, 96 inches of 2-inch-wide molding, six cup hooks, nylon fishline, assortment of nails including 3d spiral common and 6d common, staples, glue, one quart each of undercoat and finish coat paint, hammer, stapler, brushes, small handsaw.

shopping

1. Have all the plywood pieces cut from one 4×8-foot panel of ¾-inch plywood (Fig. 6-17).

2. Have lattice cut from one 4×8-foot panel (Fig. 6-18).

3. The paint is your choice.

preparation

1. Measure and mark your nail guidelines ⅜ inch in from

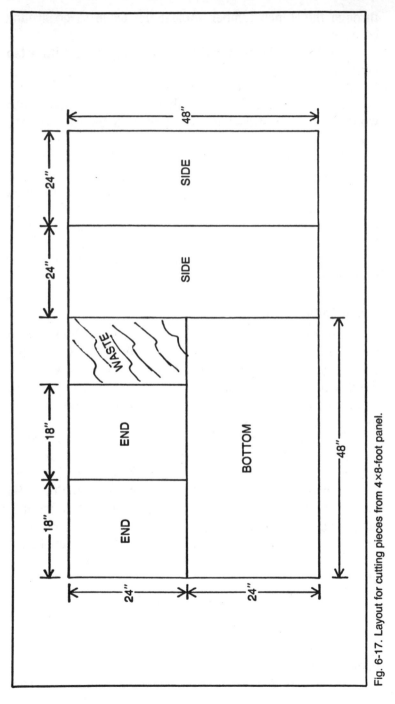

Fig. 6-17. Layout for cutting pieces from 4×8-foot panel.

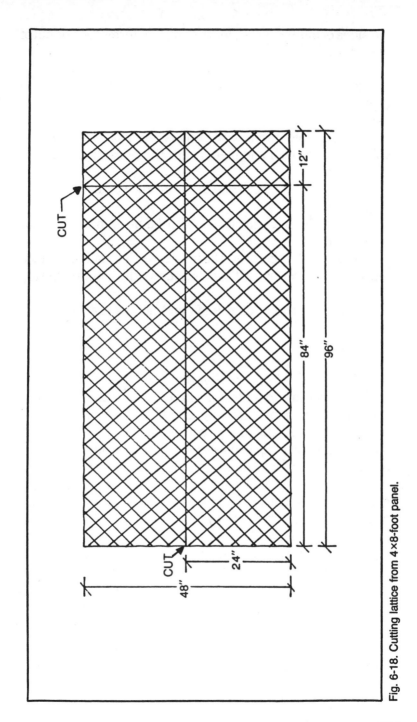

Fig. 6-18. Cutting lattice from 4×8-foot panel.

the sides of the end pieces for the box that forms the bottom of the arbor.

2. Measure and mark the placement of the lattice panel that goes on the front of the box 6 inches down from the top (Fig. 6-19).

assembly

1. Assemble the box with nails and glue. Use your 3d spiral nails through end pieces into the ends of side pieces (Fig. 6-20).

2. With 6d nails, nail one 2×4 into each corner of the box (Fig. 6-20).

3. Nail the top onto 2×4s with 6d nails in each corner (Fig. 6-19).

4. Screw the six cup hooks into the underneath side of the top, evenly spaced and in the center down the length of the top piece.

5. Staple lattice onto ends and across the front (Fig. 6-19).

finishing

1. Paint to suit your taste.

Since the arbor has no bottom, use large saucers under your potted plants to protect the floor. If you would like to use it as a planter, simply buy a piece of plywood to fit and nail it on when you make the box. Coat the inside of the arbor box with polyurethane liquid plastic. Line the bottom with gravel or pot shards before putting in your potting soil.

When selecting plants for your indoor arbor, group together species that need similar growing conditions, especially those that thrive on lots of light but need little direct sun. Use the fishline tied to the cup hooks for climbers.

This arbor was designed to frame a 48-inch window. You may change the dimensions to scale the arbor to any window you have.

Lighted Plant Stand

If you have some prize-winning house plants to be displayed, this lighted plant stand is just what you ordered. You may want to skip ahead to Chapter 8 for some details about wiring in the fluorescent fixtures.

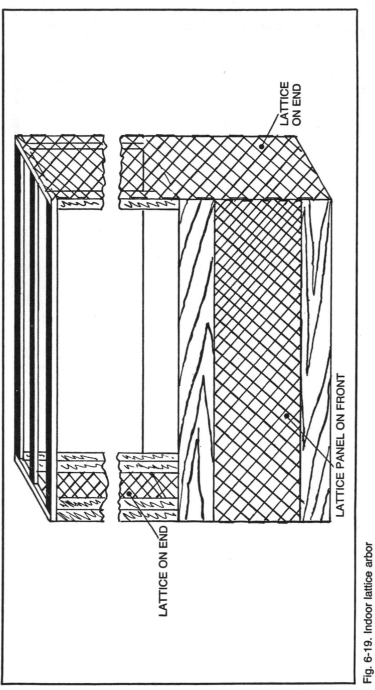

LATTICE ON END

LATTICE ON END

LATTICE PANEL ON FRONT

Fig. 6-19. Indoor lattice arbor

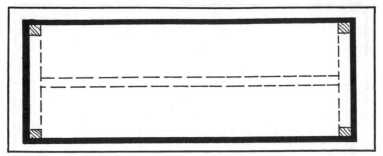

Fig. 6-20. Layout of corner 1×4s.

materials and tools

Four 12×36-inch pieces of ¾-inch interior plywood, one 36×36-inch piece of ¾-inch interior plywood, 16 corner braces (small-sized), 88 ½-inch, 8-gauge screws, two 24-inch fluorescent light fixtures, two wire nuts (solderless connectors), one 6-foot power cord with plug, four 31×7-inch white opaque plastic diffusers, 1 pint polyurethane matte varnish, screwdriver, drill, keyhole saw, wire strippers, paintbrush.

shopping

1. Buy plywood cut to size. If the lumberyard worker will make your 30×6-inch cutout in each of the four plywood sides, you can dispense with the keyhole saw and the time it will take for you to make these cuts.

preparation

1. Measure and mark the positions of all corner braces, marking the position of each screw. Use two for each corner and two for each side.

2. Measure and mark the position of the two light fixtures on the underneath side of the top (Fig. 6-21).

assembly

1. If you are making cutouts yourself, measure, mark, and then saw with a keyhole saw a 30×6-inch cutout in each of four sides. Drill a hole near one corner of the waste panel to admit the end of the saw blade.

2. Drill starter holes for screws and assemble with screws and corner braces (Fig. 6-22).

3. Drill clearance holes in plastic diffusers—six in each diffuser ¼ inch in from top and bottom edges. Secure over cutouts from inside with screws.

214

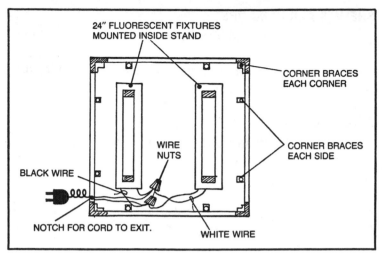

Fig. 6-21. View inside the lighted plant stand.

4. Mount fluorescent fixtures where marked.

5. Strip wires coming from the fixtures and ends of the power cord.

6. Twist white wires together with one of the wires from the power cable and secure with a wire nut.

7. Twist black wires together with other wire from the power cable and secure with a wire nut.

8. Make a small notch at the corner of one of the panels for power cord exit.

finishing

1. Give the entire structure a coat of polyurethane varnish.

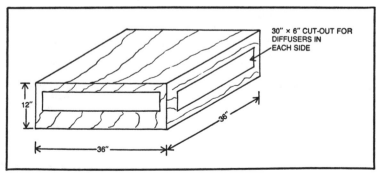

Fig. 6-22. Lighted plant stand.

SHELVES AND HANG-UPS

All kinds of shelf ideas can be used for displaying flower pots. Plants have been supported by shelves for years. Fancy shelf supports that can also be used as plant hangers have recently come into vogue.

A Shelf for Pots

Figure 6-23 illustrates this idea from which you can come up with many variations.

materials and tools

One or more 1×12 pine boards of appropriate length, two or more fancy shelf support brackets, hollow wall anchors or long wood screws, paint, keyhold saw, drill and bits, screwdriver, paintbrush.

shopping

1. Have lumber cut to suit.
2. Shop for the type of bracket shown in Fig. 6-24. They come in various finishes including gold embossed.

preparation

1. Measure diameters of pots you wish to put in the shelf. Draw circles with those diameters on the board.
2. Measure and mark carefully where you want shelves and supports to go on the wall.

Fig. 6-23. Shelf for pots.

Fig. 6-24. Ten-minute hang-ups.

assembly

1. Cut all holes in the board with a keyhole saw.

2. Locate studs in walls and screw support brackets into studs with long wood screws if possible. Otherwise, drill holes and insert the hollow wall anchors.

finishing

1. Paint shelves to match the wall or other room decor.

Ten-Minute Hang-Ups

Plant raising in pots in homes has become so popular that hardware makers have come up with a plethora of plant hangers. None takes more than 10 minutes to install. Here is a rundown on these quick-to-install plant hang-ups.

The most typical pieces of hardware for hanging plants is illustrated in Fig. 6-25. These are ceiling hangers and come in both screw-type (Fig. 6-25A) for fastening into joists and toggle bolt types (Fig. 6-25B) for use where there is no ceiling joist to tie into. To install, simply drill a starter hole or clearance hole and turn into place.

Most hardware and plant stores carry the Edward A. Designs plant holder shown in Fig. 6-26. These are made from clear plastic—platform, ring, and tube lines. These plant holders slip into the hangers discussed earlier.

Macrame hangers are easy to do yourself, but they are also available already done and ready to hang. Macrame is basically twisted rope that is looped around the pot and hung from a piece of hardware such as the screw eye or toggle bolt described earlier.

Wire is very handy for hanging plants. It comes in a wide variety of forms and sizes. Size is by gauges with 10, 12, 14, 16, and 20 the most common. Wire will either be single strand or twisted strand. The latter is probably the most used. Both are galvanized for rust resistance. The lighter gauges—18 and 20—are quite flexible and can be easily formed to hold plants. Another form of wire—usually sold as clothesline—is very handy for hanging plants; it is a plastic-coated wire. Its major advantage is that it is easy to clean. Simply wipe with a damp cloth.

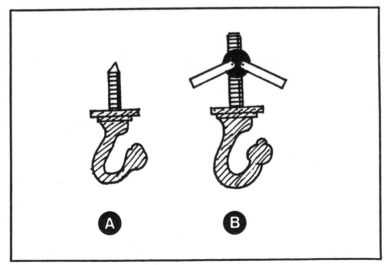

Fig. 6-25. Decorative hooks.

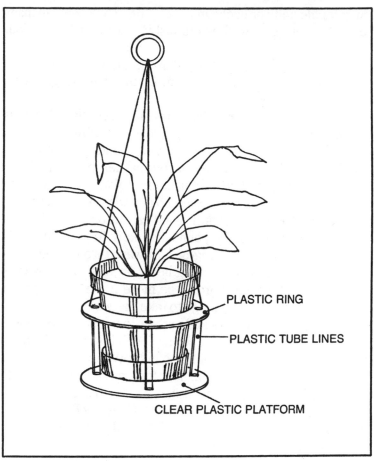

PLASTIC RING

PLASTIC TUBE LINES

CLEAR PLASTIC PLATFORM

Fig. 6-26. Edward A. Designs plant holder.

Hanging tracks are quick to install and good for four or five plants. The plants are suspended from hooks with corresonding pieces of hardware that ride along in the track. These hanging tracks come with complete installation directions.

Swivel hangers can be hooked onto just about anything you happen to have handy. Plants hung from these swivels can be rotated 360 degrees, which makes it easy to face them toward the sunlight as the day progresses.

You won't believe the variety of chains you can buy to support your plant population. Chain-hung plants can be secured to shelf support brackets used singly or in pairs and to fancy toggle bolts or hooks in the ceiling. They come in many decorator colors as well as old-fashioned brass finish. Your choices will range through single and double jack chain, straight link, twist link, sash chain, plumber's chain, bead chain, and even dog runner chain. Chain plant-hanging possibilities seem endless.

Pulley type hardware that works like venetian blinds can be used. You raise or lower the plants by pulling on a cord. The ability to lower the plants is very handy for watering.

Make sure that the material your garden is hung from can support the weight. If you are hanging a plant on a Sheetrock ceiling, for example, don't exceed 5 pounds total—plant, pot, and water. Plaster ceilings in good condition can hold a bit more. Much more than 16 pounds is likely to pull the toggle bolt used to secure your hang-up hardware through the material. Ideally, try to find a ceiling beam or joist to screw into. You can go to 20 pounds or maybe more if the screw eye or other hardware is hefty enough to take the weight. Acoustical tile ceilings are usually backed with ¾-inch plywood that will take a good-sized decorative screw eye. This type of hang-up will also support up to about 20 pounds. Where shelf support brackets are used to hang plants along a wall, these should always be anchored to a wall stud if you are hanging plants of average or large size. Here, again, don't exceed 5 pounds if you are supporting the brackets with toggle bolts into Sheetrock.

PLANTERS

Although some projects in the "boxes" section turned out to be planters, not all planters are boxes. Here are a few special planters for special purposes and boxes that are boxes plus something else.

A New Angle on Planters

As you can see when you study Fig. 6-27, none of your plants will get boxed in by this handy through-type planter. The sides are 1×12 lumber set at a 45-degree angle and supported by legs that form right triangles. Make it long or short to fit your space.

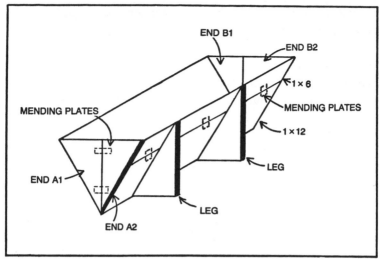

Fig. 6-27. New angle on planters.

materials and tools

Two boards 8-inches long, three 1×12 boards 48 inches long, one small can wood putty, one small can polyurethane liquid plastic, 3d casing nails and white glue, eight mending plates with small gauge ½-inch screws, hammer, nail set, glue brush, drill, screwdriver.

shopping

1. Shop for lumber such as cedar or redwood that will not need finishing or waterproofing.

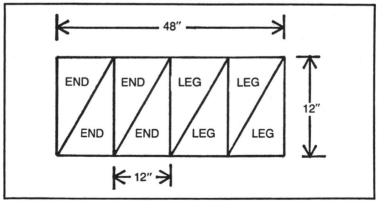

Fig. 6-28. Cutting pattern for ends and legs.

2. Have the lumber cut to your specifications.

preparation

1. Measure one of the 48-inch-long 1×12 boards off into four squares 11¼-inches on each side (Fig. 6-28). Mark a diagonal across each one of the squares.

2. Have the lumber cut into eight equal triangles as marked.

assembly

1. Spread glue along one edge each of the 1×6s and 1×12s and push firmly together. Secure with mending plate on one side only (Fig. 6-29). This makes two sides of the planter.

2. Spread glue along one edge each of four of the triangles and press together. Secure with mending plates on one side (Fig. 6-30). This makes the two ends of the planter.

3. Glue and nail ends to sides.

4. Spread glue along the hypotenuse of each of the remaining four triangles (hypotenuse is the long 16-inch side) and press firmly into place along the sides of the planter 1 foot from each end. Nail in place from the inside of the planter.

finishing

1. Caulk the crack at the bottom of the planter where two sides join with wood putty.

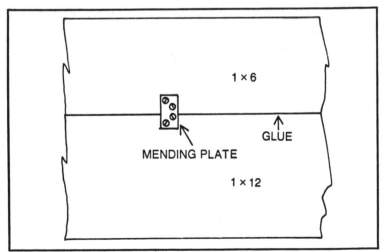

Fig. 6-29. Glue and mending plates make the sides.

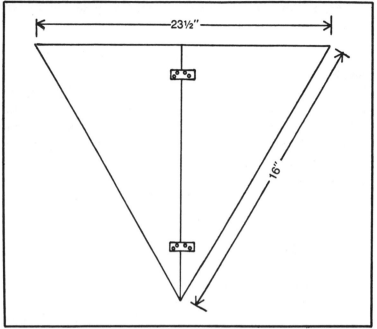

Fig. 6-30. New angle planter showing end.

2. After putty and glue are dry, coat the inside of the planter with liquid plastic.

3. Put pottery shards or gravel in the bottom of the planter and place potting soil over it.

4. Plant with long-blooming plants.

Plant Reflector Planter

This quick-to-build planter will be the envy of all your friends. The mirrors help to expand space and multiply your plants. Although we give specific dimensions, you will see in a moment how easy it is to change these to suit your space and available mirrors (Fig. 6-31).

materials and tools

Two full-length matching mirrors 16×72 inches, two pieces ¾-inch plywood 36×8 inches, two pieces ¾-inch plywood 22½×8 inches, one piece ¾-inch plywood 24×36 inches, three 2×4s 8-feet long, 3d casing nails, 10d common nails, glue, small can liquid fiberglass, paint, putty stick, sealer, sandpaper, one dozen mirror wall fasteners with screws, hammer, nail set, brushes, screwdriver.

shopping

1. Get all lumber cut to exact size as determined by the width of your mirrors.

2. Use a type of lumber that will finish well in a natural finish if you plan to varnish or stain. If you will be painting your finished planter, use less expensive plywood (but with one good side) and inexpensive 2×4s—just make sure they are number one grade, straight and true.

preparation

1. Because you will be constructing a box, measure and mark a line for your casing nails ⅜ inch in from all edges that will be glued and nailed.

2. Measure and mark positions of 2×4 columns.

assembly

1. Assemble the box with glue and casing nails (Fig. 6-31).

2. Countersink nails with the nail set. Fill with the putty stick.

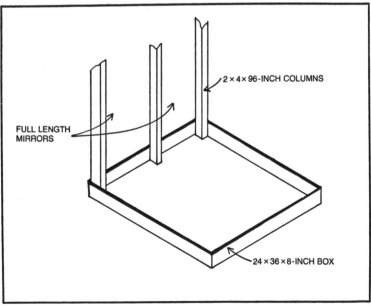

Fig. 6-31. Plant reflector planter.

3. Nail 2×4 columns in place with 10d nails (Fig. 6-31).

4. Mount mirrors in place between columns with fasteners.

finishing

1. Coat the inside of the box with liquid fiberglass. Seal the outside.

2. Paint or varnish the outside and slide the entire unit into place.

3. Place a layer of loose gravel on the bottom and pour it in the potting mixture.

Mobile Planter

Your plants can join the mobile society in this box-on-a-creeper combination (Fig. 6-32). *Creepers* are what mechanics use for rolling themselves under cars when they have to work on the underside. These creepers hold a lot of weight and roll easily on dish-shaped casters. Build the planter out of ¾-inch plywood to fit the creeper. Put your plants in pots (with saucers under them to simplify watering) and set them in the box. Fill around the pots with bark chips to make them look "planted."

materials and tools

Three 60×24-inch pieces of ¾-inch plywood, two 24×22½-inch pieces of ¾-inch plywood, mechanic's creeper, 3d casing nails, glue, paint, hammer, brushes.

shopping

1. Have plywood cut to exact sizes.

2. A creeper can be bought at an auto parts supply store, or you can advertise for a used one.

preparation

1. Measure the creeper and have the plywood box bottom and sides cut to fit.

2. Measure and mark a line for nails ⅜ inch in from the edges where nails are to be driven.

assembly

1. Assemble the box with glue and 3d casing nails.

2. Remove the headrest from the creeper.

3. Place a box on the creeper and secure with five or six 3d casing nails.

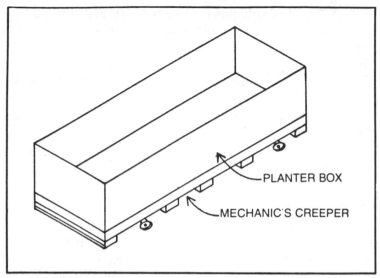

Fig. 6-32. Mobile planter.

finishing

1. Sand and seal the box.

2. Paint the box inside and out.

3. Place plants and bark chips in the box and roll to sun or shade.

CACHEPOTS

Cachepots are ornamental hiding places for flower pots. We have two suggestions for cachepots. One will give your conversations a musical background (providing there's a breeze) and the other is designed around a pun we simply couldn't resist. Would you believe an end-of-the-rainbow cachepot?

Musical Cachepot

You can cache a lot of pots in this one. It also makes an ideal summer vacation spot for your wintertime housebound plants.

materials and tools

Two 36×24-inch pieces of striated ¾-inch plywood, two 24×22½-inch pieces of ¾-inch plywood (striated), one

41×31-inch piece of ¾-inch nonstriated plywood, two 1×4s 36 inches long, two 1×4 31 inches long, three 10-foot bamboo fishing poles, 12 small corner braces, 3d casing nails, glue, paint or sealer, to suit, staples, fishline, sandpaper, hammer, screwdriver, staple gun, small handsaw, drill, small bit.

shopping

1. Have all lumber cut to exact sizes.

2. Try to get a good grade of striated plywood that will finish well to "match" the bamboo chime elements.

preparation

1. Measure and mark the bamboo fishing poles into 45 separate lengths to be cut as follows: nine pieces each 4, 6, 8, 10, and 12 inches in length.

assembly

1. Glue and nail the four sides of striated plywood together into a boxlike structure.

2. Glue and nail the plain plywood panel to make the bottom for the box. Lay it on carefully so that 3½ inches project on all four sides as shown in Fig. 6-33.

3. Using three corner braces per side, install 1×4s as the top rail on the box (Fig. 6-33).

4. Drill a small hole through the tops of each bamboo chime and cut with a saw.

5. Tie fishline through each wind chime hole and staple to the underneath side of the top rail—10 on each side with one on each of the four corners (Fig. 6-33).

finishing

1. Sand and seal.

2. Paint to suit inside and out.

3. Cache your favorite potted plants.

End-of-the-Rainbow Cachepot

This cachepot adds all the colors of the rainbow to your plants' colors. It is easy to assemble once the parts are cut and drilled.

materials and tools

Forty-four 1×2s 24 inches long, two pieces ½-inch exterior plywood 24×24 inches, two pieces ½-inch exterior plywood 24×22½ inches, eight ½-inch dowels 22½ inches

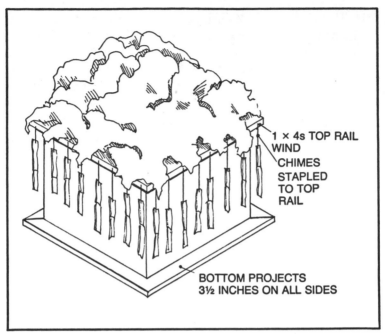

1 × 4s TOP RAIL
WIND
CHIMES
STAPLED
TO TOP
RAIL

BOTTOM PROJECTS
3½ INCHES ON ALL SIDES

Fig. 6-33. Musical cachepot.

long, 16 drapery brackets with screws, 1 quart white exterior house paint, eight small spray cans exterior paint (one each of red, orange, yellow, green, blue, indigo, violet and black), 2d casing nails, white glue, sandpaper, drill, 9/16-inch bit, hammer, screwdriver, glue and paintbrushes, ruler.

shopping

1. Get all lumber cut to exact size.

2. When shopping for the small cans of spray paint, you may have some trouble finding indigo and violet. Usually they are marketed as some shade of blue. Anyway, use a spectrum blue for your rainbow blue and then some darker shades of blue or purple for indigo and violet if need be.

preparation

1. Measure ¼ inch from the edges of plywood and mark a line to guide you in driving the 2d casing nails when assembling the cache box.

2. Measure and mark the center of each hole to be drilled in each end of the 1×2s ¾ inch from each edge and ¾ inch down from the ends.

finishing

1. Assemble four sides of plywood into the box with glue and nails. Drill holes in 1×2s as marked.

2. Paint the exterior of the box with white house paint.

3. Spray paint seven 1×2s red, seven orange, and six each of yellow, green, blue, indigo, and violet.

4. Spray paint all dowel rods black.

assembly

1. Study Figs. 6-34 and 6-35.

2. Install drapery brackets at each corner of the box's top and bottom (Fig. 6-34 and 6-35).

3. Push dowel rods through 1×2s, 11 on each side, in the sequence ROY G. BIV (i.e., red, orange, yellow, green, blue, indigo, and violet).

4. Fasten and secure all dowel rod ends into drapery brackets. For an added touch, you might set this cachepot on a mini-platform of yellow bricks.

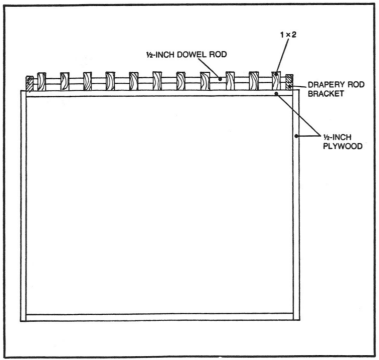

Fig. 6-34. Top view of rainbow cachepot.

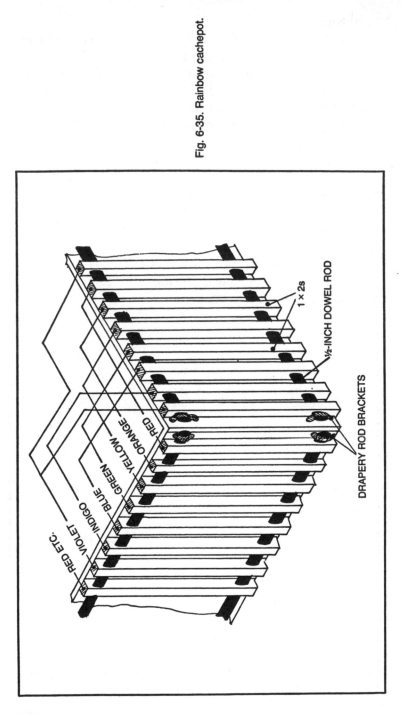

Fig. 6-35. Rainbow cachepot.

RED ETC.
VIOLET
INDIGO
BLUE
GREEN
YELLOW
ORANGE
RED

1 × 2s

½-INCH DOWEL ROD

DRAPERY ROD BRACKETS

QUICK POTTING BENCH

With the aid of a card table and a box, you can have a big potting bench that folds into a storage area only 1 foot by less than 3 feet. There is plenty of storage space in the box for your extra pots and underneath for bags of potting soil, vermiculite, and sphagnum (Fig. 6-36).

materials and tools

One 34-inch square card table with reinforced top, one piece ¾-inch exterior plywood cut to 35½×35½ inches square, one piece ¾-inch exterior plywood cut to 35½×12 inches, 2 pieces ¾-inch exterior plywood cut to 35½×12 inches, three 1×10s 34 inches long, six 1×1 cleats 9½ inches long, 3d casing nails, 10d nails, white glue, hook and eye, sunshine yellow house paint, large piano hinge, sandpaper, sealer, hammer, screwdriver, glue and paintbrushes.

shopping

1. Get all lumber cut to exact size (see below).

2. Most card tables are 34 inches square, which is what our dimensions are based on. Some, however, are only 30 inches square. If you use one of these, just scale down by 4 inches.

preparation

1. Measure your table. If it is not of the 34-inch variety, scale down your plans accordingly.

2. Measure ⅜ inch in from the edges of plywood for nail lines.

assembly

1. Glue and nail together with 3d casing nails the U-shape to form the sides and top of the storage box.

2. Glue and nail on the 35½×35½-inch back.

3. Nail in cleats to support shelves as indicated in Fig. 6-36.

4. Put 1×10 shelves in place and drive casing nails into their ends through the sides of the storage box.

5. Remove one set of legs from the card table.

6. Secure one edge of the card table to the outside edge of the bottom shelf with the piano hinge.

7. Install a hook on the top edge of the storage box and

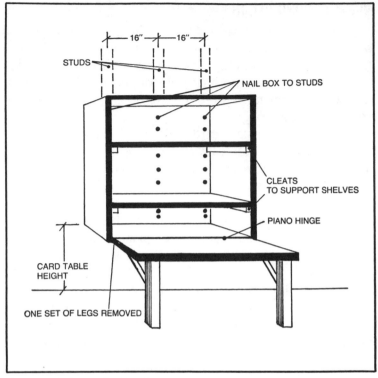

Fig. 6-36. Quick potting bench.

screw eye into the outer edge of the table. With legs folded, hook the table into "closed" position.

8. Find studs in the wall on which you are going to hang your storage box-potting table. The studs will be 16 inches on centers, so you will want to hang your box to three studs.

9. Use helpers or scrap lumber to support your box. Hang it at just the right height to accommodate the legs on the card table.

10. Line up the exact center of the box with the center stud.

11. Nail the box into place with 10d nails. Use 20 to 30 nails to make it secure.

finishing

1. Paint the entire storage box-planting bench inside and out with sunshine yellow paint.

QUICK GROW-LIGHT SETUP

Kits for making your own sawhorses are available at most lumber and discount stores. A sawhorse, with a shelf added to the crosspieces between the legs, makes an ideal grow-light setup. Add your light to the underneath side of the top crosspiece (Fig. 6-37). Paint it in attractive colors.

materials and tools

One sawhorse kit complete with brackets and 2×4 members, one 1×12 shelf cut to the length of the finished sawhorse, one fluorescent grow-light, screws, a few nails, some paint of your choice, hammer, screwdriver, drill, bit for starter holes.

shopping

1. Note exact dimensions of the sawhorse on your kit and have a 1×12 shelf board cut to fit lengthwise over the cross member. If your kit should be the type without a cross-member, just purchase four corner braces to support your shelf.

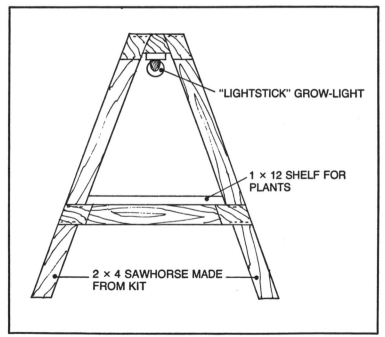

"LIGHTSTICK" GROW-LIGHT

1 × 12 SHELF FOR PLANTS

2 × 4 SAWHORSE MADE FROM KIT

Fig. 6-37. Sawhorse grow-light.

2. You do not have to purchase a grow-light as such. A fluorescent bulb is fine.

preparation

1. Measure and mark the position for the mounting light in the center of the sawhorse's top crosspiece.

assembly

1. Assemble a sawhorse according to the directions that come with the kit.

2. Mount the light on the underneath side of the top crosspiece as marked with screws provided.

3. Fasten the shelf to side crosspieces with 4d nails or with corner braces if required.

finishing

1. Paint to suit, plug it in, and let there be light.

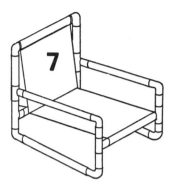

Projects for Kids

If you make items for your kids, you will become a hero in their eyes. These projects can be made easily and swiftly.

BALANCE BEAM

This beam is a mere 7 inches from the ground. You won't have to spot for the kids while they do their tricks.

materials and tools

One 4×4 8 feet long (if you don't have that much room, a 7 or 6-foot piece will have to do), six pieces of 4×4 cut into 1-foot lengths, 10 corner braces, 12 mending plates, wood screws to match, 1 piece of light upholstery plastic 14 inches wide and as long as the 4×4, staples or small tacks, glue, drill, screwdriver, ruler, marking pencil, stapler or tack hammer.

shopping

1. Have a lumberyard worker saw up your 4×4s to size.

2. You will probably need about 1 yard of the plastic. It comes in 54 and 60-inch widths; neither width is long enough to cover the beam.

3. Get your braces and mending plates in the 4-inch sizes; each half of the corner brace is 2 inches.

preparation

1. Mark the short pieces along the long edges for mending plates (Fig. 7-1).

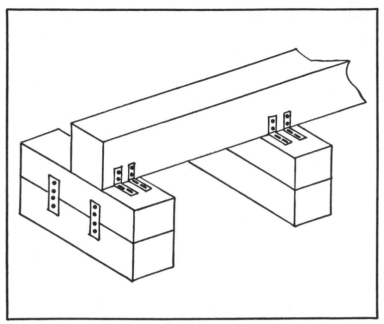

Fig. 7-1. Balance beam construction details.

2. Mark the ends of the beam for corner braces as shown.

3. Find the center of the beam. Mark 1″ each side of the center of corner braces on both sides of the beam.

4. Mark three of the short pieces on the top for corner braces to match those on the beam.

5. Cut the plastic into 16-inch-wide strips long enough to cover the beam.

6. Mark corner braces on plastic.

assembly and finishing

1. Drill holes for screws in marked places.

2. Attach mending plates to short pieces. Make three stacks of two pieces each.

3. Wrap the beam in plastic and staple or tack the plastic at close intervals along the entire seam.

4. Fold in excess as shown in Fig. 7-2 over the short ends and tack or staple those in place.

5. Set the beam on top of the short pieces. Line up the marks for corner braces and attach corner braces to all places.

6. Sand the wood. Varnish or paint if desired.

SIMPLE MINI-TRAMP

materials and tools

One tractor tire, 3½ yards heavy duck or denim material or tarp (60 inches wide), strong nylon cord, metal eyelets big enough to admit cord, heavy scissors, eyelet setter, measuring tape, ruler, marking pencil.

shopping

1. Get your secondhand tractor tire at a truck and tractor supply store.

2. Because tractor tires vary in size, it is impossible to give exact measurements for material patterns and cord requirements. Thirty feet of cord should be about right.

3. If you have an old tarp in good condition, use it.

preparation

1. Set the tire on top of the tarp. Draw the circle on the tarp.

2. Measure 2½ inches and draw a bigger circle around the one you have.

3. Repeat step 1 and 2 for a second circle.

4. Two inches in from the edge, mark a circle at 3-inch intervals. Repeat with the other circle.

assembly and finishing

1. Set eyelets on the marks on both circles.

2. Place the tire on one circle and put the other circle on top of the tire.

3. Lace a cord through the first eyelet and then lash the circles together (Fig. 7-3).

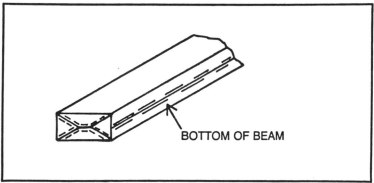

BOTTOM OF BEAM

Fig. 7-2. Covering beam with plastic.

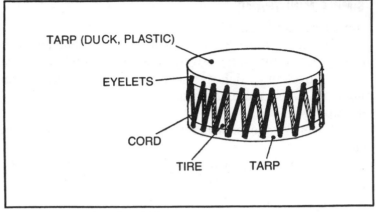

Fig. 7-3. Construction of a mini-tramp.

SIMPLE BARRÉ

materials and tools

One piece of banister 4 or more feet long, two brackets, screws to fit brackets, large mirror (optional), hammer, screwdriver, marking pencil, ruler, drill.

shopping

Have a piece of banister railing, the wooden kind, cut to your measurements.

preparation

1. Locate the studs on the wall for which the barré is destined.

2. Measure the wall to see how long the barré can be.

3. On the two studs that are the right distance apart for the barré, mark the position of the banister brackets—including screw holes. The barré should be about chest height to a child.

assembly and finishing

1. Attach brackets to the wall on places marked.

2. Attach banister to brackets according to directions with the banister/bracket package.

3. Sand and wax (Fig. 7-4).

4. Hang a large mirror on the opposite wall or directly behind the barré.

5. If the mirror is behind the barré, hang brackets first, then the mirror, and finally the banister.

TUMBLING MAT

materials and tools

One foam pad 26 inches wide and 5 or 6 feet long, 4 yards of light upholstery plastic or material, Velcro fastening tape (optional), scissors, yardstick, sewing machine and needle and thread.

shopping

1. You can usually find the 1-inch thick foam on rolls. Have it cut to size to fit your needs.

2. If you find a ready-cut pad that varies slightly from the given measurements, use it if it is not less than 24 inches wide or more than 30 inches wide.

3. You can substitute heavy duck, denim, or even sheeting for the plastic of the cover if you don't mind washing the cover occasionally.

preparation

1. Cut two pieces of material the length plus 2 inches of your pad and the width plus 2 inches.

2. If you are using material or plastic that is wide enough, you may cut only one piece—2 inches longer and 1½-2 inches wider than the pad.

assembly and finishing

1. Sew plastic together along one short side and two long sides, with the wrong side of the plastic out, and make a seam about ⅝ inch wide.

2. When using wide material or plastic, fold material in half lengthwise and sew one short end and the long side up (Fig. 7-5).

3. Turn it right side out and insert a pad.

4. Sew closed.

5. If you are using material and want the cover to be easily removed, sew two strips of Velcro fastening tape to the inside of the free edges (Fig. 7-6).

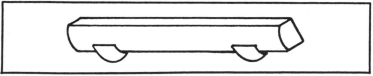

Fig. 7-4. Banister barré.

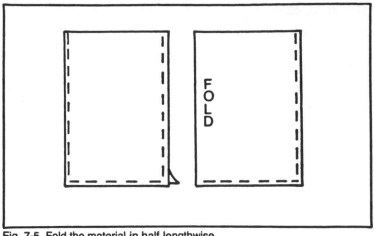

Fig. 7-5. Fold the material in half lengthwise.

OUTDOOR TURNING BAR

materials and tools

One 4×4 4½ feet long or whatever is shoulder high to your child, one piece of 2×4 6 inches long, one heavy-duty closet pole and brackets (3 feet long), four or more heavy-duty gym set anchors, wood screws, creosote (optional), small sack of ready-mix cement and sand (optional), spade, fence post setter (optional), drill, screwdriver, paintbrush (optional), pan to mix concrete (optional).

shopping

1. Get the sturdiest closet pole and brackets available.
2. Have the pole cut to a 3-foot length.
3. Have the rest of the lumber cut to size.

preparation

1. Find a place alongside your house (on grass or sand) that will be suitable for the turning bar.
2. Measure a yard from the house and mark. Mark another 4 inches. Draw a 4½-inch square at that place.
3. Mark for closet pole brackets at one end of your 4×4 and at one end of the 2×4.

assembly and finishing

1. Dig a 6-inch hole on your square.
2. Optional—paint one end (about 6 inches up) of your 4×4 with creosote.

3. Attach gym anchors to your 4×4 following directions on the package.

4. Optional—mix up some concrete and sand with some water. Pour a bit in the bottom of the hole.

5. Set in the 4×4 and secure gym anchors.

6. Optional—pour in more concrete mix to fill the hole.

7. Fill in the hole with earth. Tamp down well.

8. Fasten brackets to the 4×4 and 2×4 on the marked places. Drill starter holes first to make the job easier.

9. Nail or screw 2×4 to the wall directly in line with the 4×4, so the brackets are level with each other.

10. Insert a closet rod (Fig. 7-7).

HOPSCOTCH RUGS

Most kids like to play hopscotch. In areas where the children are confined indoors for long periods, hopscotch mats or rugs are ideal.

"Skinny Sidewalk" Hopscotch Rug

One strip of indoor/outdoor carpeting 2 feet wide and as long as you have room (5-foot minimum) in a dark red or blue, one roll of narrow (1-1½-inch-wide) aluminum tape, some cardboard or heavy paper (optional), scissors, measuring tape, ruler, marking pencil, stapler, needle (optional).

shopping

1. Carpeting usually comes in 6-foot widths, so buy 24 inches or 2 running feet.

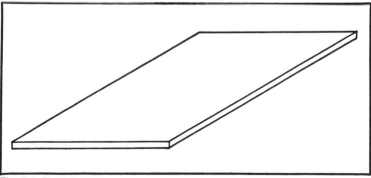

Fig. 7-6. Tumbling mat.

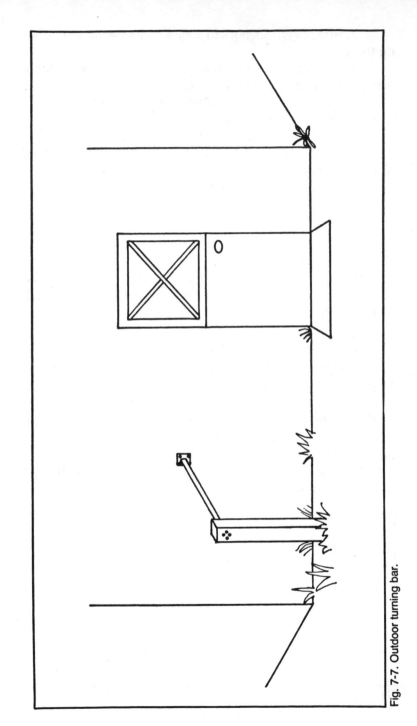

Fig. 7-7. Outdoor turning bar.

preparation

1. We will mark for the "skinny sidewalk" version of the hopscotch game, but basically the marking procedure is the same.

2. Find the center of each short end of your rug and mark it.

3. Measure in 2 inches from each edge, the long ones, and mark at each end.

4. Measure off 5 inches at each short end and mark again.

5. Connect marks to form lines (Fig. 7-8).

6. Put down strips of the aluminum tape you have cut to size on the lines and form a grid pattern.

7. With chalk or pencil, draw numerals in the center of boxes and write the word "start" at one 5-inch margin end and the word "out" at the other.

8. Cut strips of aluminum tape and follow the outlines for numerals and letters. Make the numerals as squared as

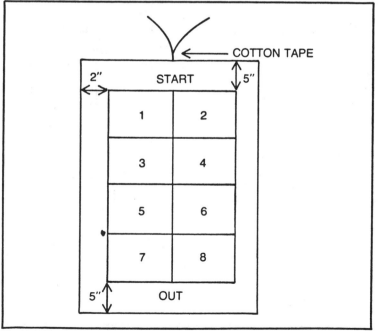

Fig. 7-8. Hopscotch rug with "skinny sidewalk" hopscotch.

possible and use block letters. These are easier to do with tape.

9. Sew the cotton tape to the center of one long edge. Sew in the center of the tape. This step is optional.

10. You can bind the edges of the rug in aluminum tape, too, but it is not necessary.

All the other versions of hopscotch are made in the same way. You can use plastic tape if you prefer. Just make sure the color contrasts well, and that the lines will be thick enough to be easily seen. Make sure the tape sticks well. Rolling a small paint roller or brayer over each strip is ideal.

Note the other versions of the basic hopscotch game (Figs. 7-9A through 7-9F). You might put a different version

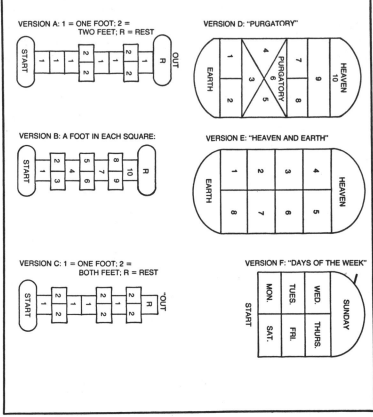

Fig. 7-9. Hopscotch patterns.

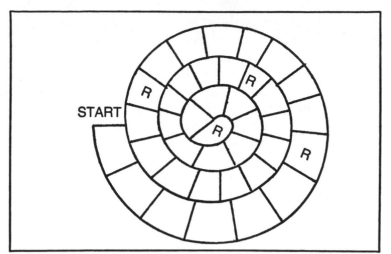

Fig. 7-10. Square hopscotch rug shaped like a snail.

on the flip side of your hopscotch rug, or you might like to
have two or three to decorate the room. If you want to use
them as rugs, omit the tape.

Square Hopscotch Rug
materials and tools
One piece of carpeting about 5 to 6 feet square, aluminum
or plastic tape, scissors, pencil, string and large carpet tack,
ruler.
shopping
Same as for the "skinny sidewalk" rug.
preparation
1. Find the center of your rug by drawing in the diagonals.

2. Using the string, arrange it in the pattern shown in Fig.
7-10.

3. Draw in a line with chalk or pencil.

4. Follow the line with tape.

5. Measure off 5-inch segments and make your lines
across to form little rectangles.

6. Draw the letter "R" in some of the rectangles—about
six or seven—and outline with tape.

7. Letter in the word "start."

To play the game, the player hops around the whole snail on one floor, but is allowed to rest in the places marked with an "R." For each successfully completed turn, the player may throw a rock or small token such as a poker chip from the start position. The rectangle that it lands in is then declared to belong to the player. He may use it as a resting place.

The token remains in the spot. The opponent(s) have to jump across the chamber—on one foot—without stepping on a line.

STORAGE SOLUTIONS

Children need storages areas for their playthings. Here are some suitable projects.

Storage Tower

materials and tools

Beer cartons, strapping tape, sealer, enamel paint, staples, staple gun, scissors, ruler, pencil, paintbrush, paint roller.

shopping

1. Ask people at a brewery or beer distributor if you can buy some used or new cartons.

preparation

No measuring or marking necessary.

assembly and finishing

1. Wipe the boxes clean with a damp cloth or sponge.

2. Use four, five, or six cartons for a stack. You can make double stacks or triple stacks.

3. Staple the cartons together long sides to long sides, with the original tops of the cartons forming the fronts.

4. Reinforce the stack with tape along sides (Fig. 7-11).

5. Seal the cartons and let dry.

6. Paint and let dry; touch up if necessary.

7. You can tie the stacks(s) into the wall with some tacks driven through the back of the stack(s) inside into the wall.

Open Front Tower

materials and tools

Frozen chicken boxes, strapping tape, adhesive-backed

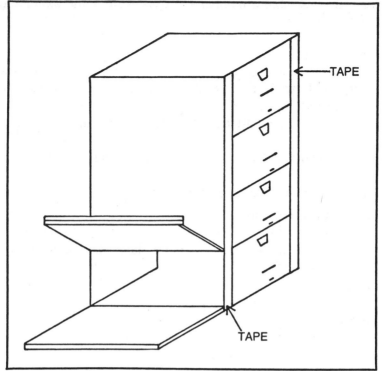

Fig. 7-11. Storage tower.

vinyl (about 3¼ yards per box if you want to cover the inside
and outside and ¾ yard if you cover only the sides, plus an
extra ⅔-yard strip for the top, staples, staple gun, scissors,
ruler, pencil.

shopping

1. Obtain some frozen chicken boxes—24 × 16 × 11
inches.

preparation

1. If you are going to use the adhesive-backed vinyl, cut a
strip 70 inches long and 16 inches wide and a strip 16×24
inches for each box.

assembly and finishing

1. Clean out the boxes by washing them with a sponge
and soapy water. Hang them out to dry.

2. When thoroughly dry, line your boxes with the
adhesive-backed vinyl.

247

3. Assemble a number of boxes—the same as for the storage tower.

4. With long sides together, staple the boxes together into a tower.

5. Reinforce sides with strapping tape along narrow sides, with two bands to each side about 2 inches in from the edges (Fig. 7-12).

6. Cover the outside of the boxes with adhesive-backed vinyl.

7. You might tie the tower into the wall with tacks.

Quick Version of the Open Front Tower

materials and tools

Same as for the open front tower, but omit adhesive-backed vinyl and add 1½-inch-wide plastic tape in a favorite color if desired.

shopping

Same as discussed earlier.

preparation

None.

assembly and finishing

1. Follow steps 1, 3, 4, and 5 for the open front tower (Fig. 7-12).

2. Bind the front edges of the tower with plastic tape if desired.

3. Tie into the wall with tacks if you like.

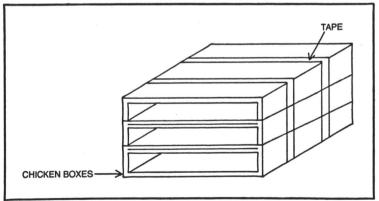

Fig. 7-12. Open front tower.

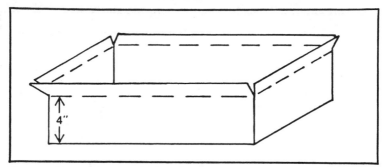

Fig. 7-13. Preparing to cut the box down to fit under-bed clearance.

Under-Bed Storage Boxes

materials and tools

Six frozen chicken boxes for each single bed: 2-inch-wide reinforcing, plastic, or aluminum tape, 1-foot-long heavy cord for each box, adhesive-backed vinyl (optional), scissors, ruler, straightedge, sharp knife.

shopping

Same as for the open front tower.

preparation

1. Measure the clearance between the bottom of your child's bedsprings and the floor. Deduct ¾ inch. You will probably come up with about 4 inches.

2. On each of your six chicken boxes, measure up 4 inches from the bottom of the boxes at each corner. Draw a line connecting them.

assembly and finishing

1. Split each corner down to the mark with your sharp knife.

2. Using your straightedge as a guide, score along each line on both sides (Fig. 7-13).

3. Cut off on scored lines.

4. Reinforce upright joints with the tape.

5. Bind raw edges with the tape.

6. Find the center on the long edge of the box. Punch two holes 2 inches from the center on each side—two holes per box.

7. Thread cord through holes and tie firmly.

8. Put the lid on the box (Fig. 7-14).

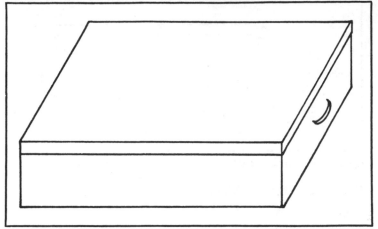

Fig. 7-14. Under-bed storage boxes.

9. If you like, cover the boxes with adhesive-backed vinyl inside and outside. It is a good idea to cover the outside bottom of the boxes, too, for extra strength.

Wooden Under-Bed Storage Boxes for 5-Inch Clearance

Two pieces of ½-inch plywood 16×24 inches (bottom and lid), two pieces of ½-inch plywood 4×15 inches (short sides), two pieces of ½-inch-thick plywood 4×24 inches (front and back), four small plywood scraps, four glides, 2d nails, sandpaper, two pairs of butt hinges per box, hardware for hinges, paint, glue, drawer pull or knob with screws, adhesive-backed vinyl (optional), hammer, screwdriver, ruler, marking pencil, scissors (optional).

shopping

1. For each box you want, have the lumberyard cut your plywood in the pieces described. One 4×8 sheet will give you four boxes.

preparation

1. On one of the 4×24-inch pieces, mark the center front for the knob or pull (Fig. 7-15).

2. On one of the 16×24 pieces, mark the position of butt hinges about 3 inches in from corners.

3. Match the hinge markings on the remaining 24×4-inch piece.

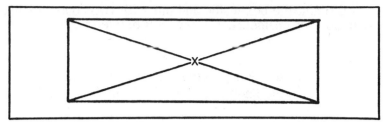
Fig. 7-15. Marking for handle.

assembly

1. Drill a hole for the knob and starter holes for screws on butt hinges.

2. Nail your 15×4 boards between your 25×4 boards to form a frame (Fig. 7-16).

3. Nail your unmarked 24×16 board on top. Make sure that the markings for the hinges are on the other side of the 24×4 piece.

4. Glue the four plywood scraps in the corners of the box on the inside.

5. Attach hinges to the back of the box.

6. Attach hinges to the lid.

finishing

1. Sand the box inside and out.

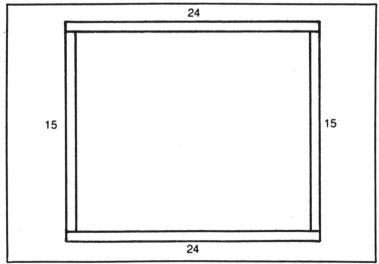
Fig. 7-16. Construction details for under-bed storage boxes.

2. Paint the box inside and out with two coats of latex semigloss or enamel. Let it dry well between coats.

3. Line the box with adhesive-backed vinyl or shelf paper at the bottom and sides and the inside lid if desired (optional).

4. Attach the glides to the corner at the bottom.

5. Attach the knob or pull to the front (Fig. 7-17).

Simple Shelf Unit

This is one of the easiest shelving units to construct and, if you make it out of particle board, one of the cheapest. It is quite sturdy and roomy.

materials

Six 1×8 boards of ⅜-inch-thick particle board (frame and shelves), three 1×8 boards of ⅜-inch-thick particle board (spacers) 11⅝ inches long, 2d nails, sealer, paint, 23 feet of ⅜-inch trim (flat or rounded), small finishing nails, wood putty (optional), sandpaper, hammer, ruler, marking pencil, knife (optional) saw, paint roller.

shopping

1. When you buy your particle board shelves, inspect the corners and make sure they have not been knocked off. Particle board tends to crumble at places of great wear.

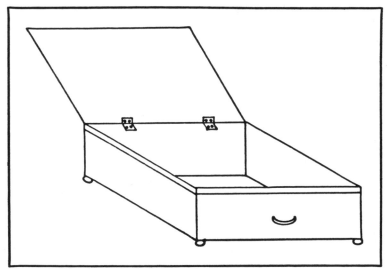

Fig. 7-17. Wooden under-bed storage box.

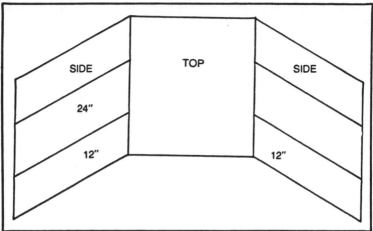

Fig. 7-18. Simple shelf unit—making the U-frame.

preparation

    1. Mark two of your long boards 12 and 24 inches.

    2. Mark the remaining four boards at 18 inches.

assembly

    1. Nail one board of the 36-inch kind between two of the other boards to form a U-frame (Fig. 7-18).

    2. Nail the next 36-inch board inside the "U" at the 12-inch mark.

    3. Nail the next 36-inch board inside the "U" at the 24-inch mark.

    4. Nail the last long board across the top of the structure.

    5. Set in your short 1×8 pieces at the 18-inch marks and nail in place as spacers.

    6. Cut the trim into six 36-inch-long pieces and four 8-inch-long ones, plus three 11⅝-inch-long ones.

    7. Apply to edges as shown using small nails (Fig. 7-19).

finishing

    1. Sand the structure thoroughly.

    2. Seal well with sealer.

    3. Apply two coats of paint using a roller. See Fig. 7-20.

Three "Bs" Storage Units

    These units are made with beer cartons, bricks, and boards.

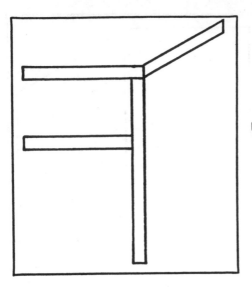

Fig. 7-19. Putting on trim.

materials and tools

As many 12×1 boards as you like or need—either regular lumber or particle board; enough bricks or cement blocks to support the boards in 12-inch-high stacks, as many beer cartons as you can accommodate (17½ to 18 inches of shelf space are needed for each one), sandpaper, sealer, paint, epoxy or mortar (optional), paintbrush, roller, ruler, marking pencil, putty knife and bucket (optional—for mortar only).

shopping

1. Particle board shelves will do very nicely.

2. You can use 1×1-foot cement blocks.

3. You can intersperse the beer cartons with open storage space, so consider this when you get your cartons.

preparation

1. Mark your boards for the brick supports. If you use particle board, you need a support about every 3 feet or so.

2. Measure and mark where the shelves will be on the wall.

assembly and finishing

1. Sand your shelves if they are lumber.

2. Seal the shelves and boxes.

3. Paint the shelves.

4. Paint the boxes.

254

5. If you are going to use epoxied stacks of bricks, do the epoxying now.

6. If you use mortar, get the ready-mix kind and add water to it in a bucket. Apply the mortar with a putty knife. Make sure the surfaces are fairly level before you set the next brick on top.

7. Assemble bricks and boards.

8. Set in boxes with the tops facing the front (Fig.7-21).

On-Door Storage

While there are all kinds of hooks and gadgets available to hang things from doors, you can make a customized version for greater versatility and usefulness. It is inexpensive and quick to make.

materials and tools

One piece of ½-inch pegboard 6 inches narrower than the width of the door and 78 inches long (that will be somewhere between 18×78 inches and 28×78 inches, depending on your

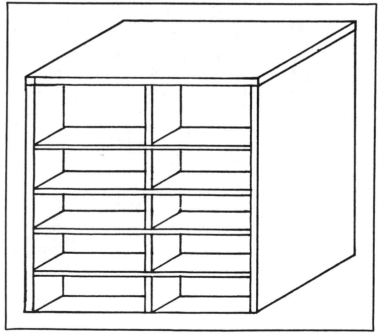

Fig. 7-20. Simple shelf unit.

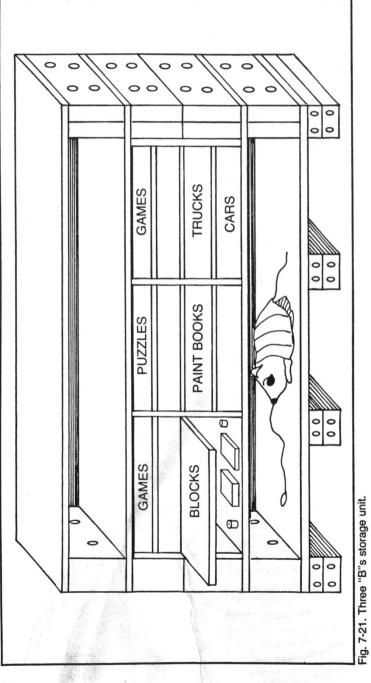

Fig. 7-21. Three "B"s storage unit.

door), two pieces of 1×1 as wide as your pegboard (between 18-28 inches), wood screws 1¼ inches long, 2d nails, paint (optional), pegboard, hangers, spice trays, clips, four small corner braces, drill, hammer, ruler, marking pencil, paintbrush (optional).

shopping

1. Get appropriate hangers.
2. Have pegboard and 1×1s cut to size at the lumberyard.

preparation

1. Measure and mark the door frame 6 inches in from the doorknob edge.
2. Mark your short 1×1s ½ inch in from the end and then every 3 inches.
3. Mark 1×1s for corner braces (Fig. 7-22).

assembly and finishing

1. Drill holes in short 1×1s.
2. Screw 1×1s to the door frame's top and bottom.
3. Attach long 1×1s between short 1×1s. Nail and reinforce with small corner braces.
4. Nail or screw pegboard over the frame.
5. Paint if desired (optional).
6. Attach hardware hangers and trays (Fig. 7-23).

Simplest Pocket Storage System

This one is especially nice for babies if hung by the crib or for toddlers when dangled from a low window casing.

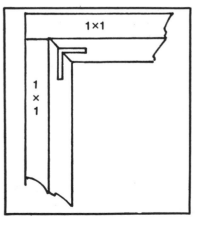

Fig. 7-22. Marking 1×1s for corner braces.

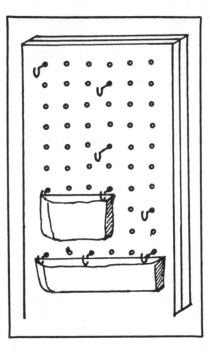

Fig. 7-23. On-door storage unit.

materials and tools

One strip of denim or duck 54 inches long and 10 inches wide, one strip of denim or duck 84 inches long and 7 inches wide (pieced), (1 yard of 54-inch-wide materials), five medium-sized drawer pulls and matching hardware, iron-on decals or fabric crayons (optional), thread, measuring tape, marking chalk or pencil, needle, sewing machine, scissors, ruler, pins, iron and ironing board, drill, screwdriver.

shopping

1. You can buy either plain-colored or printed fabric.

2. You can buy the background (the short strip) in a plain color (⅓ yard—54 inches wide) and the pocket strip in a matching print (½ yard—54 inches wide).

3. Buy drawer pulls that are 1-1½ inches in diameter.

preparation

1. Mark fabric according to dimensions given.

2. Cut in strips.

3. Mark ¼ inch from the long edges and again 1 inch from the long edges.

4. On 7-inch strips, mark 9-inch intervals along the long edges.

5. On a 10-inch strip, mark 6-inch intervals along the long edges (Fig. 7-24).

6. Measure and cut five pieces of fabric 6 inches long and 2 inches wide.

assembly and finishing

1. Fold and crease edges with your iron along 1 and ¼-inch marks on all strips.

2. Fold short 6-inch strips in half, lengthwise, then fold again in half and press.

3. Sew together the two 7-inch strips along the short edges, unfolding and matching creases as you go.

4. Stitch along the bottom of the hem on the wrong side on the short (10-inch) strip at the top and bottom of the strip.

5. Stitch down the hem along one edge of the long pieced strip. Make sure your 9-inch markings remain visible.

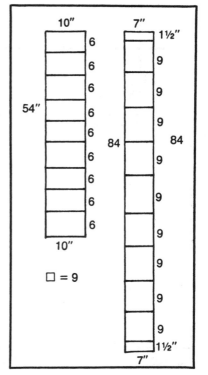

Fig. 7-24. Measuring and marking for the simplest pocket system.

6. Pin the long strip to the shorter strip with side edges matching lower hems evenly (the hem on the longer strip is only folded—not stitched in yet).

7. Pin the 9-inch marks to your 6-inch marks on the shorter strip. Pin the top and bottom, forming pockets.

8. Stitch down along outer edges and along pin markings. Stitch each seam twice, going over the top edge several times to reinforce (Fig. 7-25).

9. Make folds in pockets as shown in Fig. 7-26 and pin down.

10. Stitch across the bottom—forming hem and attaching one strip to the other in one operation. Stitch again ½ inch up from the seam.

11. Stitch your short strips down along each long edge.

12. Fold strips in half and sew one at each end, one in the middle and one each at the 13¼-inch marks (Fig. 7-27).

13. Mark the wall above the crib for knobs. Make starter holes.

14. Attach knobs to the wall with screws that come with the knobs.

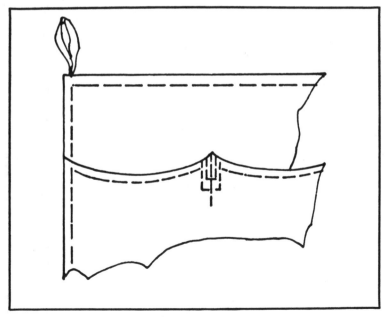

Fig. 7-25. Securing top edges of pockets.

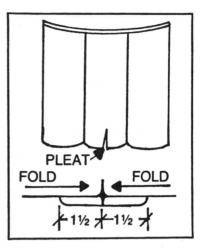

Fig. 7-26. Making folds to form pleats in pocket bottoms.

PLEAT
FOLD → ← FOLD
1½ — 1½

15. If desired, decorate pockets with decals or fabric crayons.

Larger Pocket Storage System

materials and tools

One piece of canvas, duck, or denim 48 inches wide and 2 yards long, heavy eyelets, thread, hooks, scissors, ruler, marking pencil, sewing machine, needle, pins, eyelet setter, drill (optional).

shopping

Same as for simplest pocket storage system.

preparation

1. Mark off and cut one piece of denim 48×32 inches.

2. Mark off ½ inch from the top and bottom and then 2½ inches from that mark.

3. Mark off ½ inch and 1 inch from each long edge.

4. Press along marked lines.

5. Lay out the pockets on remaining fabric as in Fig. 7-28.

6. Mark ½ inch on each pocket edge and press.

assembly and finishing

1. Stitch top and bottom hems on the background piece along creases.

2. Stitch along narrow side hems.

3. Lay pocket pieces on the background and mark lightly around them.

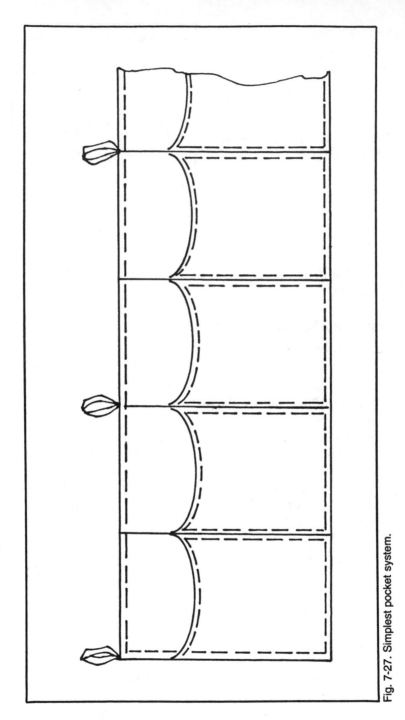

Fig. 7-27. Simplest pocket system.

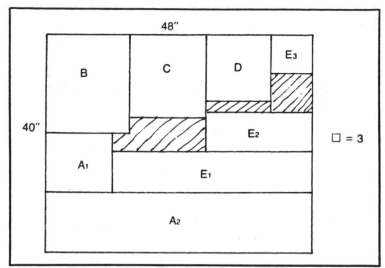

Fig. 7-28. Fabric layout for the large pocket system.

4. Remove pocket pieces and draw a chalk line ¾ inch to the inside of your marks.

5. Stitch across the top hems of all pocket pieces.

6. Pin pockets in place on the background piece on inner chalk lines. Your pockets will be slightly larger than the markings.

7. Stitch in place, twice around, reinforcing at ends with several stitchings.

8. Stitch at marked intervals on pocket strips as well, twice up and down. Reinforce with extra stitching at the tip.

9. Set eyelets, one in each corner and then at 4-inch intervals into the top and bottom hem, and center them between the top edge and bottom of the hem.

10. Hold your denim up to the wall and mark through each eyelet, top and bottom.

11. Attach hooks to marked places.

12. Hang the pocket system (Fig. 7-29).

Door-Hung System

materials and tools

Two-and-a-half yards of 48-inch-wide fabric (denim, duck, or such), two pieces of 1×1 78 inches long, two pieces of

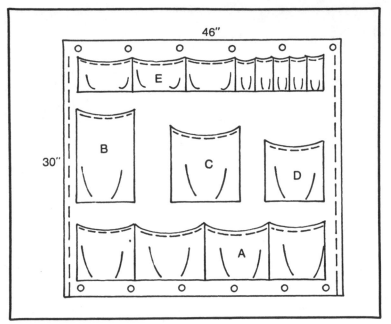

Fig. 7-29. Large pocket storage system.

1×1 20 inches long, staples, 1¼-inch-long wood screws, corner braces (optional), stapler, measuring tape, ruler, pencil, scissors, screwdriver, drill.

shopping

Same as for other pocket systems.

preparation

1. Cut two strips of fabric 48×24 inches (to be pieced).

2. Following the layout in Fig. 7-30, mark and cut pockets and pocket strips.

assembly and finishing

1. Piece the two large pieces so they will measure 96×24 inches.

2. Measure and cut off a 14-inch strip so that you will have an 82×24-inch-long strip left. Keep the 14-inch strip for a pocket strip.

3. Turn up 2 inches top and bottom (24-inch edges)—first 1 inch then the next—and press. Stitch in place.

4. Turn under long edges first 1 inch, then the second, and stitch.

264

5. Mark around the pockets on large strip. Mark again ¾ inch in from the first marks.

6. Attach pockets and strips. Stitching around each pocket twice and reinforce ends by stitching over them three or four times for ½ inch or so.

7. For the pocket strips, sew along indicated lines twice, again reinforcing with overstitching on tops as you did for pockets.

8. Drill through short ends of 1×1 for screws, with the first set in ½ inch from each edge and the next at 3-inch intervals.

9. Screw 1×1s to the top and bottom of the door.

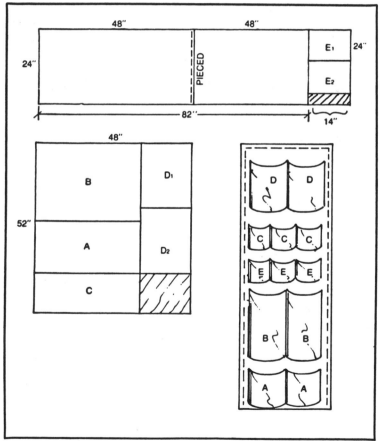

Fig. 7-30. Fabric layout and construction details for door-hung system.

10. Put long pieces of 1×1s in between, attaching with nails to crosspieces. Reinforce with corner braces if desired (Fig. 7-31).

11. Staple the pocket system to the 1×1 frame all around. Keep staples ½ inch in from the hem edges and no more than ¾ inch apart.

Ceiling Storage Unit

materials and tools

Nylon netting (1 yard and 80 inches wide), nylon cord, swivel hooks and hardware, thread, scissors, sewing machine, needle and thread, drill.

shopping

1. The nylon net is readily available and quite inexpensive. It comes in many colors.

2. Use nylon cord in a matching color, or white will do fine.

3. Use the kind of hooks that are designed for hanging baskets.

preparation

1. Measure off the center of the material and fold lengthwise.

2. Measure off 1 inch along the short edges, top and bottom, and then 3 more inches. Repeat with long edges.

3. Press.

4. Measure off four, 5½-foot lengths of cord and cut.

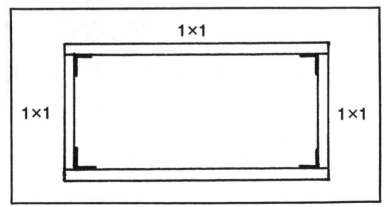

Fig. 7-31. 1×1 framing detail.

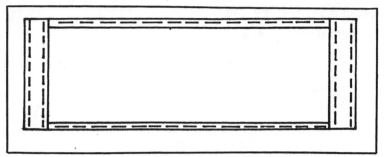

Fig. 7-32. Construction details for the ceiling storage unit.

assembly and finishing

1. Stitch to form the hem's top and bottom. Stitch side hems, leaving ends open.

2. Thread cord through hems (Fig. 7-32).

3. Mark for your four swivel hooks on the ceiling. They should be arranged in a rectangle 24×28 or thereabouts.

4. With a helper, hold up netting by the cords to check the amount of room. If it is too shallow, bring the hooks closer together; if too deep, move the hooks apart.

5. Put in the hooks.

6. Tie cords to hooks.

7. Now you have a place for balls that roll everywhere (Fig. 7-33).

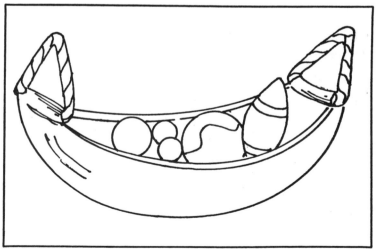

Fig. 7-33. Balls can be stored in the unit.

Bathtub Toy Storage Bag

materials and tools

One yard of nylon net, cord, one swivel hook. Tools are the same as for the ceiling storage unit.

shopping

Same as for the ceiling storage unit.

preparation

1. Fold in half crosswise.
2. Measure down 3 inches from the top.

assembly and finishing

1. Sew the folded nylon net into a rectangle (Fig. 7-34).
2. Turn down 3-inch hem and sew, leaving an opening.
3. Insert the cord (you will need 4 yards). Tie the ends into a double knot.
4. Mark for the hook in the ceiling. Drill a starter hole and screw in the hook.
5. Hang the bag (Fig. 7-35). You can do without the hook and hang the bag from the shower.

EASELS

Easels can be used to support an artist's canvas. They may easily double as bulletin boards.

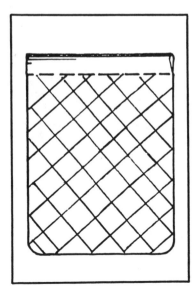

Fig. 7-34. Construction details for the bathtub toy storage bag.

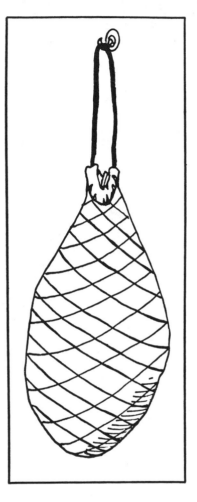

Fig. 7-35. Bathtub toy storage bag.

Wall-Hung Easel

materials and tools

One piece of 30×20 ⅜-inch particle board or ½-inch plywood, four pieces of 2×4 about 8 inches long, one large spring clip paper holder or two medium ones, heavy picture wire or rope, 1-inch screws, decorative wall hook, plastic spice shelf and hardware (optional), sealer and paint (optional), ruler, marking pencil, drill, screwdriver.

shopping

1. Particle board will do well and be cheaper than plywood. Seal and paint the particle board for best results.

preparation

   1. Mark two holes in the top of the board—2 inches in from the sides and 2 inches down from the top edge.

   2. Mark two holes in the bottom of the board—9½ inches from the side and 2 inches from the bottom (Fig. 7-36).

   3. Mark the top of the board center.

assembly and finishing

   1. Drill holes in marked places.

   2. Attach 2×4 pieces to board with screws.

   3. Attach a second set of 2×4 pieces on top of the first in the same manner.

   4. Seal the board.

   5. Paint the board if desired.

   6. Thread rope or wire through the holes on top.

   7. Attach a spring clip to the center of the board on top, 2 inches down from the edge, using screws (Fig. 7-37).

   8. Mark the wall for a hook or hooks on a stud.

   9. Attach a spice rack through the holes in the bottom of the board.

   10. Hang the easel from the hook.

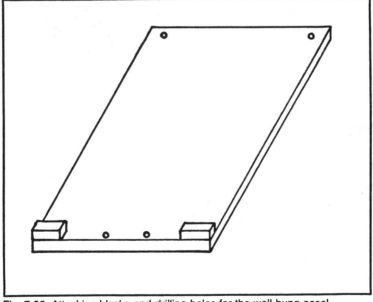

Fig. 7-36. Attaching blocks and drilling holes for the wall-hung easel.

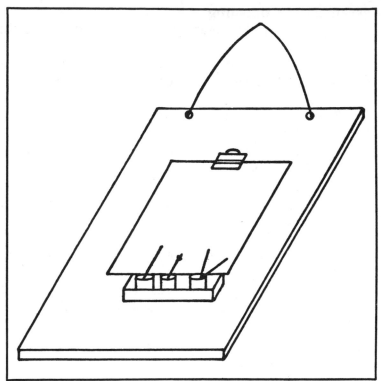

Fig. 7-37. Finished wall-hung easel.

Easel Built for Two

materials and tools

Two pieces of hardboard or plywood 20×30 inches (½-inch), four pieces of 1×4 4½ feet long, four pieces of 1×2 20 inches long, two 3-inch butt hinges and hardware, 18 inches of light metal chain, two plastic spice trays, sandpaper, sealer and paint, white glue, four small screws, four spring clips, wire brads (number 18 ½-inch length) for the hardboard or 2d nails for the plywood, hammer, screwdriver, paintbrush or roller, marking pencil, ruler, drill.

shopping

1. Have lumber cut to specifications.

preparation

It is faster to measure and mark while you assemble rather than to do it first.

assembly and finishing

1. Glue and nail (or brad if you use the hardboard) 1×2s to the short edges of panels (Fig. 7-38).

2. Attach panels to 1×4s, 1×2 side up, with long edges flush with outer edges of 1×4s and the top of panel and 1×4s even (Fig. 7-39).

3. Mark for butt hinges on top of the 1×4s (Fig. 7-40). Drill starter holes.

4. Attach a 9-inch length of chain to each 1×4, 14 inches down from the top.

5. Attach hardware for the removable spice rack on bottom 1×2s, 5 inches in from each side edge, or so the spice rack will be centered.

6. Sand well all over.

7. Seal and paint. Let dry thoroughly between sealing and painting.

8. Fasten two spring clips, to the top of each side onto the 1×2s, about 6½ inches in from each side. Use small screws or nails (Fig. 7-41).

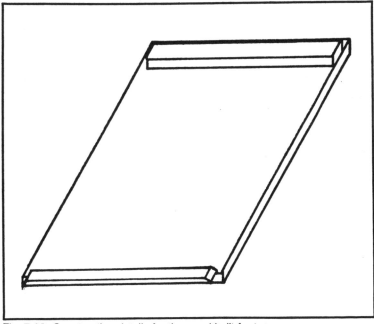

Fig. 7-38. Construction details for the easel built for two.

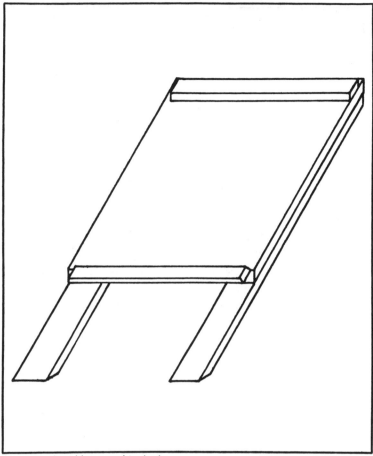
Fig. 7-39. Attaching panel to 1×4s.

Instant Wonder Easel

materials and tools

One piece of heavy cardboard 24×60 or so or one cardboard carton about 30×24 inches, adhesive-backed vinyl or paint, two extra-large heavy rubber bands or two pieces of narrow elastic sewn or stapled together into loops, ruler, marking pencil, scissors, knife, ice pick or steel knitting needle.

shopping

1. Find an appropriate carton.
2. You will need 5 yards of vinyl 18 inches wide.

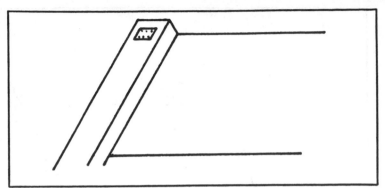

Fig. 7-40. Hinge detail.

preparation, assembly, and finishing

1. If you are using a carton, remove two adjacent sides from the box. Leave one corner intact (Fig. 7-42).

2. If you use a flat sheet of cardboard, crease down the center, after drawing a line and scoring with your knife and straightedge, to form two 24×30 sides. These are attached to each other on the top.

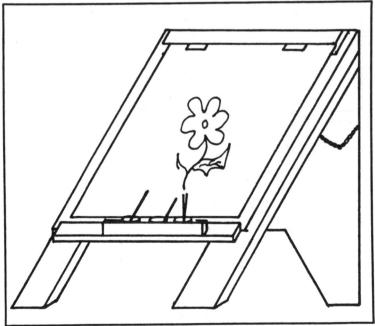

Fig. 7-41. Finished easel.

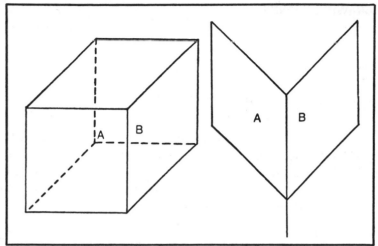

Fig. 7-42. Cutting a carton for the instant wonder easel.

3. Cover both sides with adhesive-backed vinyl, front and back.

4. You may paint the cardboard instead, though painting takes more time and tends to be messy.

5. Punch a hole into each side, about 10 inches from the top edge and 1½ inches in from the side edge (Fig. 7-43).

6. Slide one rubber band or elastic loop over the side and push up toward the top.

7. Thread the cord through the holes and tie. Slip on a second rubber band or elastic loop (Fig. 7-43).

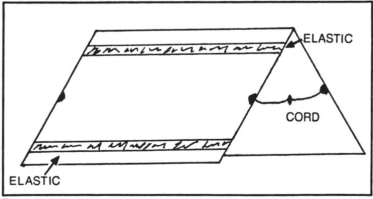

Fig. 7-43. Instant wonder easel.

DRAWING BOARDS

You don't have to be an artist or draftsperson to appreciate the convenience of a drawing board. The boards have many uses.

Quick and Easy Drawing Board

materials and tools

One panel of roughly 18×24 inches ½-inch marine plywood, wood sealer and clear plastic spray or 1½ yards of adhesive-backed vinyl, two 50-inch lengths of ¾-inch-wide elastic, sandpaper, scissors, measuring tape, needle and heavy thread, hammer, and tacks.

shopping

1. You can use ordinary plywood as well as the marine kind.

2. You can substitute particle board, but the surface will not be as smooth.

preparation

1. If you are going to use the adhesive-backed vinyl, measure and mark it to fit the board covering both sides.

2. Measure and cut elastic to size.

assembly and finishing

1. Sand the board.

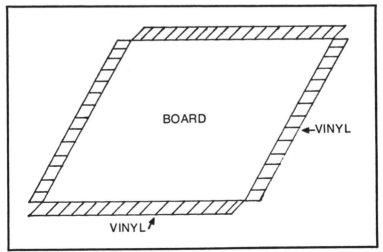

Fig. 7-44. Covering the drawing board with vinyl.

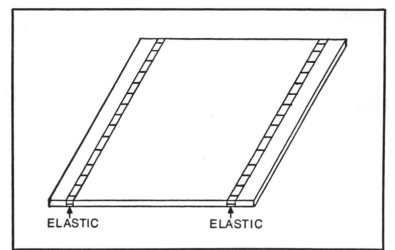
Fig. 7-45. Attaching elastic bands.

2. Seal wood and let dry.

3. Cover with clear plastic spray.

or

Cover the board with adhesive-backed vinyl on both sides after sanding (Fig. 7-44).

4. Sew together the ends of the elastic to form loops.

5. Tack an elastic loop to each end of the board, fastening it down top and bottom as shown in Fig. 7-45.

Deluxe Drawing Board with a Stand

A stand and a pencil/eraser catcher at the bottom of the board will transform the quick and easy model into the deluxe version.

materials and tools

Two pieces of 2×4 18 inches long or one 4×4 of the same length, two small mending plates (if you use the 2×4s), small screws, glue, sandpaper, sealer, hammer, screwdriver, drill (optional).

shopping

If you don't have any scraps, buy the lumber as specified and have it cut. If you do have scraps, use up the 2×4 pieces. They don't need to be that length; anything down to 14 inches and up to 24 inches will do.

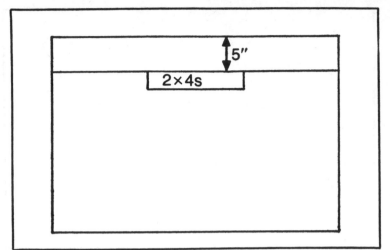

Fig. 7-46. Drawing board stand detail—marking position of 2×4s.

preparation

1. Mark down 5 inches from one long edge of the board.

2. Lay 2×4 or 4×4 even with the line, so the top of the lumber is level with the line. Draw around the lumber (Fig. 7-46).

assembly and finishing

1. Attach the 2×4s one to the other with mending plates (Fig. 7-47).

2. Spread glue inside the marked area on the drawing board.

3. Set the lumber on top. Weight it down with heavy books or weights.

4. Along the lower edge of the board, nail and glue a 24-inch-long piece of 1-inch-wide quarter round.

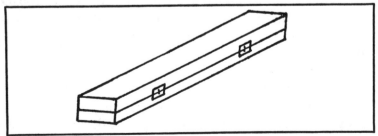

Fig. 7-47. Drawing board stand detail.

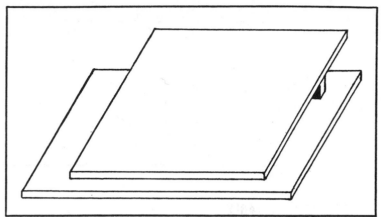

Fig. 7-48. Drawing board stand with pencil/eraser catcher.

5. Sand and seal the stand and pencil/eraser catcher (Fig. 7-48).

CLAY WORKBOARD

materials and tools

One board 18×24 or 18×18 or two pieces of heavy cardboard of the same dimensions, ¾ yard of firmly woven fabric (duck or canvas is best, but firm doubled sheeting will do), masking tape, staples or tacks, scissors, ruler, measuring tape, pencil, staple gun or tack hammer.

shopping

None

preparation

1. Cut fabric 1½ inches larger than your board all around. If your board is 18×24 inches, cut material to 19½×25½. For an 18×18 board, cut material 19½×19½.

assembly and finishing

1. Lay material flat on the table and cover with the board or stacked pieces of cardboard (Fig. 7-49).

2. Bring the material's edges up. Fold the edge under and staple or tack in place, starting in the center of each side (Figs. 7-50 and 7-51).

3. Pull corners taut and anchor with double staples or several tacks. Reinforce corners and edges with masking tape.

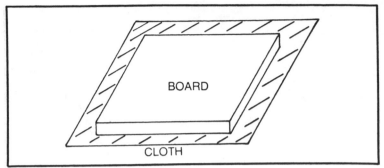

Fig. 7-49. Clay workboard.

STORE-AND-PLAY TABLE

The compartment in this table provides a storage area for cars, crayons, or games.

materials and tools

One piece of ½-inch-thick plywood 20×36 inches, two pieces 7×36 inches and ½ inch thick, two pieces 7×19 inches and ½ inch thick, two pieces of 2×2 36 inches long, four pieces of 2×2 17 inches long, four pieces of 2×4 18 inches long, 2d nails, sandpaper, glue, sealer, paint, 10 small corner braces, three small butt hinges, two flat hooks/eyes, ruler, pencil, hammer, paintbrushes, drill, screwdriver.

shopping

1. Have the lumber cut to specifications.

preparation and assembly

1. Lay out your 2×2s into a frame as shown in Fig. 7-52.
2. Nail and glue pieces together. Let glue set.

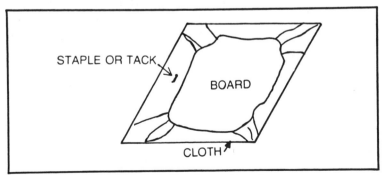

Fig. 7-50. Construction details for the clay workboard.

280

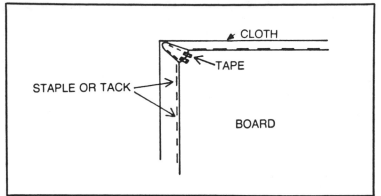

Fig. 7-51. More construction details for the clay workboard.

3. Mark all corners for corner braces.

4. Drill starter holes.

5. Put on corner braces.

6. Nail the large piece of plywood to the frame.

7. Nail and glue the remaining plywood pieces to the large piece to form a box.

8. Nail and glue the 2×4 pieces, one to each corner, as shown in Fig. 7-53 to form legs.

9. Attach the remaining large piece of plywood to the box with butt hinges (Fig. 7-53).

10. Sand thoroughly inside and out.

11. Seal inside and out. Allow for drying.

12. Paint inside and out. Allow for drying.

13. Attach flat hooks and eyes to the front (Fig. 7-53).

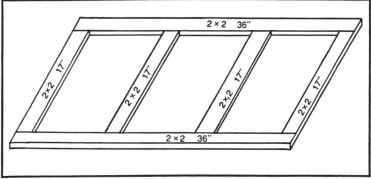

Fig. 7-52. Constructing and attaching the frame for the store-and-play table.

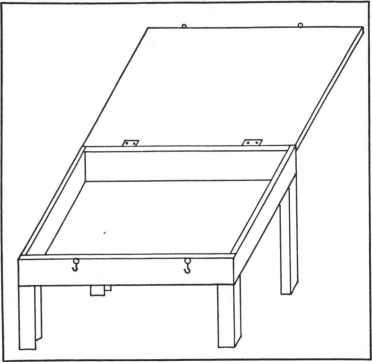

Fig. 7-53. Store-and-play table.

SAND TABLE

This is basically an indoor sandbox to be used when the snow, sleet, and rain outside make the use of the outdoor store-and-play model impractical. It can also be used as a place for building with blocks, making candles, or casting plaster. It can be easily converted into the store-and-play type.

materials and tools

Materials are the same as for the store-and-play table plus heavy plastic, tape, and staples. Tools are the same as for store-and-play table plus scissors and staple gun.

shopping

1. Use marine plywood.

2. Get enough heavy plastic to make two liners for the box—that is, two sheets 52×36 inches. These sheets may be pieced and then held together with tape.

3. Apply a coat of polyurethane varnish over the paint. You can use floor and deck enamel topped with some of the acrylic floor finish that gives a tough cover coat.

preparation and assembly

Follow instructions given for store-and-play table.

finishing

1. Follow steps given for finishing store-and-play table.

2. Line the inside of the table with plastic. Lay out sheets, one on top of the other, centered in the box.

3. Staple the center. Put in a row of staples to each side (Fig. 7-54).

4. Staple around the side edges of the bottom panel.

5. Bring up plastic over side panels and staple each center.

6. From each center, staple toward the corners.

7. In corners, fold in excess plastic and staple through all thicknesses. Do not cut or trim. If it is hard to staple (it shouldn't be), simply fold the excess out toward each side and staple that way. You can cover the inside of the box with adhesive-backed vinyl topped by a layer of plastic.

TOY STORAGE IDEAS

We prefer shelves instead of boxes. There are times, though, when it is desirable to stuff toys out of sight as quickly as possible. Here are some toy storage ideas.

Mobile Toy Box

This toy box is ideal for blocks and other building materials.

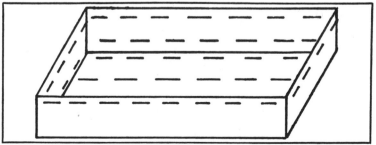

Fig. 7-54. Putting in plastic liner for the sand table.

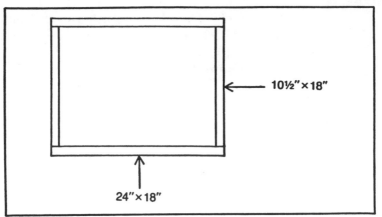

Fig. 7-55. Mobile toy cart—framing details.

materials and tools

One piece 24×12 inches of ¾-inch plywood, two pieces of ¾-inch-thick plywood 18×24 inches, two pieces of ¾-inch-thick plywood 10½×18 inches, two pieces of 1×2 12 inches long, two strips of ¾-inch trim 24 inches long, heavy duck or denim 26×17 inches, 3d nails, four 2-inch casters, fusing tape, sandpaper, sealer, paint, hammer, ruler, marking pencil, staple gun (optional), scissors, needle and thread, paintbrush, iron, ironing board, screwdriver, drill.

shopping

1. You can get a cheap grade of plywood if you seal well and cover with two coats of enamel paint.

2. You can get a solid color fabric to match or contrast. If you happen to have some leftover drapery or bedspread fabric, use it as long as it is firmly woven.

3. Have lumber cut to size.

preparation

1. Mark off 1 inch on each 26-inch edge of material.

2. Mark off ¾ inch on each of the remaining two edges and another ¾ inch from that mark.

assembly

1. Nail your 10½×18-inch pieces between your 24×18 pieces to form a frame (Fig. 7-55).

2. Mark for corner braces 2 inches down from the top—one brace to each corner.

284

3. Drill starter holes if desired.

4. Install corner braces.

5. Nail a 24×12-inch piece on top of the framing.

6. Mark for four corner braces in the center of each side as shown in Fig. 7-56 and on the bottom piece.

7. Install corner braces.

8. Nail 1×2 pieces to the bottom of the box on the outside.

9. Attach casters, one to each corner, on top of the 1×2s.

finishing

10. Sand the box inside and out. Sand trim pieces as well.

11. Seal box and trim pieces. Allow for drying.

12. Paint box and trim pieces. Let them dry thoroughly.

13. Cut fusing tape to fit the sides of the material. Fold along marked lines along the long edges. Fuse the tape between the fabric with an iron according to the directions on the fusing tape.

14. Fold in the first one ¾ inch along remaining edges and press, then fold again ¾ inch, insert fusing tape, and fuse.

15. Tack or staple one long edge of material to one painted trim piece (Fig. 7-57).

16. Tack the other long edge to the long edge of the box. Cover with trim piece. Nail down (Figs. 7-58 and 7-59).

Four-for-One Toy Box Cart

materials and tools

One piece of ¾-inch plywood 36×25 inches, two pieces of 1×2 36 inches long, 2 pieces of quarter round 1½ inches

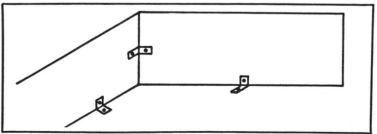

Fig. 7-56. Mobile toy cart—bracing details.

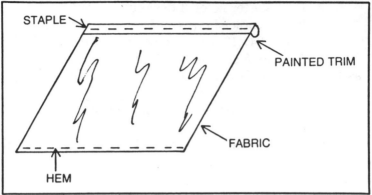

Fig. 7-57. Mobile toy cart—stapling the cover to trim.

wide and 36 inches long, two pieces of quarter round 1½ inches wide and 22 inches long, four beer cartons, 4d finishing nails, ½-inch-long tacks, four 2-inch casters and hardware, paint, sealer, sandpaper, two ½-inch screw eyes, ⅜-inch rope (1 yard), hammer, drill (optional), ruler, marking pencil, paintbrush.

shopping

1. Get enough paint for two good coats. Get a good brand

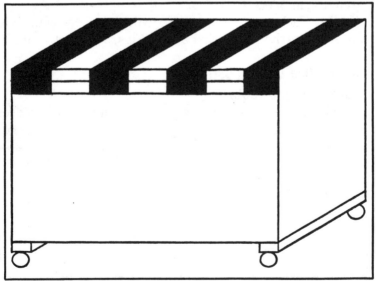

Fig. 7-58. Mobile toy cart closed.

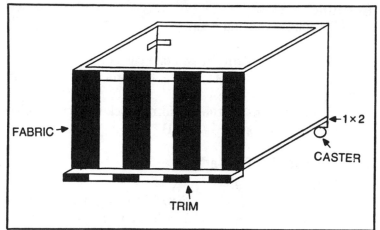

Fig. 7-59. Mobile toy cart open.

latex in a darker color to get a really nice finish—dark red, blue, green, or brown are all good.

preparation

1. On one of the 25-inch edges, mark the center—1 inch in from the edge. Mark again 2 inches from that mark on both sides of the mark.

assembly

1. Nail 1×2s to the long edges of the board sides even.

2. Trim the edges, letting the trim project ¾ inch above the plywood on the side that does not have the 1×2s.

3. Install casters in all corners on 1×2s.

4. Install screw eyes on marks (Fig. 7-60).

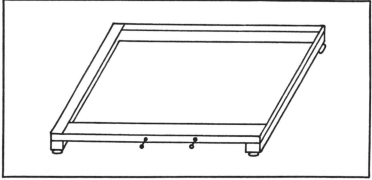

Fig. 7-60. Four-in-one toy box cart platform.

finishing

1. Sand wood and seal.
2. Seal cartons.
3. Paint the platform and one carton.
4. Paint the other three cartons. Let them dry thoroughly.
5. Set cartons on the platform. Tack bottoms in place from inside of cartons (Fig. 7-61).

Double-Decker Toy Box Cart

materials and tools

Two pieces of plywood 25×36 inches and ¾ inch thick, two pieces of plywood 22×25 inches and ¾ inch thick, two pieces of 1×2 36 inches long, four pieces of 1×2 3 inches long, two pieces of 1×2 10 inches long, four 3-inch casters, 4d nails, ½-inch tacks, paint, sandpaper, sealer, eight corner braces, eight beer cartons, hammer, screwdriver, ruler, marking pencil, drill, paintbrush.

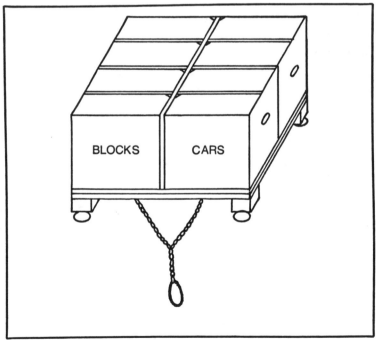

Fig. 7-61. Four-in-one toy box cart.

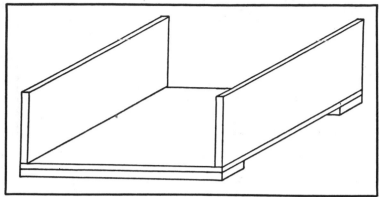

Fig. 7-62. Construction details for double-decker toy box cart.

shopping

1. Have all lumber cut to size.

2. Follow suggestions for the four-in-one cart

preparation, assembly, and finishing

1. Nail your 36-inch-long 1×2s along the edges of one of your 36×25 boards, with edges flush.

2. Nail one of the 22×25-inch boards to each end of the 36×25-inch board, with the 1×2s facing down (Fig. 7-62).

3. Nail the remaining 36×25-inch board in between the 25×22-inch boards on top to form a rectangle frame.

4. Mark for corner braces in each corner, 1 inch down from the top and 1 inch up from the bottom.

5. Measure and mark 3 inches down from the top of the short sides. Draw a line. Mark a line 7½ inches in from the side edges and again ¾ inch in from the last mark.

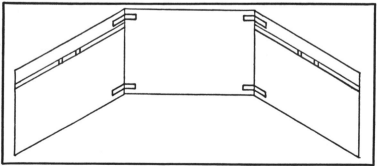

Fig. 7-63. Measuring and marking details.

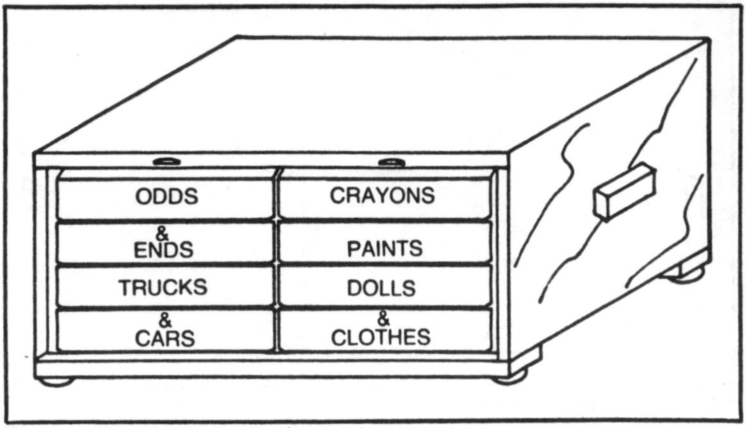

Fig. 7-64. Double-decker toy box cart.

6. Draw another line 1½ inches below the one you have. Mark as above. Trace out rectangles between the marks from the top line to bottom line (Fig. 7-63).

7. Attach corner braces.

8. Attach casters to the bottom of the cart.

9. Nail one of your 3-inch 1×2 pieces to each of the rectangles you marked on the side panels.

10. Nail your 10-inch 1×2s across the short pieces to form the handle.

11. Sand inside and out. Seal.

12. Seal the cartons.

13. Paint the cart. Let it dry thoroughly.

14. Paint cartons, two or three per 10-minute segment, depending on how fast you are.

15. Put four cartons on the cart and tack to the cart, with the top facing and the bottom in (you actually tack through one long side).

16. Stack the remaining four cartons on top of the others in the same manner. These will remain removable (Fig. 7-64).

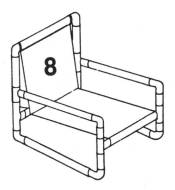

Lighting Projects

Think about your lighting needs and pick those projects that will do the most for you, your rooms, and your possessions. Here is some general information that will help you.

Plan your lighting projects one room at a time. Keep in mind what activities will go on in the room. Remember that placement of light is just as important as the amount of light. You will need high levels of illumination placed close to kitchen or workshop areas, studio, study, sewing, drawing, and writing areas. If you read in bed, you will need a well-placed bright light. Other activities will require lower, softer, and more subdued light levels.

INCANDESCENT AND FLUORESCENT LIGHT

Those projects that use *incandescent* light bulbs will give you few problems with bulb supply sources. All incandescent light bulbs give out the same quality of light—not so with *fluorescent* bulbs. Fluorescent lighting comes in many hues and in so-called "warm" and "cool" qualities.

You can buy fluorescent light bulbs that mimic the warm-hued quality of incandescent light. GTE Sylvania makes an "incandescent-fluorescent" lamp. Incandescent light is usually described as "warm" in color.

The General Electric Company markets four regular "white" fluorescent lamps designated CW (cool white), CWX (cool white deluxe), WW (warm white), and WWX (warm white deluxe). The difference is in the psychological effect created by the dominant color range radiated by the various lamps. "Warm" white will have a predominance of red, orange, and yellow colors in its "white" light. "Cool" lamps will produce more light in the green to violet end of the spectrum.

Colored objects and surfaces will change in appearance quite markedly depending on the intensity and color quality of the light illuminating them. Incandescent lighting is quite deficient in blue-green-violet light and will tend to accent the red-orange-yellow "warm" range. Cool colors are grayed out by both incandescent and warm fluorescent lamps, although the WWX lamp will render colors better. Similarly, the CWX will do a better job with colors than the CW. These deluxe lamps do not emit as high a percentage of yellow and green light as the WW and CW do. This lowers their overall lighting efficiency, because the eyes are most sensitive to yellow and green light. The WW and CW lamps will give you more light per watt.

You can create a cool, daylight atmosphere with good color renditions using CWX lamps; CW lamps will produce cool atmosphere at high efficiency. The WWX lamps offer a warm atmosphere with good color rendition; WW lamps will produce the warm atmosphere at high efficiency.

The best of both lighting worlds can sometimes be obtained by using fluorescent light as the main source and incandescent light for "fill-in" light. If you want contrast in your mixed lighting, use CW or CWX fluorescent. If you want a blending of the two, use the WWX or WW lamps.

PRECAUTIONS

Don't be afraid of the electrical wiring involved. Electricity is simple. Electrical wiring jobs require careful thought. We will guide you step-by-step through the basic wiring procedures needed for these projects. Electricity, comes from your utility company through your electric meter to your main switch box. It is split there into different fused circuits that go to various light fixtures and wall plug outlets. There is always a switch—on the wall or on the light fixture or appliance—that must be turned on to close the electrical circuit and start the current flow.

The two simple precautions you must follow are these:

●*Always disconnect and/or unplug the device on which you are working.* Remove the fuse or turn off the circuit breaker. Make absolutely certain that the power is off before working on the project.

●*Never stand in a wet area when working with anything electrical.* Don't even insert an insulated electrical plug into a wall outlet while standing in a damp area.

All wire connections must be made inside the service box that you will find behind any light fixture or wall plug. Electrical wires (called conductors) are color-codes. Hook-ups are as easy as connecting black to black, white to white, red to red, green to green, or bare to bare wires.

Conductors come in three basic types. The size of wire depends on the amount of current a circuit is supposed to carry. The bigger the wire, the more current the circuit can safely handle. The three types of conductors are:

●Two-wire (one black and one white).

●Two-wire with a bare grounding wire (also one black and one white).

●Three-wire (black, white, and red) plus grounding wire.

WIRE CONNECTING AND SPLICING

The basic tools you will need for connecting and splicing wires in the upcoming projects are a knife or wire stripper, a small screwdriver, and long-nose pliers.

Removing Insulation

Before electrical wires can be spliced together or connected to a switch, socket, or any other device, the insulation has to be removed from one end of the wire. See Fig. 8-1 for the right and wrong way to remove the insulation. Do not cut the insulation at right angles to the wire as shown in Fig. 8-1A. This is likely to nick the soft copper wire and cause it to

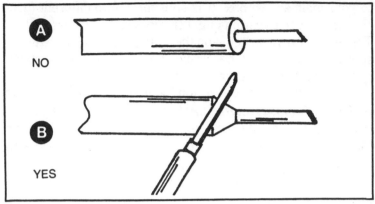

Fig. 8-1. Improper and proper ways to remove insulation.

break when being twisted. Hold knife or wire strippers at an angle, as shown in Fig. 8-1B, so that the insulation is cut at an angle of about 45 degrees to the wire. When the insulation has been peeled away, be sure the wire is clean and bare by scraping it lightly with a knife blade.

Connecting Wires to Terminals

Use the long-nose pliers to make a loop in the wire to fit around the connecting terminal. Always loop the wire clockwise, which is the direction that the terminal screw threads. If the wire is stranded, twist the strands together before forming the loop. If the end of the wire runs out beyond the screw, do not cut if off. Instead, wrap it around the terminal screw another time or two. Tighten down the screw, keeping all the wire or wires contained underneath the screwhead (Fig. 8-2).

Splicing One Wire to Another

In order to splice wire to wire, first hook the two bare wires together (Fig. 8-3A). Twist together tightly six to eight turns (Fig. 8-3B). It is best to then solder the finished joint if you have a soldering gun.

Clean both wire and solder. Use only rosin core solder (never use acid) for electrical work. Apply the hot tip of the soldering gun to the wire joint—not to the solder. Let the joint

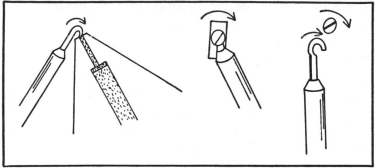

Fig. 8-2. Connecting wires to terminals.

get hot enough to melt the solder. Let the solder flow into the joint (Fig. 8-3C).

You can skip the solder if you have made a tight joint. You must, however, tape the joint after soldering or splicing to add insulation equal to the original insulation. Use electrical plastic tape and make at least three or four turns around the joint,

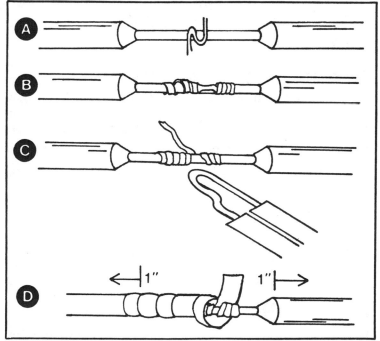

Fig. 8-3. Splicing, soldering, and taping wires.

beginning 1 inch from the insulation cut and extending 1 inch past the cut (Fig. 8-3D).

Using Solderless Connectors

You can buy solderless connectors to match wire of almost any size. To use them, place your scraped wires side by side (Fig. 8-4A). Then you simply screw the connector down over the wires to hold them together firmly (Fig. 8-4B). Make sure that the insulated cover of the connector covers up all bare wires. If any uninsulated wire sticks out from under the connector cover after you have installed it, remove the connector, clip off the wire, and reinstall the connector.

CEILING LIGHT PROJECTS

Ceiling lights are often limited to the location of the built-in overhead outlet box, which is usually situated in the middle of the room where light is least needed. The center of the room is a good location for some overall lighting, but specific areas of light are usually needed somewhere around the periphery of a room. Our first ceiling light project fulfills such a need.

Skylight for Drawing Board or Indoor Garden

The imitation skylight in Fig. 8-5 will provide good "north light" at any time of day for drawing, painting, or doing hobby work over a workbench. Its power source is a wall receptacle. The perforated hardboard used on the triangular

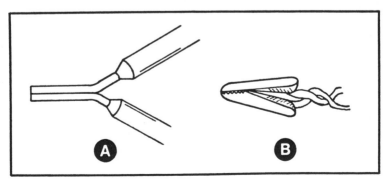

Fig. 8-4. Using solderless connectors.

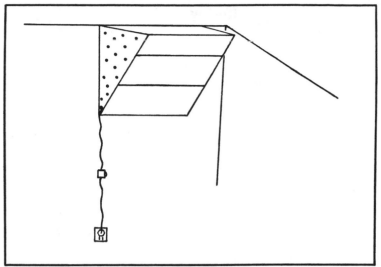

Fig. 8-5. Skylight for drawing board, workbench, or indoor garden.

sides provides ventilation for the light bulbs and a handy place to hang tools and equipment.

materials and tools

Two 1×2s cut 33 inches long, two 1×2s cut 24 inches long, two 1×2s cut 22½ inches long, two 1×2s cut 21½ inches long, two 1×1s cut 21 inches long, one 24×24-inch piece of perforated hardboard cut into two equal right triangles, one piece frosted acrylic cut to 31×21 inches, three fluorescent strip fixtures, one cord switch, one dead-front male plug, two or three solderless connectors, 6 to 15 feet of number 16 two or three-wire lamp cord (length depending on distance to nearest outlet from skylight installation), 10 hollow wall anchor fasteners, six 2-inch × number 10 flathead screws, screwdriver, drill with small bits, knife or wire cutters and stripper, miter box, small saw.

shopping

1. Have a lumberyard worker cut all materials to exact size.

2. Purchase all hardware. Make sure you obtain a three-way cord and plug if your fluorescent fixtures have grounding connection (usually a green wire in addition to the black and white "hot" (and neutral wires).

preparation and mitering

1. Place both ends of the two 33-inch 1×2s into a miter box and cut with a saw at a 45-degree angle.

2. Using Figs. 8-6, 8-7, and 8-8 as guides, place 1×2s on the wall and ceiling. Mark for position and drilling of holes for hollow wall anchor fasteners.

3. Drill the 1×2s, wall, and ceiling for fasteners according to the instructions that come with the fasteners.

assembly

1. Fasten 1×2s to the wall and ceiling.

2. Attach two fluorescent fixtures to the wall and one to the ceiling (Fig. 8-8). Use wall fasteners unless studs or joists are encountered; then you can use screws.

3. Use solderless connectors to connect the three black leads from the light fixtures to one wire of the lamp cord. Connect the three white leads to the other wire of the lamp

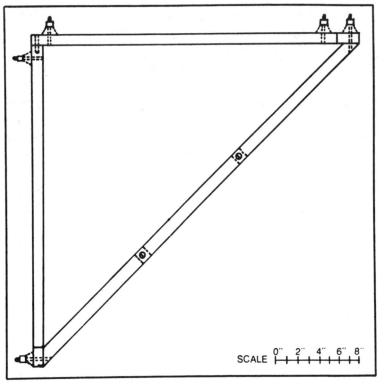

Fig. 8-6. Side view of skylight construction.

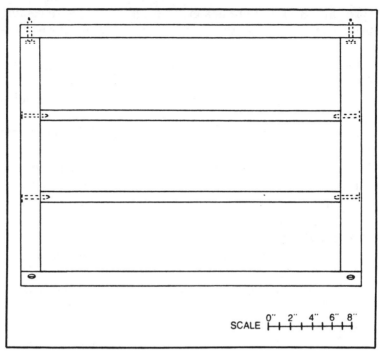

SCALE 0" 2" 4" 6" 8"

Fig. 8-7. Front view of skylight construction.

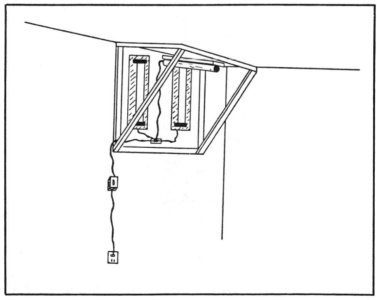

Fig. 8-8. Attaching fluorescent fixtures to the wall and ceiling.

cord (Fig. 8-9). If there is a green or grounding wire coming from each fixture, use the third solderless connector to combine these three leads. Connect them to the ground wire in the lamp cord. Drape the cord out one side of the frame (Fig. 8-8).

4. Using Figs. 8-6 and 8-7 as guides, drill starter holes for 1×1 grid members.

5. Install a frosted acrylic sheet behind 1×1s and screw the 1×1s in place.

6. With a saw, notch one angle of one of the perforated hardboard pieces for the lamp cord. Install both with screws.

7. Take the cord switch apart with a screwdriver.

8. Split the cord wire as shown in Fig. 8-10A and cut one wire only (Fig. 8-10B).

9. Place the wire in the half of the cord switch without the wheel (Fig. 8-10C).

10. Press halves together (Fig. 8-10D). Points inside will pierce the insulation and make contact with copper inside the cut wire.

11. Replace the nut into the switch and tighten the screw until both halves are securely fastened together.

12. Remove screws from the front of your dead-front plug. Take off the thick cap so the plug is opened (Fig. 8-11).

13. Insert the lamp cord into the cap. You may need to loosen the screws on top of the plug.

14. Strip wires and secure to screws or pressure slots.

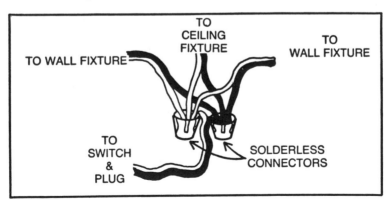

Fig. 8-9. All wires of the same color go into the same solderless connectors (also called wire nuts).

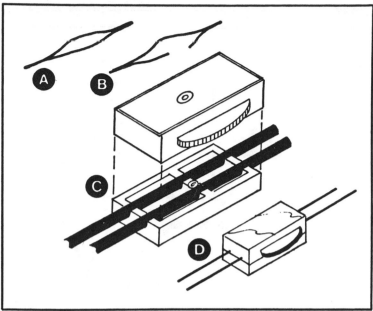

Fig. 8-10. Wiring a cord switch.

15. Close the plug and secure with screws in front. Tighten the screws on top of the plug.

finishing

No finishing is really necessary, unless you would like to paint the perforated hardboard sides to match the colors of your walls and ceiling.

Chandelier

This project uses a cluster of ceiling fixtures, hung as illustrated in Fig. 8-12, and gives plenty of light for reading or

Fig. 8-11. Open dead-front plug.

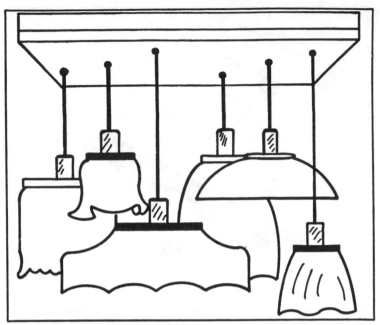

Fig. 8-12. The cluster of fixtures makes a nice chandelier.

sewing a fine seam. With each fixture sporting only a 60-watt bulb, 240 watts of incandescent light will be produced by the chandelier. By using sockets with switches on them, you can turn off light you don't need or adjust it. Fixtures can be the cheap dimestore type or Tiffany glass.

materials and tools

Two 1×2s 24 inches long, two 1×2s 21 inches long, one 24×24-inch piece of ⅜-inch plywood, 12 feet of number 14 two-wire lamp cord, six solderless connectors, six wood screws, four toggle bolts, six electrical sockets with switch, six uno-type shade holders, six assorted glass shades, six 60 to 100-watt plain or decorative bulbs, drill, hammer, small nails, glue, screwdriver, wire cutters and strippers.

shopping

1. Have the lumber dealer cut all materials to exact size.

2. Choose glass shades that can hang within the 2 by 2-foot chandelier area without bumping into one another. Remember that they will hang at different heights as shown in Fig. 8-12.

preparation

1. Measure, mark, and cut a 12-foot length of lamp cord into six unequal lengths, depending on the size and spacing of the fixtures to be hung.

2. Measure and mark for drilling the 2×2-foot plywood sheet.

3. Drill holes of slightly larger diameter than the lamp cord where marked on the plywood sheet.

assembly

1. Make a frame of 1×2s as shown in Fig. 8-13. Make sure the frame fits flush with the outside edge of the plywood. Use glue and 8d casing or finishing nails to secure the frame together. Drill for toggle bolts.

2. Pry apart sockets and attach one end of the lamp cord wires to the screw terminals inside the sockets. Replace the end piece (Fig. 8-14).

3. Thread the cord through the hole in the plywood sheet and make an "underwriter's" knot in the other end (Fig. 8-14).

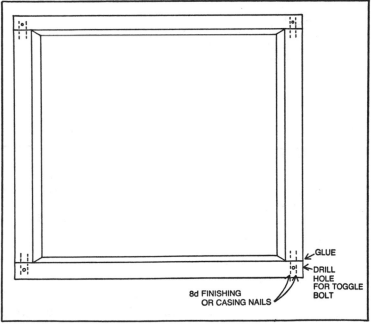

Fig. 8-13. The 2×4 frame for the chandelier.

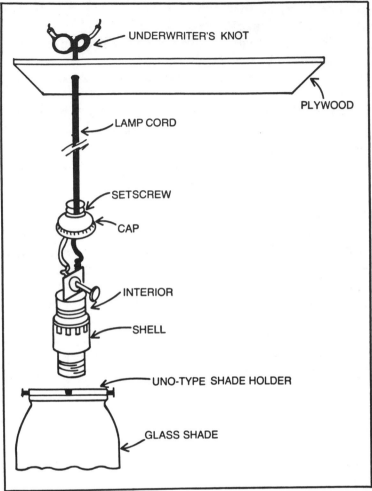

Fig. 8-14. Wiring socket to power cord.

4. Strip the insulation from the ends of wires on the other side of the knot.

5. Fasten the frame to the ceiling around the old light fixture with toggle bolts.

6. Remove the old light fixture. Be sure to trip the circuit breaker or unscrew the fuse on that light circuit.

7. Raise plywood with wired sockets near to the frame and wire in to the ceiling box with solderless connectors (Fig. 8-15).

8. Raise the plywood flush with the frame and attach to the frame with wood screws.

9. Rim each socket with the shade holder and shade.

10. Screw in light bulbs.

finishing

If attractive wood was chosen for the plywood sheet, you may finish the wood in natural tones by simply waxing it or giving it a light coat of varnish. It can also be painted to match the color of the ceiling.

WALL LIGHT PROJECTS

Lights in the center of the ceiling tend to make areas around the walls of a room dim. Eyestrain and fatigue can result when too much contrast is present in a lighted room. Wall lights help by putting more light where and when you need it for reading or working. Our first wall light project is a quick valance-type installation. You can make many variations. A typical installation is shown in Fig. 8-16.

Shielded Valance-Type Wall Light

A wall bracket that is just a shield parallel to the wall is constructed and fitted over a single strip fluorescent fixture mounted horizontally along one wall. It is similar to a valance,

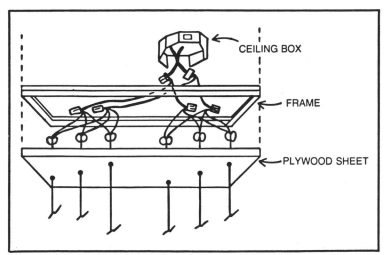

Fig. 8-15. Wiring the chandelier into the ceiling box.

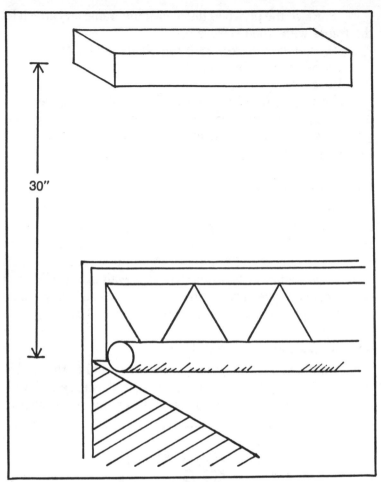

Fig. 8-16. Typical installation of valance lighting.

except the light source is farther from the ceiling and light is distributed evenly around the room. The fixture can be as low as 6 feet above the floor. It should be about 30 inches from the reading or work surface. The installation is ideal for placement over a bed to provide both a reading light and general room illumination.

materials and tools

One 2×2 cut 72 inches long, one 1×8 cut 72 inches long, two 1×8s cut 9 inches long, one fluorescent 40-watt strip fixture, 12 flathead 1-inch, number 5 wood screws, four wall anchors, ½-pint flat white paint, sandpaper, sealer, screwdriver, drill with bits for wall anchors and starting holes for number 5 screws, paintbrush.

shopping

1. Have all lumber cut to exact size.

2. Purchase a fluorescent fixture with the power cord already wired in. If the power cord is exceptionally short, you may need to purchase a 6 or 9-foot extension cord to reach a wall plug.

preparation

1. Measure 30 inches up from the bed or table surface. Draw a line 72 inches long parallel to the floor.

2. Drill four holes in the 2×2—3 inches and 9 inches from each end—big enough to slip the wall anchors through (Fig. 8-17).

3. Place the 2×2 along the line on the wall. Mark the wall for anchor holes. Remove the 2×2 and drill holes in the wall.

4. Paint one side of 1×8×72-inch board with flat white paint after sanding and sealing.

assembly

1. Place the 2×2 in position along the wall and secure it with four wall anchors.

2. Secure the fluorescent fixture to the 2×2 with hardware (Fig. 8-18).

3. Drill starter holes in 1×8×9-inch end pieces and fasten to the 2×2 and 1×8×72-inch board (Fig. 8-18 and 8-19).

finishing

If you like natural wood finishes and you choose a wood that goes well with the woodwork in the room or the furnishings, finish your valance-type wall light with clear shellac or a

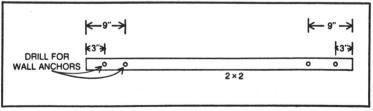

Fig. 8-17. Marking and drilling for hollow wall anchors.

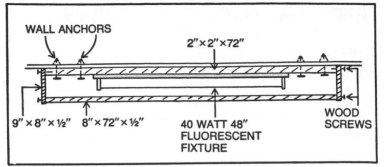

Fig. 8-18. Top view of the shielded wall lighting.

light varnish. Otherwise, paint to match and blend in with the wall color.

A Lighted Valance

A natural place for a wall light is in a valance above a window. The preceding instructions will apply for this type of wall light with the following changes:

1. The light fixture should be at least 10 inches below the ceiling.

2. The fixture should be 3 to 4 inches out from the top of

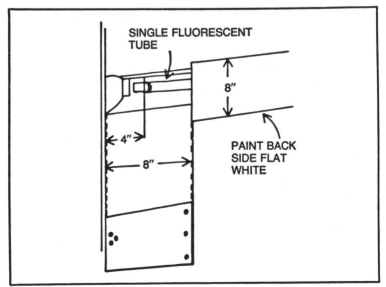

Fig. 8-19. End view of the shielded wall lighting.

the wall and away from the tops of any draperies. The light might fade the tops of some colored fabrics if placed too close to the fluorescent tubes.

3. If you want to keep light off the ceiling and direct it down the length of the drapes, fasten a top board onto the valance between the shield and the wall with corner brackets (Fig. 8-20).

Cabinet and Shelf Lighting

For bright lighting of kitchen counters and other shelves, you can use the basic valance-type light in still another variation (Fig. 8-21A).

1. Install a 2×2 strip of wood a little longer than the fluorescent fixture you plan to use on the wall at the back of the cabinet or just under the shelf.

2. Add an apron, hung by corner brackets or chair braces, to hide the strip light. If the cabinet is metal, you can drill holes through its bottom to take bolts for fixing the apron in place. Remember to paint the backside of the apron with flat white paint before installing it.

The apron can be placed along the shelf's front edge, but the light will be softer if you locate the apron close to the light (Fig. 8-21B).

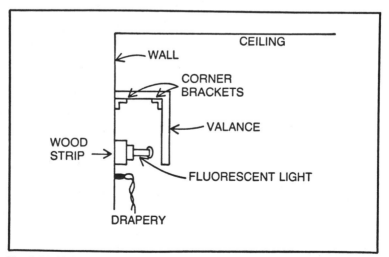

Fig. 8-20. Valance light over draperies.

Skylight for a Wall

Fluorescent strip lights can be mounted vertically on a wall to brighten up a windowless area. Figures 8-22 and 8-23 give details for this unusual but simple lighting project.

materials and tools

Two boards 1×6×96 inches, three 1×1s 96 inches long, one ⅛-inch-thick frosted acrylic plastic panel 24×96 inches, two 6-foot-long commercial fluorescent light fixtures, one power cord, 12 toggle bolts, screws or hollow wall anchors to fasten the fixtures to the wall, glue, polyvinyl resin white glue (8 ounces), two or three solderless connectors, about 12 corner braces, screwdriver, drill, wire cutters and strippers, small brush for spreading glue, plumb line, ruler, C-clamps.

shopping

1. Have the lumber dealer cut all material to exact size.

2. Have someone with a routing device make a groove ⅛ inch deep and ⅛ inch wide along the inside front edge of both 1×6s to hold the acrylic panel.

3. Buy and install the 1×6s before you buy the acrylic panel, so you can get it cut to fit exactly.

4. If fluorescent fixtures have three wires, buy a three-wire grounded power cord; if there are two wires, buy a two-wire cord.

preparation

1. Measure the floor to ceiling distance at the place where you will install your light. Use this dimension when having the lumber—1×6s and 1×1s—cut. Have the grooves in the 1×6s routed in about ¼ inch from the inside front edge of each board.

2. After the 1×6s have been installed, measure the distance between the two and add the depth of each groove to get the exact width of the acrylic panel. Have it cut to this exact width and to the length of the actual floor to ceiling measurement—the same length as the 1×6s.

3. Carefully measure and mark the vertical lines on your frosted acrylic panel for gluing on the 1×1s, so they are evenly spaced approximately 6 inches apart.

assembly

1. Using a plumb line from the ceiling, fasten the 1×6s to

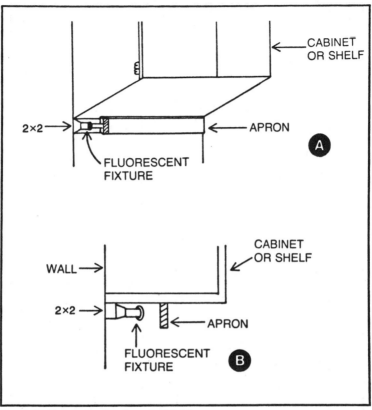

Fig. 8-21. Detail of cabinet or shelf lighting.

the wall with corner braces, screws, and hollow wall anchors or expansion shields if it is a masonry wall. See Fig. 8-24 for details on using expansion shields.

2. Spread glue along vertical lines marked on the frosted acrylic panel and along one side of the 1×1s. Use a brush and spread the glue evenly. Be sure all surfaces you are gluing are clean and dry.

3. Place 1×1s along lines and clamp with C-clamps at each end. Tighten the C-clamps for moderate pressure—firm but not too tight. Place some weights along the lengths of the 1×1s.

4. Mount the two fluorescent fixtures on the wall between the 1×6s. You can probably find two studs within the 2-foot space between the 1×6s to which fixtures can be

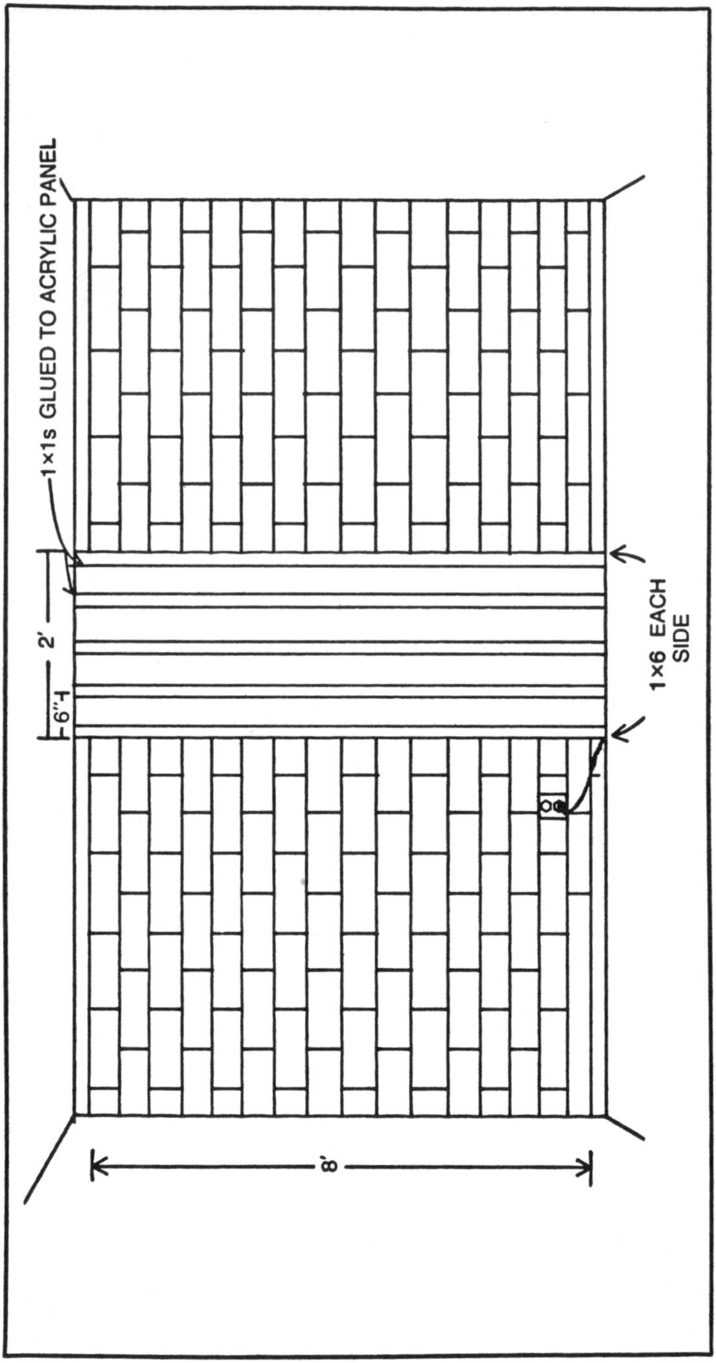

Fig. 8-22. Front view of wall skylight.

1×1s GLUED TO ACRYLIC PANEL

1×6 EACH SIDE

2'

6"

8'

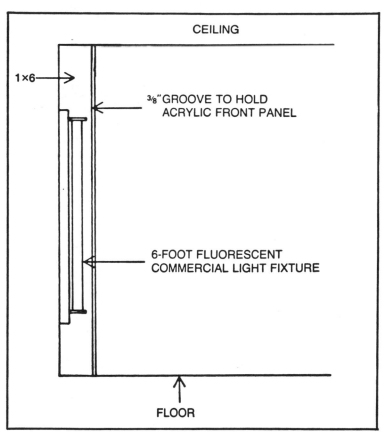

Fig. 8-23. Side view of wall skylight.

fastened if you have a hollow wall. Knock on the wall with your fist. Where the wall sounds solid or less hollow, there will likely be a wall stud. You can then screw the fixtures through the wall to the stud with the hardware that comes with the fixtures. If you can't find the wall studs, mount the fixtures with hollow wall anchors or with expansion shields if the wall is masonry (Fig. 8-24).

   5. Drill a small hole in the side of one of the 1×6s—the one closest to the nearest power outlet—and thread the power cord through. Connect the power cord to wires coming from the fixtures. All black wires go together with one of the wires on the power cord, and all the white wires go together with the other wire of the power cord. Use solderless connec-

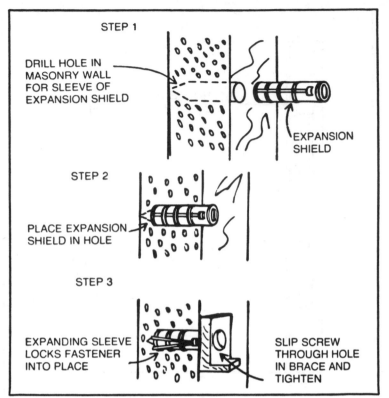

STEP 1

DRILL HOLE IN
MASONRY WALL
FOR SLEEVE OF
EXPANSION SHIELD

EXPANSION
SHIELD

STEP 2

PLACE EXPANSION
SHIELD IN HOLE

STEP 3

EXPANDING SLEEVE
LOCKS FASTENER
INTO PLACE

SLIP SCREW
THROUGH HOLE
IN BRACE AND
TIGHTEN

Fig. 8-24. Detail of masonry wall anchor installation.

tors to tie together each group of wires. If there is a third green wire (the ground wire), fasten it to the ground connection on the power cord.

6. After glue is thoroughly dry on 1 × 1s and the acrylic panel, install the panel between the 1×6s by flexing it slightly and slipping it into the grooves on the inside front edges of the boards. To change fluorescent tubes, you can remove the front panel by gently snapping it out of the grooves.

finishing

1. Leave the wood natural and protect it with a thin coat of liquid plastic, or stain the wood with a light stain to match the woodwork in the room.

Inexpensive Track Lighting

This inexpensive track lighting gives you the ultimate in

light control. A little 1×4 lumber, a shower rod, and some clamp-on light fixtures are all it takes, plus a few minutes of your time. See Fig. 8-25.

materials and tools

One piece of pine lumber 1×4×60 inches, two pieces of pine lumber 1×4×4 inches, one 1-inch square chrome shower rod, two or more clamp-on reflector light fixtures with colored reflectors to match room decor, six number 8 flathead wood screws 1¼ inches long, four toggle bolts or expansion shields with screws if the wall is masonry, 1 pint flat paint to match the color of the reflectors, screwdriver, drill, paintbrush.

shopping

1. Have pine lumber cut to size.

2. Shop for light fixtures and paint at the same time, so you can match the color of the paint to the color of the reflectors on the clamp-on fixtures.

preparation

None to do.

assembly

1. Construct a U-shaped bracket from the three pieces of pine. Put it together with wood screws.

2. Paint and allow to dry.

3. Mount shower rod brackets on the inside of one end of the U-shaped pin bracket and insert the shower rod.

4. Slip the other shower rod bracket over the other end of the shower rod. Position it on the inside of the other end of the wood bracket and fasten in place, so the shower rod is secure.

5. Position on the wall and mark and drill holes for toggle bolts. Insert the toggle bolts and secure them to the wall.

6. Clamp light fixtures onto the shower rod and plug in to nearby outlets. Use an extension cord with multiple outlets if outlets are not nearby.

finishing

1. Use paint to touch up heads of toggle bolts and places where paint flaked off due to drilling.

FLOOR LAMP PROJECTS

Floor lamps are fun to make and useful as reading lamps.

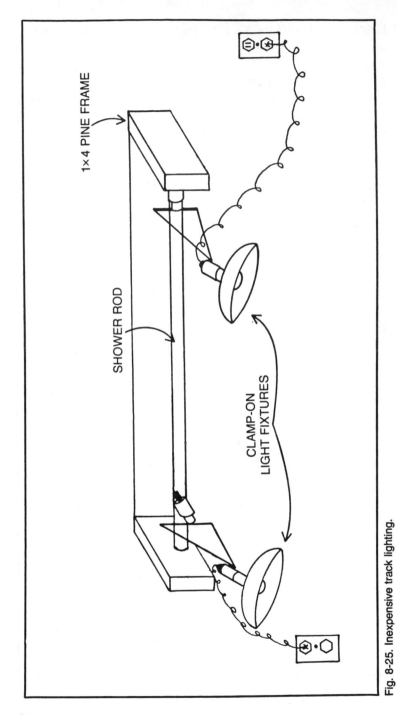

1×4 PINE FRAME

SHOWER ROD

CLAMP-ON
LIGHT FIXTURES

Fig. 8-25. Inexpensive track lighting.

316

Here are three interesting, unusual, and practical floor lamp projects.

A Versatile Floor Lamp

This beautiful floor lamp consists of a wood frame and a plain electrical socket into which may be screwed various incandescent light bulbs. Figure 8-26 shows the lamp with an 8-inch globe bulb screwed into the socket. A 150-watt reflector floodlight will give lots of indirect, soft light. A regular 200-watt bulb with a clamp-on conventional lampshade can be used for a more conventional look.

materials and tools

Two 1×12×48-inch boards, one 1×12 cut to 8½×17 inches, one 48-inch strip of corner molding, one lamp socket with built-in switch, one 9-foot power cord with plug, one 8-inch globe bulb or other bulb of your choice, small assortment of 8d casing nails, wood putty stick, white glue, hammer, wire cutters and strippers, screwdriver.

shopping

1. Have lumber cut to size.

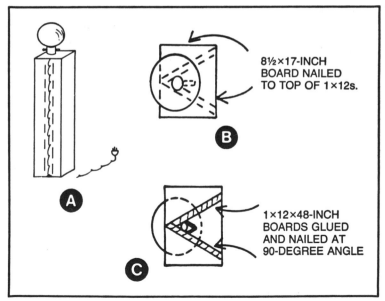

8½×17-INCH BOARD NAILED TO TOP OF 1×12s.

1×12×48-INCH BOARDS GLUED AND NAILED AT 90-DEGREE ANGLE

Fig. 8-26. Details of the pedestal floor lamp.

preparation

    1. None necessary.

assembly

    1. Drive 12 casing nails along one edge of one of the 1×12×48-inch boards ⅜ inch in from the edge of the board. Drive them just far enough to protrude about ⅛ inch from the other side of the board.

    2. Spread white glue along the edge where the casing nails protrude and along one 48-inch end of the other 1×12×48-inch board.

    3. Press together and nail securely, making a 90-degree stand (Fig. 8-26C.) Countersink nails.

    4. Glue and nail the top board (8½×17-inch 1×12) to the stand you have just made. Countersink the nails.

    5. Drill a ⅝-inch hole centered 3 inches from one edge and 8½ inches from each end of the top board.

    6. Thread the power cord through the hole and into the bottom of the socket. Take the socket apart and wire as shown in Fig. 8-14.

    7. Reassemble the socket, remove the setscrew from the cap, and fit the small end of the cap into the hole on top of the top board. Glue the cap into place.

    8. Glue a corner molding strip in place over the power cord on the inside corner of the stand. Use a few 2d finishing nails to hold the strip in place while the glue is drying.

finishing

    1. Fill in all countersunk nail holes with a putty stick; let dry.

    2. Lightly sand the entire lamp base, including the top.

    3. Finish in natural wood or paint to match other furnishings.

    4. Screw in the decorative light bulb of your choice.

Pedestal Floor Lamp

    This pedestal floor lamp is made for showing off a favorite piece of pottery or glass vase. The lamp also brightens the corner where it is located.

materials and tools

    Four pieces of ¾ inch plywood cut 15×40 inches, eight

pieces of 1×1 cut 13 inches long, one hardboard piece 14 inches square, one clamp-on utility light with reflector shade, one square of ¼-inch-thick opaque glass or acrylic (dimensions to be determined when project is complete), small box of 3d finishing nails, white glue, sandpaper, primer and paint, veneer to cover the edges of exposed plywood, hammer.

shopping

1. Have plywood and hardboard cut to the exact size. A large hole should be cut in the center of the piece of hardboard to hold a utility light.

preparation

1. Center 1×1s (cleats) on plywood side pieces ¼ inch from the top edge and mark around.

2. Measure 24 inches below top cleats (1×1s) and mark the position for remaining cleats.

assembly

1. Place cleats on marked positions and secure in place with finishing nails.

2. Nail three sides together with butt joints (edge along side) to make a box.

3. Place the utility lamp into the hole in the hardboard and slide into place on lower cleats.

4. Nail the fourth side on to close the box.

5. Cover exposed edges of plywood with veneer.

6. Prime and paint all exterior surfaces and the tops of the top cleats.

finishing

1. Place the utility light in the hole in the shelf. Thread the power cord out through the groove in the side of the pedestal.

2. Carefully measure the top of the completed pedestal box for frosted glass or acrylic. Have it cut to size. Put it in place (Fig. 8-27).

Black Box Floor Lamp

This floor lamp "grows" out of a black box into an assortment of electrical elements to bloom with light. Designers would call this floor lamp "organic."

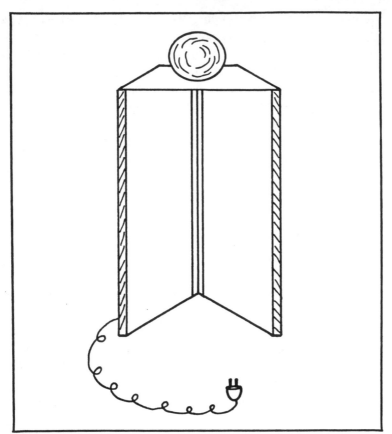

Fig. 8-27. Pedestal floor lamp.

materials and tools

Four 9×9-inch pieces of ½-inch plywood and two pieces 8×9 inches, 72 casing nails, white glue, nine 8×2½×3-inch bricks, three one-hold straps for securing conduit, three ½-inch flathead wood screws, one 9-foot length conduit or pipe with ⅜-inch outside diameter, one 15-foot length power cord with plug, one brass pull-chain socket (ivory), three ivory current taps, six ivory socket adapters, six tubular 40-watt incandescent light bulbs, one 60-watt globe-type incandescent light bulb, ½ pint of black paint, hammer, screwdriver, paintbrush, wire cutters and stripper.

shopping

1. Have plywood cut to size.

2. Purchase remaining supplies at a paint and hardware store. If ⅜-inch conduit is a rare item in your neighborhood, go to a plumbing supply store and buy regular metal pipe of that size.

3. Have the pipe bent into a graceful curve somewhat like that shown in Fig. 8-28.

preparation

1. Measure and mark lines on one side of each plywood piece ½ inch in from all edges.

assembly

1. Assemble five sides of the plywood box using casing nails with marked lines as guides.

2. Stack the bricks inside the box and nail on the other side.

3. Secure the lower 8 inches of conduit to the box with one-hole straps and screws.

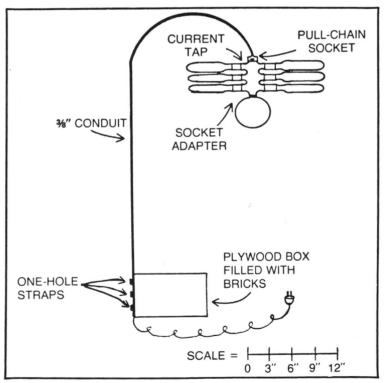

Fig. 8-28. Black box floor lamp.

4. Thread the power cord through the conduit and wire into the pull-chain socket. See Fig. 8-14.

5. Push the wired socket onto the end of the conduit. Fasten it in place with a setscrew on the socket.

6. Screw all three current taps together and into the socket.

7. Plug socket adapters into current taps.

8. Screw tubular light bulbs into adapter sockets.

9. Screw a globe-type bulb into the end current tap socket.

finishing

1. Paint the plywood box black.

TABLE LAMPS

Table lamps can be made out of tail pipe tubing, large covered baskets, and imported wood canisters.

Table Lamp Made from Tail Pipe Tubing

This table lamp made from flexible tail pipe tubing features six light bulbs stemming from a double socket with current taps, socket adapters, and decorative light bulbs (Fig. 8-29).

materials and tools

Four-foot length of tail pipe tubing of 1½-inch diameter, 9-foot length of power cord with plug, one light socket with push-type off-on switch, one double socket, two current taps, four socket adapters, six 60-watt decorative bulbs, screwdriver, wire cutters and strippers.

shopping

1. Tail pipe tubing may be purchased at any auto parts supply store. Length is not critical.

preparation

None to be done.

assembly

1. Curl the tubing into a whimsical shape that suits your fancy.

2. Thread the power cord through the tubing.

3. Wire the single socket to the end of the power cord (Fig. 8-14).

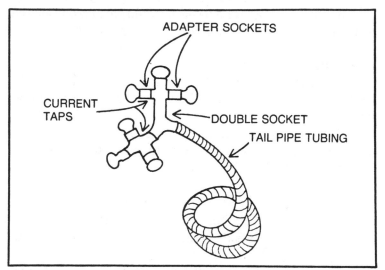

Fig. 8-29. Table lamp made from tail pipe tubing.

4. Press-fit the socket into the end of the tubing.

5. Screw in a double socket.

6. Screw in current taps, insert socket adapters, and install 60-watt decorative bulbs.

finishing

None to be done.

A Basketful of Light

A large covered basket with a handle is ideal for this table lamp. You can make your own adaptation, though, of almost any basket you have.

materials and tools

The basket of your choice, threaded rod to extend at least 6 inches above the basket handle, three locknuts and washers, one harp, one finial, one 6-foot power cord with plug, one lampshade of your choice, screwdriver, drill, small wrench or pliers, wire cutters and strippers.

shopping

1. Obtain a basket. Go to a hardware store and buy the lamp parts.

2. The threaded rod should be $\frac{3}{8}$-inch diameter to screw into the socket. Get suitable locknuts and washers.

3. The lampshade and basket should balance one another as far as size is concerned. If you use a fancy basket, you may want to consider a plain lampshade and vice versa.

preparation

1. Measure the basket and the shade carefully. Pick a length of threaded rod that will give you a nicely proportioned lamp.

2. If much of the threaded rod shows above the basket and below the shade, you may want to purchase a brass sleeve to slip over the threaded rod.

assembly

1. Drill a hole through the basket handle, straight down through the lid and the bottom of the basket, big enough to accommodate the threaded rod (and brass sleeve if you use one).

2. Insert the threaded rod through the handle—top and bottom.

3. Slip the washer on the bottom of the threaded rod and screw on the locknut.

4. Spin the locknut onto the threaded rod at the top. Insert the harp and washers and another locknut, but do not tighten yet (Fig. 8-30).

5. Thread the power cord up through the threaded rod and wire into the socket (Fig. 8-14).

6. Screw the socket cap onto the threaded rod. Tighten the screws around the harp, so the harp is held firmly in place.

7. Pull the power cord back through the rod until the shell of the socket can be force-fitted into the cap.

8. Push the bottom of the basket into a slightly concave shape if necessary to accommodate a ⅛-inch clearance for the bottom washer and locknut. Make a slight nick at one edge of the basket bottom, if necessary, for the power cord.

9. Secure the shade to the top of the harp with the finial.

finishing

None necessary.

Mushroom Table Lamp

If you can stretch your imagination, you are ready to combine an imported wooden canister with an antique frosted

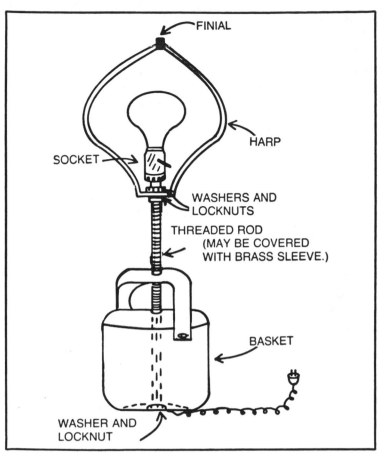

Fig. 8-30. Detail of basket light.

ceiling-fixture type light globe and grow your own mushroom that glows in the dark. The globe goes upside down on the top of the canister.

materials and tools

One imported wood canister and one antique frosted light globe of the right scale and dimension to fit into one another, one porcelain light fixture with pull-chain switch, one power cord with plug, two rubber grommets, screwdriver, drill, wire cutters and strippers.

shopping

1. Shop for an ornate frosted globe light fixture and a wooden canister to fit it and set it off.

preparation

None required.

assembly

1. Secure the porcelain fixture to the bottom of the canister with short screws (Fig. 8-31).

2. Drill small holes at the base of the canister on opposite sides. Thread power cord through one and the pull-chain through the other after inserting rubber grommets.

3. Fasten power cord wires to terminals on the porcelain fixture.

4. Screw in the light bulb and place globe in place over it.

finishing

None required.

Ice Mold Lamp

Hollow plastic ice molds sold by restaurant supply stores make attractive table and shelf lights. The molds come in all forms. You may prefer swans, but we like mermaids. The base illustrated in Fig. 8-32 will take any of the regular ice molds.

materials and tools

One wooden block 1×5×8 inches, one porcelain socket with pull-chain switch, one power cord with plug, one double socket, two 40-watt light bulbs, one or more plastic ice molds, screwdriver, wire cutters and strippers.

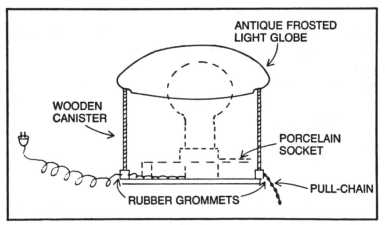

Fig. 8-31. Mushroom table lamp.

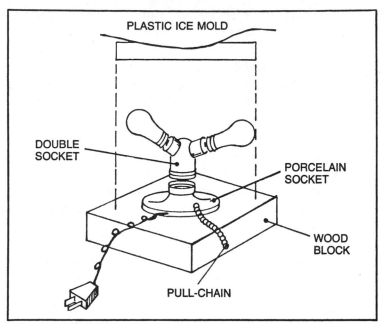

Fig. 8-32. Base for ice mold lamps.

shopping

1. Before you buy a wooden block, be sure and look in your lumber dealer's wood scraps pile. You may find something exotic on which to "base" your mermaid.

preparation

1. Be sure the ice mold you buy is wide and deep enough to fit over the light bulbs onto the base.

assembly

1. Fasten the porcelain socket in the middle of the wood block base with screws.

2. Fasten power cord wires to terminals on the porcelain socket.

3. Screw in double socket and light bulbs.

finishing

1. Put the ice mold in place over the light source. Make small notches in the bottom of the ice mold for the power cord and pull-chain switch.

2. For interesting decorative effects, colored light bulbs can be used. Don't hesitate to experiment. Do not use high

wattage bulbs, however, because the plastic used in ice molds is not designed to stand excessive heat.

Light from Scrap Lumber

Some of our most attractive table lamps have been made from scrap lumber. Check your neighborhood lumberyard for scraps.

materials and tools

Fourteen to 24 odds-and-ends pieces of lumber scraps, threaded rod of appropriate length and ⅜-inch diameter, two sets locknuts and washers, one socket with three-way switch, one harp, one finial, screwdriver, small wrench, drill, long drill bit, large size C clamp.

shopping

1. Unless you plan to make several lamps, don't buy long drill bits. Try to borrow or rent bits from a tool rental place.

preparation

You may want to spend some time sanding the scraps of wood you will be using before you assemble them.

assembly

1. Experiment with placing the wood scraps one on top of another in slightly staggered fashion somewhat like Fig. 8-33 suggests. When you have something that pleases you, take hold of the top and bottom wood pieces, press, and flip the whole pile upside down.

2. Take the top piece, which will be the bottom piece of your lamp, and coat its top side with glue. "Butter the underside of the next piece with glue and stick the two together. Continue in this manner until the whole pile of scraps is glued together.

3. Place your lamp base inside the jaws of the large C clamp and tighten down—adjusting any wayward pieces as you go—until the entire pile of wood scraps is firmly held by the clamp. Set aside to dry thoroughly.

4. After the glue has set, drill a cord hole through the center of the lamp base with a long drill bit.

5. Insert a threaded rod through the hole and set washers and locknuts in place. Do not tighten them yet.

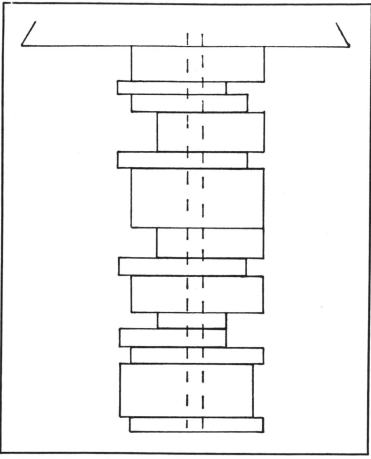

Fig. 8-33. Light made from scrap lumber.

6. Slip the harp on top of the threaded rod and screw the socket cap on loosely at the very top.

7. Thread the power cord through the rod and socket cap. Wire into the socket (Fig. 8-14).

8. Pull the interior of the socket down into the cap. Slip the shell down and force-fit into place.

9. Tighten all locknuts with a wrench.

10. Screw a three-way light bulb into the socket. Secure the shade to the harp with a finial.

finishing

1. Sand off excess glue. Apply an appropriate finish.

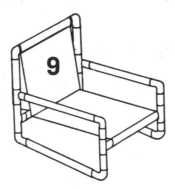

Rest and Relaxation Projects

Make the most of your free time and create some items that will provide comfort. Pillows are ideal projects.

PILLOWS FILLED WITH SHREDDED MATERIALS

There are two kinds of *pillows* you can make—those that have solid foam bases and those that are filled with shredded materials.

Loose-Fill Cushions
materials and tools

One piece of firmly woven material for lining 34×25 inches, one piece of covering material, 1 medium sack of fiberfill or shredded foam, 14-inch Velcro fastening tape or 14 inch zipper (optional), thread, scissors, needle, sewing machine, pins, measuring tape, chalk.

shopping

1. These simple cushions look best if they are made of fabric in a solid or vivid color.

2. For the inside cover you can use unbleached muslin or any other inexpensive firm cotton. Old sheets are great. When you use any leftover material, make sure the color and/or print does not show through the outside cover.

preparation

1. Cut your lining fabric into 25×34 inches.

2. Do the same for the cover material.

assembly and finishing

1. Fold the lining in half—that is into a 25×17 rectangle and stitch one short side (1-inch seam). Stitch twice.

2. Repeat the same step with the cover material. Stitch once.

3. Fill the lining with fiberfill or shredded foam.

4. After filling the inner bag, sew it shut. Pull the outer covering over the cushion, right side out, and sew shut. You can put a zipper in the end seam or two strips of Velcro fastening tape to make removal of the cover for washing easier.

cover with zipper

1. Fold the cover material in half—25×17-inch rectangle.

2. Sew one short end closed—1½ inches at either end (Fig. 9-1). Finger-press or iron the rest of the seam.

3. Insert the zipper between stitching. Baste or pin, right side up, naturally.

4. Stitch in the zipper. Open the zipper.

5. Turn inside out and stitch open sides. Turn again.

6. Put on over the cushion.

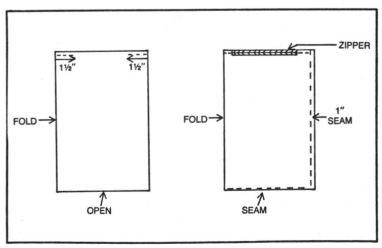

Fig. 9-1. Construction details for the pillow cover with zipper.

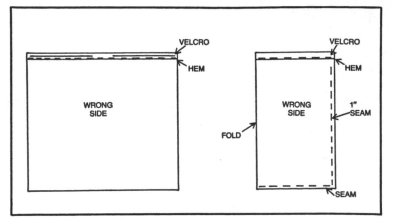

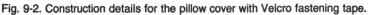

Fig. 9-2. Construction details for the pillow cover with Velcro fastening tape.

cover with Velcro fastening tape

1. Turn up a 1-inch hem along one 34-inch edge and stitch.

2. Cut a strip of Velcro fastening tape 14 inches long. Separate it.

3. Sew or glue the Velcro fastening tape to the hem on the inside. Set the strips in 1½ inches from the ends and 2 inches apart in the middle.

4. Fold the cover in half between the strips.

5. Stitch the open end (Fig. 9-2).

Chair Cushions for Seats and Backs

Measure your chair seat from back to front and from side to side. Do the same for the back. Add 2 inches to all measurements and cut (Fig. 9-3).

materials and tools

One piece of lining fabric and one of cover fabric 34×20 inches (18×16 inches the finished size), one piece of cover and one of lining fabric 18×24 inches (11×16 inches the finished size) one piece of 15-inch Velcro fastening tape or 14-inch zipper, one piece of 14-inch Velcro fastening tape or 12-inch zipper, six pieces of matching tape or ribbon 16 inches long each, heavy thread, one package of fiberfill or shredded foam fill, measuring tape, chalk, pins, scissors, sewing machine, needle.

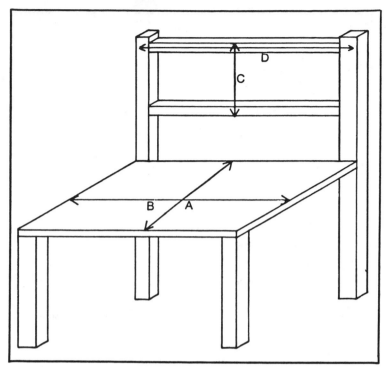

Fig. 9-3. Measuring the chair for chair cushions.

shopping

1. Buy buttons.

2. Instead of buying tape or ribbon, you can make ties out of your own cover material by cutting 2-inch-wide strips for the required lengths, folding them in half, then in half again lengthwise, and stitching along each edge (Fig. 9-4).

preparation

1. Follow directions for loose-fill cushions.

assembly

1. Follow directions for either zipper-closed cushions or Velcro fastening tape-closed ones. Set in 3 inches from each edge.

finishing

1. Fold tape, ribbon, or self-fabric tapes in half.

2. Sew through the center to the corners of the cushions—two at the wider end of the seat cushion and one in each corner of the back cushion.

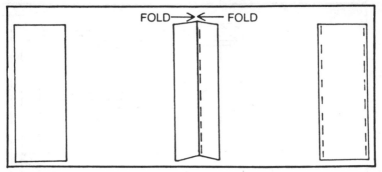

Fig. 9-4. Folding and stitching strips.

Floor Cushions

materials and tools

One piece of lining and one piece of cover fabric 36×54 inches (34×24 inches finished), four medium-sized bags of shredded foam, one piece of decorative cord (3½ yards), thread, scissors, sewing machine, chalk, pins, needle.

shopping

1. Same as for loose-fill cushions.

preparation

Same as for loose-fill cushions.

assembly

Same as for loose-fill cushions.

finishing

Same as for loose-fill cushions. Plus, sew the cord all around the outer edge of the pillow. Be careful to catch in only one edge on the side that has the fastening (Fig. 9-5). These

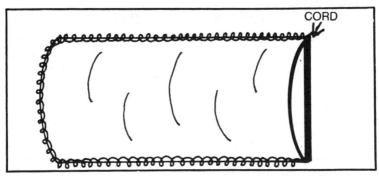

Fig. 9-5. Pillow outlined with cord.

floor pillows should be stuffed quite well. Because the size of shredded foam bags vary, you might need three or more.

Cushion Seat

materials and tools

Two pieces of lining fabric 48×58 inches (44×26 finished size of cushion), two pieces of cover fabric 48×58 inches, 7 yards of decorative cord, 10 bags of shredded foam or more, thread. Tools are the same as for the loose-fill cushions.

shopping

1. Obtain some heavy upholstery fabric, corduroy, or plush.

2. Get more foam than you think you will need.

preparation

Same as for loose-fill cushions.

assembly and finishing

Same as for loose-fill cushions. These cushions should be packed as firmly as possible with the fill to give them a "furniture" look (Fig. 9-6).

Loose-Fill Bolster

materials and tools

One piece of fabric 32×18 inches for lining plus two circles 11 inches in diameter, one piece of fabric 40×18

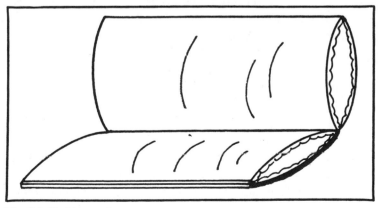

Fig. 9-6. Cushion seat.

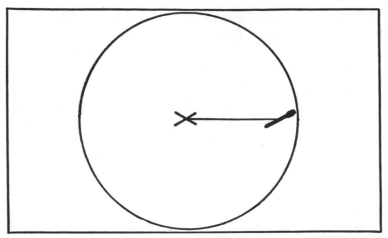

Fig. 9-7. Drawing a circle with string and pencil.

inches for cover, two pieces of ¼-inch-wide cord 10 inches each, thread, one-two sacks of foam, scissors, sewing machine, needle, measuring tape, chalk, pins, tack, pencil or compass, iron.

shopping

1. A softer fabric looks best for this kind of bolster—not too heavy in weight.

preparation

1. Cut the pieces of fabric as described.

2. To cut circles, use a compass set at 2½ inches for the radius.

3. If you don't have a compass, you can use an object with the required measurements and draw around it—a small bowl or saucer might do.

4. Another possibility is to tie a pencil to a piece of string, measure off 2½ inches, and tack the string down. Use the pencil to draw a circle (Fig. 9-7).

assembly

1. Fold the rectangle in half the long way and stitch. Stitch the seam again.

2. Pin one circle along one open edge, ½-inch seam, gathering in the long tube to fit. Stitch twice.

3. Stuff the tube according to the directions in Chapter 3.

4. Pin the remaining circle onto the open edge and sew by machine or by hand. Stitch twice around.

5. On each short end of the cover piece, turn down ¼ inch and press.

6. Turn down ½ inch and press again.

7. Stitch in the hem.

8. Sew up the long edge. Stitch twice but leave the hemmed ends open.

9. Insert the cord in the hems.

10. Pull over the bolster form, draw together tightly, and tie firmly (Fig. 9-8).

FOAM FORMS

You have probably seen foam that is cut into pillow forms of every description and thickness—from the 1½-inch-thick 9×9 square to oblong cushions and so forth that range up to 4 inches thick. You can also get wedge-shaped bolsters, square bolsters, and round bolsters in various lengths, diameters, and widths. You may get pads or mattresses that come in thicknesses from 1 to 6 inches and can be bought 24 to 39 inches wide. You may buy foam as rolled goods. These rolls vary from an 18-inch width to a 54-inch width.

You can buy most of these materials through the catalog departments of Sears, Montgomery Ward, or Penney's.

Foam Form Pillow

materials and tools

One foam form 20×20 inches and 4 inches thick, two pieces of fabric 21×21 inches, four strips of fabric 20½×5 inches, one zipper 18 inches long or one strip of Velcro

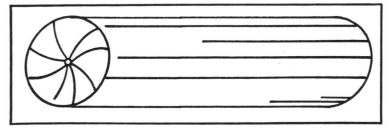

Fig. 9-8. Loose-fill bolster.

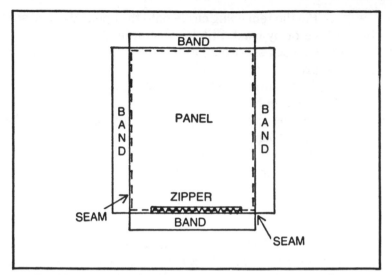

Fig. 9-9. Foam form pillow construction and zipper placement.

fastening tape 18 inches long, thread, measuring tape, chalk, pins, needle, scissors, sewing machine.

shopping

1. You have the option of using an inner cover with foam forms if you want one. It helps to preserve the foam, though it is not absolutely necessary. You need the same amount of material as you do for the cover.

2. We recommend heavier double knits for the covers, because the fitting is so much easier.

preparation

1. Cut out your pieces of material as directed.

assembly and finishing

1. Sew one 5-inch band to one side of the square piece. Repeat with the two other bands, making ½-inch seams.

2. Sew the fourth band 2½ inches on each side and leave the center open (Fig. 9-9).

3. Pin in the zipper on the right side and sew in. Open the zipper.

or

3A. Pin in Velcro fastening tape strips and sew or glue.

4. Sew together short 5-inch ends of strips with ½-inch seams.

338

5. Sew the other square on top of the bands, matching short seams to corners (Fig. 9-10).

6. Turn and put on the form.

Sit-n-Lean Pillow Combo

This is the first way that you can combine pillows into furniture—with or without wooden bases.

materials and tools

Two foam forms 24 inches square and 4 inches thick, two 22-inch zippers or Velcro fastening tape, four squares of fabric 25×25 inches, eight strips of fabric 5 inches wide and 25 inches long, one piece of fabric 10 inches wide and 24 inches long, 2 yards of heavy knit (54-60 inches wide) or 3 yards of other kinds of material (36-48 inches) all together, thread, measuring tape, scissors, pins, needle, sewing machine, chalk.

shopping

Follow instructions for foam form pillow.

preparation

1. Measure and mark your material to correspond to the layout given for your fabric (Fig. 9-10).

2. Cut out.

assembly and finishing

1. Follow steps 1-4 for the foam form pillow.

2. Fold the 10×24-inch piece in half lengthwise. Stitch a ½-inch seam each short end. Turn.

3. Note the free edges of the piece in the seam as you

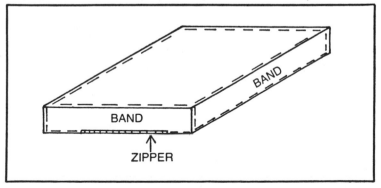

Fig. 9-10. Foam form pillow finishing.

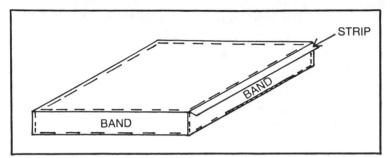

Fig. 9-11. Sit-n-lean pillow combo—sewing in the hinge strip.

attach the top square to the band. The strip should be on the same side and above the zipper (Fig. 9-11).

4. Sew the rest of the square to the band, matching corners and seams.

5. Repeat step 1 (i.e., steps 1-4 foam form).

6. Attach fold edge of 10×24-inch piece to the second cover in the same manner as in step 3 (Fig. 9-12).

7. Finish as in step 4 (Fig. 9-13).

Lean and Lounge Combo

materials and tools

Three foam forms 24×24×4 inches, six squares of 25×25-inch fabric, 12 strips of 5×25-inch fabric, two strips of fabric 10×24 inches long, (3 yards of double knit 54-60 inches wide or 4½ yards of 48-inch material), thread, scissors, needle, sewing machine, tape measure, pins, chalk.

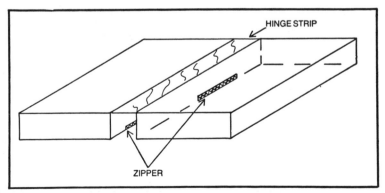

Fig. 9-12. Sit-n-lean pillow combo detail.

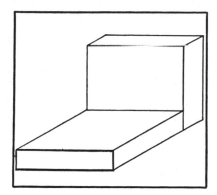

Fig. 9-13. Sit-n-lean pillow combo.

shopping

Same as above.

preparation

1. Follow layouts given for your material width (Fig. 9-14).

2. Cut out.

assembly and finishing

1. Follow assembly instructions for sit-n-lean pillow combo exactly.

2. Repeat the procedure for the third pillow (Figs. 9-15 and 9-16).

Fig. 9-14. Layout for fabric for lean and lounge combo.

60″			
25 × 25	25 × 25	10 × 24	
25 × 25	25 × 25	10 × 24	
25 × 25	25 × 25	5 × 25	5 × 25
5×25	5×25	5 ×	5 × 25
5×25	5×25		
5×25	5×25		
5×25	5×25	//////	

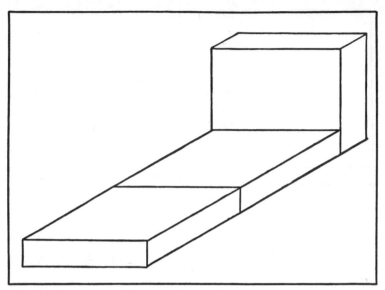

Fig. 9-15. Open lean and lounge pillow combo.

Pillow-for-All-Uses Combo

materials and tools

Four foam forms 21×14×3 inches, four 12-inch zippers or four 12-inch Velcro fastening tape strips, eight pieces of fabric 22×15 inches, eight strips of fabric 4×22 inches, eight strips of fabric 4×15 inches, three strips of fabric 7×14 inches, thread, measuring tape, chalk, scissors, sewing machine, needle, chalk, pins.

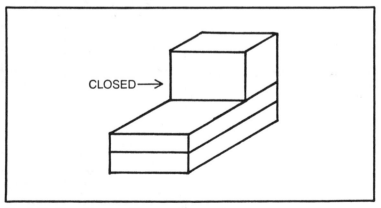

Fig. 9-16. Closed lean and lounge pillow combo.

shopping

1. You can cover two of the pillows in one pattern and/or color and the other two in a contrasting pattern or color.

2. If you plan to take this combo outdoors and in your car, consider making the cover out of medium weight upholstery plastic.

preparation

1. Follow layouts given for your width of material in Fig. 9-17.

2. Cut out.

assembly and finishing

1. Follow instructions for assembling the sit-n-lean combo.

2. Repeat for the third and fourth pillows.

3. Hinge the two combos together with another of the 2×16 bands. All the zippers and the hinges will go into the 15-inch sides (Figs. 9-18 and 9-19).

Hassock

materials and tools

Four 24×24×5-inch foam forms, two 22-inch-long zippers or Velcro fastening tape strips, eight pieces of fabric

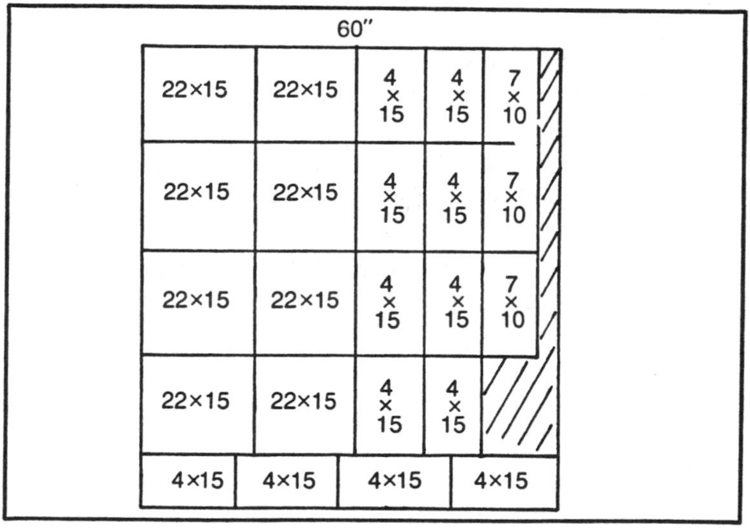

Fig. 9-17. Fabric layout for the pillow-for-all-uses combo.

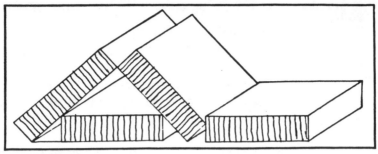

Fig. 9-18. Sample setup for the pillow-for-all-uses combo.

25×25 inches, 16 strips of fabric 6×25 inches, two pieces of 3- or 4-inch webbing 98 inches long, two buckles to match, eyelets, thread, measuring tape, scissors, eyelet setter, needle, pins, chalk, sewing machine.

shopping

 1. You can usually pick up the webbing in an upholstery shop. You can even order it from Sears.

 2. You can also work with the plastic webbing that you normally use to replace the seat of your lawn chairs, which can be bought at your local discount or hardware store. You can omit the eyelets.

preparation

 1. Follow the layout given in Fig. 9-14.

 2. Cut out fabric.

assembly and finishing

 1. Follow assembly directions given for the foam form pillow.

 2. Attach a buckle to one end of the webbing.

 3. Make three or four eyelets, 2 inches apart, at the other end.

 4. Narrowly hem the end of the webbing if you are using the upholstery variety.

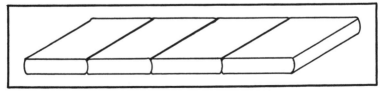

Fig. 9-19. Open pillow for-all-uses combo.

5. Stack your finished pillows and strap them together with your webbing belts (Fig. 9-20).

Pillow Headboard
materials and tools
Two foam forms 24×20×3 inches, one brass or wood drapery rod with decorative ends 54 inches long, hardware to hang the rod, brackets for rod, four 25×21-inch pieces of fabric, four 21×4-inch pieces, four 25×4-inch pieces and six 6×4-inch pieces (2 yards of fabric altogether) two 16-inch zippers, thread, ruler, measuring tape, scissors, marking pencil, chalk, pins, needle, sewing machine, screwdriver, drill (optional).

shopping
1. Get the kind of rod that goes well with the other things in your bedroom. You might paint or stain a rod to match.

2. You can cover the rod with matching fabric.

3. Fabric can either match your bedspread or contrast.

4. You can use knit, but it is best to match the fabric to that already in the room. Consider sheeting that is easy to handle and looks good. Towels are another solution.

preparation
1. Lay out the material as in Fig. 9-21.

2. Mark and cut pieces.

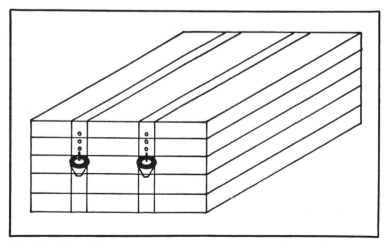

Fig. 9-20. Hassock.

25×21	25×21	4×21	4×21
25×21	25×21	4×21	4×21
4×25	4×25	6×4	
4×25	4×25	6×4	
6×4 6×4 6×4 6×4			

60″ WIDE   1⅞ YDS

Fig. 9-21. Fabric layout for pillow headboard.

3. Mark for drapery rod brackets on the wall above the bed. If you can find studs, that's fine. If not, you will have to use molley bolts instead of simple screws.

assembly and finishing

1. Follow assembly directions given for foam form pillows—steps 1-4.

2. Fold the 6×4-inch pieces in 1 inch from each end. Fold in half (Fig. 9-22). Stitch on both edges.

3. Sew one of the folded strips to the free rectangle ½ inch in from the corner, folding in half to form a loop (Fig. 9-23).

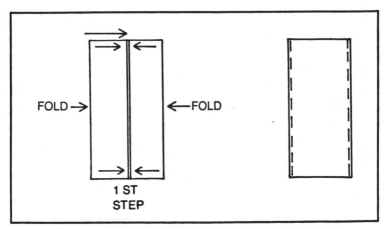

FOLD →   ← FOLD

1 ST
STEP

Fig. 9-22. Folding and stitching strips for loops.

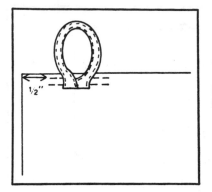

Fig. 9-23. Sewing loops to the corner of the rectangle.

4. Repeat this procedure, sewing another loop in the other corner of the 25-inch-long side, and lastly a third in the center at 12½ inches in from the side.

5. Finish the pillow by sewing the top piece with loops to the pillow. Remember to keep the loops between the top and bottom of the pillow—on the inside (right side) as you sew on the wrong side (Fig. 9-24).

6. Repeat for the second pillow.

7. Slip loops over the drapery rod and hang in brackets (Fig. 9-25).

This method of covering pillow forms applies equally to covering pads or mattresses. The only difference is the size and shape of the pieces. Because most pads come in 75-inch lengths and are 30 inches wide, you can usually cover a pad with 3 yards of 60-inch material. A 28-inch zipper at one of the

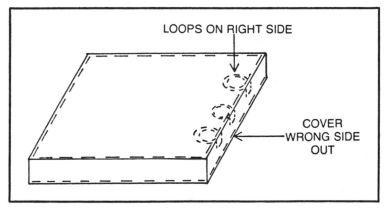

Fig. 9-24. Finishing pillow with loops.

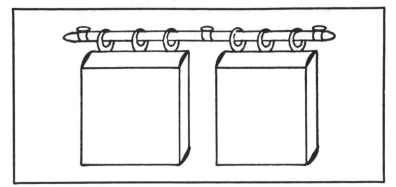
Fig. 9-25. Pillow headboard.

short ends will be ample. You can get these extra long zippers in upholstery stores. A 28-inch strip of Velcro fastening tape will do equally well and save you that extra stop.

The fun begins when you use pads and pillows together. Here is a two pads, three pillows combo that is nice to sit and lounge on and presents comfortable "crash" pads for two overnight guests.

Two Pads, Three Pillows Combo
materials and tools

Two foam form pads 30×75×5 inches, three foam form pillows 24×21×3 inches, two 4-inch buckles, one drapery rod 75 inches long with decorative ends, brackets for rod, hardware, four pieces of fabric 31×76 inches, four pieces 76×6 inches, four pieces 31×6 inches, six 25×22-inch pieces, six 25×4-inch pieces, six 22×4-inch pieces, nine 6×4-inch pieces, two 28-inch zippers or Velcro fastening tape strips, three 18-inch zippers or Velcro fastening tape strips, thread, 6 yards of webbing, sewing machine, measuring tape, needles, pins, chalk, scissors, pencil, ruler, screwdriver, drill (optional).

shopping

1. You will need about 9 yards of 60-inch knit material or 12 yards of 54 or 48-inch material.

2. When you buy the brackets for the drapery rod, buy two small support brackets to go between the pillows instead of the usual center support.

3. Follow the suggestions given for the pillow headboard.

preparation

1. Follow the layout for cutting fabric pieces (Fig. 9-26).

2. Follow all measuring and marking directions for the pillow headboard.

assembly

1. Follow assembly directions given for the pillow headboard.

2. Follow directions given for assembly of the foam form pillow for the pads.

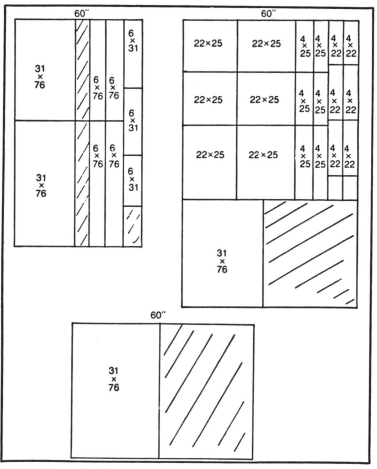

Fig. 9-26. Layout for fabric for two pads and three-pillows combo.

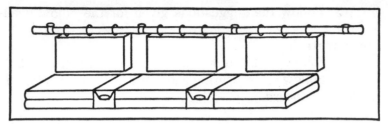

Fig. 9-27. Two pads and three pillows combination.

3. Follow assembly steps 1-4 for the hassock.

4. Stack mattresses and strap together as shown in Fig. 9-27.

5. Hang the drapery rod above the mattresses (Fig. 9-27).

Round Pillows

materials and tools

One round foam form 16 inches in diameter, one 10-inch zipper or strip of Velcro fastening tape, two fabric circles 17½ inches in diameter (knit fabric), thread, measuring tape, chalk, string, pencil, tack, sewing machine, needle.

shopping

1. Same as for the other foam forms.

2. Some of the round forms are slanted. They are about 4 inches thick in the center and taper out to 2 inches along the edges. The assembly instructions are for this particular kind of cushion.

3. If you buy or have the round kind of form that is equally thick throughout, follow the layout and instructions given in the assembly steps. The yardage will be the same, and you can use woven instead of knit fabric.

preparation

1. Make yourself a large compass by measuring off 8¾ inches on your string after you have tied your pencil to it.

2. Tack the string to the material with your large tack and draw your circle. Repeat for the second circle.

or

1A. Make a compass in the same way, but measure off 8¼ inches.

350

2A. Same as step 2.

3A. Cut a strip of fabric 1 inch wider than the thickness of your cushion (4 inches for a 3-inch thickness) and 52½ inches long.

assembly

1. Sew together the two circles for 4 inches. Leave open for 10 inches and sew another 4 inches. Backstitch or tie off the thread.

2. Insert zipper or Velcro fastening tape strips into the opening. Sew or glue.

open zipper

3. Finish sewing the two circles together. Turn and put on the foam form.

1A. Sew the strip to one of the circles for 4 inches. Leave an opening 10 inches long and sew for another 4 inches. Tie threads at both ends of the opening (½-inch seam).

2A. Insert the zipper or Velcro fastening tape strips and sew or glue. Open zipper.

3A. Finish the attaching band to the circle, leaving the ½-inch end of the band free at each side.

4A. Sew ends of band together (½-inch seam).

5A. Sew the second circle to the band all around. Turn and put on the form (Fig. 9-28).

BOLSTERS

People tend to not work with bolsters, even though they feel perfectly capable of dealing with pillows or pads. Cylindrical, wedge-shaped, and square bolsters are available.

Bolster covers have to fit well. You usually sit or lie on a pad, which somewhat squashes the foam form and/or stretches the fabric. The same is true with pillows. The function of bolsters is more decorative, serving to delineate space, though they are also used as armrests, backrests, or as backdrops for smaller cushions.

You can use knit fabric to get a clinging fit. Another method is to make your cover very small. It will be a struggle to put it on, but the fabric will stretch a bit. To help you get the cover on the bolster easier, you may want to dampen the cover.

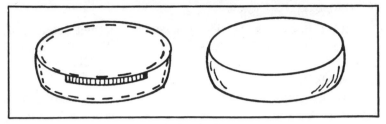

Fig. 9-28. Round cushion construction details.

Round or Cylindrical Bolster

materials and tools

One round bolster foam form 9 inches in diameter and 30 inches long, one 18-inch-long zipper or Velcro fastening tape strip, two fabric circles 9½ inches in diameter, one strip of fabric 30×29 inches (1 yard of fabric altogether), thread, scissors, sewing machine, needle, pins, chalk, string, pencil, tack.

shopping

Same as for the foam form pillow.

preparation

1. Draw two 9½-inch circles following the instructions given in the preparation section for the round pillow.

2. Cut one strip of 29×30-inch fabric.

assembly and finishing

1. Fold 29×30-inch strip in half (30×14½).

2. Sew ½-inch seam 6 inches up from each end. Tie the threads.

3. Insert the zipper or Velcro fastening tape strips. Sew. Open the zipper.

4. Sew circles to each end of the tube. Turn and put on the form (Fig. 9-29).

Alternate Method

There is an alternate way to make round bolster covers, which is the one we used when we made the shredded foam bolster.

shopping

Same as the above plus string and two covered buttons 1-1½ inches in diameter.

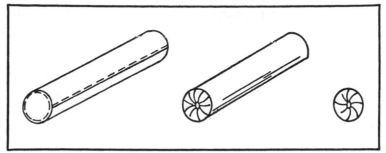

Fig. 9-29. Round bolster construction details.

preparation
1. Cut one single 29×40-inch strip—no circles.
assembly and finishing
1. Make a ½-inch hem across both short ends.

2. Sew a ½-inch seam 6 inches up from the hem stitching on each side (14½×40). Tie ends of threads.

3. Insert a zipper or Velcro fastening tape strips and sew in place. Turn right side out.

4. Insert the string in each hem. Pull as tightly as possible. Tie securely.

5. Whip open edges together. Sew a covered button over the tiny remaining opening at each end (Fig. 9-29).

Square or Rectangular Bolsters
materials and tools
One square bolster foam form 9×9×36, one 24-inch zipper or Velcro fastening tape strip, one piece of fabric 37×37 inches, two fabric squares 10×10 inches, thread, measuring tape, scissors, needle, sewing machine, chalk.
shopping
Same as for the other foam forms. You will need 1¼ yards of 48, 54, or 60-inch fabric.
preparation
1. Mark and cut material as indicated.
assembly
1. Fold a 37-inch square in half (37×18½). Sew up 6½ inches from each end—½-inch seam.

2. Insert a zipper or Velcro fastening tape strips—sew in. Open the zipper.

3. Pin a 10-inch square to one end of the tube, so the seam falls in the center of one side (Fig. 9-30). Sew in with ½-inch seam.

4. Repeat with the other square. Turn and put on the foam form with the zipper on the bottom surface.

Wedge-Shaped Bolster

materials and tools

One wedge-shaped bolster form 36 inches long, 12 inches high, 9 inches deep at bottom, and 5 inches deep on top; one 24-inch zipper or Velcro fastening tape strip; one strip of fabric 37×39½ inches and two wedge-shaped pieces 13×10 inches trimmed to fit the wedge, thread, scissors, sewing machine, chalk, pins, needle, measuring tape.

shopping

Same as for other foam forms.

preparation

1. Copy the wedge shape pictured in Fig. 9-31 on heavy paper in acutal size. Cut out.

2. Using the piece of paper as a pattern, cut out two pieces of fabric. Make sure you have a right and a left piece (Fig. 9-32).

3. Cut out a 37×39½-inch piece.

assembly and finishing

1. Fold a 37×39½-inch piece in half (19¾×37 inches). Sew up 6½ inches from each end—½-inch seam. Tie threads.

2. Insert a zipper or Velcro fastening tape strip. Sew in. Open the zipper.

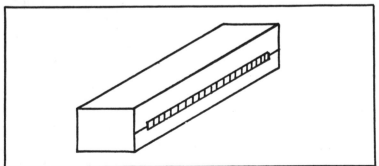

Fig. 9-30. Square bolster.

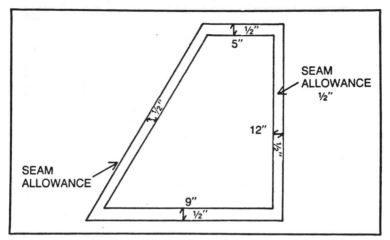

Fig. 9-31. Pattern for cutting wedge-shaped piece.

3. Center the seam on a 9-inch side of the wedge piece. Pin the rest of the wedge to the tube. Use a ½-inch seam stitch.

4. Repeat with the other wedge-shaped piece. Turn and put on the foam form (Fig. 9-33).

There is usually no problem in keeping pads in place, because they are heavy and rest on their largest surfaces. You can use the belting technique to combine two or more pads into a unit. If your pad seems to have a tendency to slide, anchor it by attaching fabric strips to the lower back corner

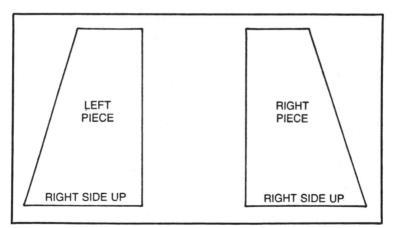

Fig. 9-32. Cutting a right and a left wedge-shaped piece for the bolster.

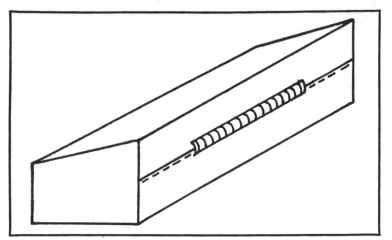
Fig. 9-33. Zipper and seam detail for wedge-shaped bolster.

and the center of the back. Tack the strips to the back or bottom of the base. If you have a backrest piece or pieces, you can tie the strips of the pad to them.

If the pillows are small, rearrange them whenever you feel you need to interfere with their natural bent. For larger cushions, you can also use ties in the corners, the two top ones or, if you prefer, in all four corners. Self-fabric ties look best, but tape ties in a matching color are fine, too. Ribbon ties are good if you use sturdy ribbon. You can hang the back cushions from a rod or, if you prefer, from some decorative hooks.

Another method can be used when the backrest consists of posts or poles. It is called the double-back solution.

Double-Back Cushion Covers
materials and tools
One 24×24×4-inch cushion (foam form or fiberfill) and cover, one extra 25×25-inch panel. Tools are the same as for cushions, plus an iron.
shopping
Follow instructions for the foam form or fiberfill.
preparation
1. Cut one extra piece 25×25 inches.
2. Turn under ½ inch all around the piece and press.

3. Turn up another ½ inch along one edge, press again, and stitch all across.

assembly

1. Pin the piece to the back of the finished pillow. The cover is right side out. Pin the new piece on top, right side up.

2. Stitch a new piece to the cover ¼ inch from the edge all around and then stitch again ⅛ inch from the edge (Fig. 9-34).

Alternate Method

materials and tools

One piece of fabric 52×26 inches, one piece of fabric 26×26, 18-inch zipper or Velcro fastening tape, thread, two-three bags of fiberfill or shredded foam, measuring tape, pins, sewing machine, needle, chalk, iron.

shopping

Same as for the other fiberfill pillows.

preparation

1. Turn up ½ inch at one edge of the 26×26-inch piece, press, turn up another ½ inch, press again, and stitch.

2. Sew this panel to the big piece of fabric, with the right side of the smaller piece up (right side of the big piece to the wrong side of the small piece) (Fig. 9-35).

3. Fold the large piece in half.

4. Sew up 3 inches on each end of one side. Tie the threads.

5. Insert the zipper or Velcro fastening tape strips.

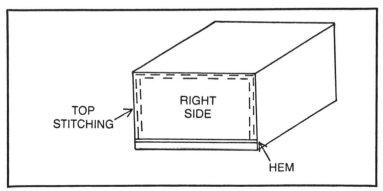

Fig. 9-34. Top stitching outer back flap to the back panel.

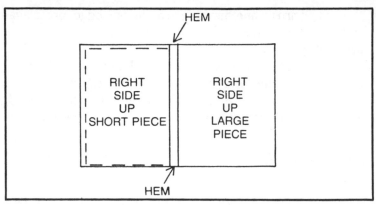

Fig. 9-35. Attaching extra panel to the large cover piece.

½-inch seam, including the extra panel in the seam. Open the zipper.

6. Sew the other two seams including the third panel.

7. Turn and put on the pillow.

8. Slip the pocket formed by the extra panel over the posts or poles of your wooden or metal bases (Fig. 9-36). This method can be used equally well with foam forms. Just attach the extra panel in three of the seams that adjoin the bands. Hem the fourth, leaving it free to form the pocket.

COUCHES AND BEDS

Couches and beds are easy and quick to build if you are willing to use innovative ideas along with some of the pillows, cushions, and pads suggested in the preceding section.

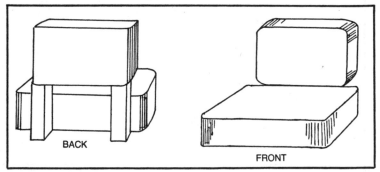

Fig. 9-36. Pillows on posts.

Love Seat-Sized Couch

A box, a few slats, and some pillows make for comfortable rest and relaxation.

materials and tools

Four cushions approximately 24 inches square, two pieces of ¾-inch plywood 48×12 inches, two pieces of ¾-inch plywood 18½×12 inches, one piece of ¾-inch plywood 48×20 inches, four 1×6s 36 inches long, 16 1⅜-inch lag screws, 3d casing nails, white glue, putty stick, clear varnish, hammer, nail set, adjustable wrench, drill and bit for lag screw clearance and pilot holes, ruler, marking pencil.

shopping

1. Shop for a good grade plywood for the box base with some nice grain that will look good under your cushions.

2. If you use store-bought pillows, shop for the fluffiest ones you can find.

preparation

1. Measure and mark the nail guideline ⅜ inch in from the edges of plywood that will form the five-sided box.

2. Mark lag screw clearance holes in a staggered pattern as shown in Fig. 9-37.

assembly

1. Construct a five-sided box as shown in Fig. 9-38 with casing nails and glue.

2. Countersink nailheads with a nail set and cover the heads with putty.

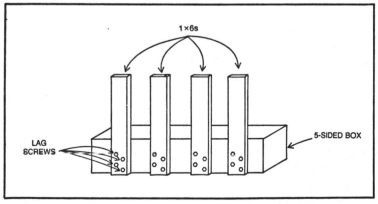

Fig. 9-37. Detail showing pattern of lag screw clearance holes.

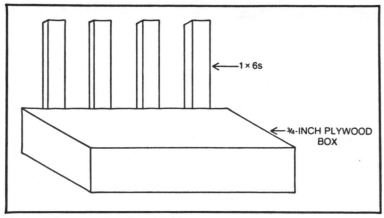

Fig. 9-38. Love seat is a five-sided box.

3. Drill clearance holes in 1×6s as marked, then drill pilot holes into the back of the box base.

4. Insert lag screws and turn to a tight fit with the wrench.

finishing

1. Coat with clear varnish. When dry, install pillows.

Pine Platform/Pad and Pillow Haven

Figure 9-39 shows a rest and relaxation area with a built-in look. The base is a platform of knotty pine with a double bed-sized pad or mattress with plenty of space left over for fun and games on the night table extension. Make it a game table, a snack table, a book repository, or even just a clutter cache.

materials and tools

One pad or mattress 54×75 inches, one assortment of pillows and cushions, 22 pieces 1×6 tongue-and-groove knotty pine flooring 54 inches long, nine 2×4s of knotty pine 120 inches long, six 2×4s of knotty pine 54 inches long, corrugated fasteners, 4d and 8d spiral nails, clear liquid plastic, hammer, ruler, marking pencil.

shopping

1. Get all lumber cut to exact lengths.

preparation

1. None necessary.

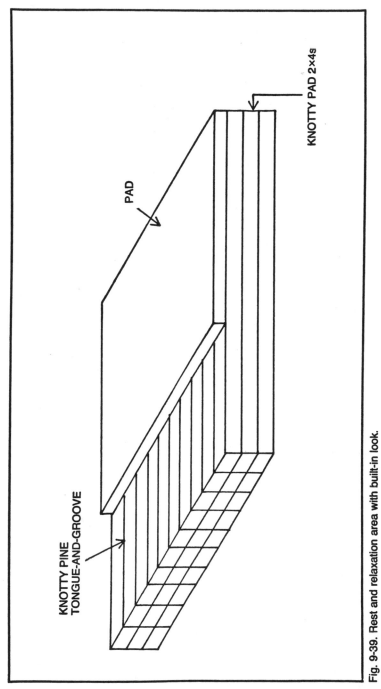

KNOTTY PAD 2×4s

PAD

KNOTTY PINE
TONGUE-AND-GROOVE

Fig. 9-39. Rest and relaxation area with built-in look.

assembly

1. Lay 120-inch 2×4s side by side in three groups of three each and fasten together with corrugated fasteners on one side only.

2. Turn each group on end and space 26¼ inches apart on centers (Fig. 9-40).

3. Lay 1×6s across and secure with 4d spiral flooring nails.

4. Lay 54 inch 2×4s side by side in two groups of three each and fasten together with corrugated fasteners.

5. Turn each group on end. Place at the "head" and "foot" of the main platform structure and secure by driving 8d nails into the ends of the 2×4 platform supporting the structure.

finishing

1. Coat the entire platform with two coats of clear liquid plastic.

2. When dry, furnish with pad, cushions, pillows, games, snacks, and your favorite books.

Ceiling-Hung Bed

Some people like to float on a water bed. How about floating on air with this swing bed hung from the ceiling? A single-bed pad or mattress rests on a flush door supported by four porch swing chains (Fig. 9-41).

Ceiling joists must be located. Large screw eyes are screwed in firmly. Pillows and cushions may be stowed aboard to match the mattress or pad cover.

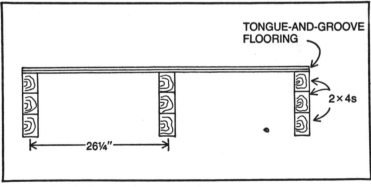

Fig. 9-40. Two-by-four members 26¼ inches on centers.

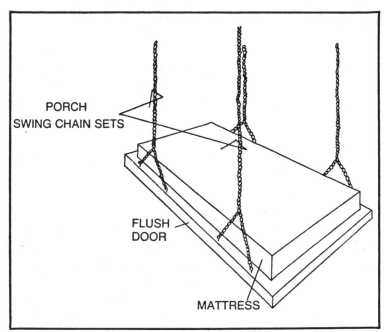

Fig. 9-41. Ceiling-hung bed.

materials and tools

Four sets of porch swing chains, one 80×36-inch flush door, eight medium screw eyes for fastening the chain to the door, four large screw eyes for anchoring bed to ceiling joists, pads and pillows of your choice, clear varnish, Drill with bit for starter holes in door and ceiling joists, wrench for turning screw eyes, ruler, marking pencil.

shopping

1. A ready-to-finish Philippine mahogany flush door with a hollow core makes a good platform for your swinging bed. It is among the least expensive flush doors.

preparation

1. Locate ceiling joists and carefully mark the ceiling for drilling of starter holes for large screw eyes.

2. Measure bottom "Y" of porch swing chains and mark edges of the flush door for starter holes for medium-size screw eyes.

assembly

1. Drill starter holes for large screw eyes in ceiling joists

and turn the screw eyes into place with a wrench.

2. Hang the four sets of swing chains from the ceiling screw eyes.

3. Drill starter holes where marked on the solid edges of the door and insert screw eyes. Fasten them with a wrench.

4. Hang the bed by slipping the chain into one set of screw eyes at a time.

finishing

1. Use two coats of clear varnish to finish the door. Load on a pad or mattress and cushions.

Wall-Hung Indoor Hammock

This indoor hammock can be hung from the studs of any interior wall or from ceiling joists. Either way, use a short length of welded machine chain in the wall or ceiling hooks and tie marine rope onto that (Fig. 9-42). The frame is of 2×4 construction. Webbing is bought and installed from a rewebbing kit sold for the repair of outdoor aluminum lawn furniture.

materials and tools

Two 2×4s 74 inches long, two 2×4s 17 inches long, corrugated fasteners, two short lengths of welded machine

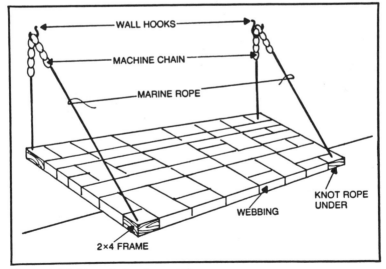

Fig. 9-42. Wall-hung indoor hammock.

chain, four lengths marine rope to hang the hammock about 12 to 18 inches off the floor, one rewebbing kit for large aluminum chaise lounge, two large screw eyes, drill with bits for starter holes and ½-inch bit for rope holes in the hammock frame, tools for rewebbing suggested in the kit, ruler.

shopping

1. Get 2×4s cut exactly to size.
2. Choose webbing to suit the room decor.

preparation

1. Locate studs in the wall or joists in the ceiling and mark for starter holes for large screw eyes.
2. Measure and mark centers for ½-inch holes to be drilled in the four corners of the 2×4 frame 1½ inches in from the edges of the frame.

assembly

1. Lay out 2×4s in the frame pattern shown in Fig. 9-43. Secure the frame together with corrugated fasteners.
2. Drill holes as marked on the four corners of the frame.
4. Drill starter holes for the large screw eyes in studs or joists and insert screw eyes. Secure them with a wrench.
5. Hang the chain over screw eyes and splice the rope securely to both ends of each chain.
6. Thread the rope through holes in the frame and secure by tying knots into the end of the rope under the frame. Adjust knots to the level frame.
7. Install webbing on the frame according to instructions in the rewebbing kit.

finishing

1. Just climb aboard with your favorite book or magazine and a few pillows.

BENCHES AND RACKS

These projects are complementary. They are ideal when you want to "get away from it all."

Jail-Cot Bunk

This little bunk can be tucked away in the corner of a den or other small room.

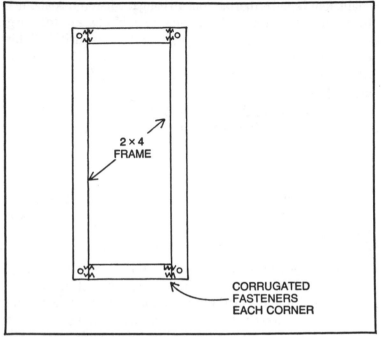

Fig. 9-43. Frame secured with corrugated fasteners.

materials and tools

Four 1×6 tongue-and-groove boards 74 inches long, four 2×4s 18 inches long, one 2×4 72 inches long, four large screw eyes, two 32-inch lengths of 1-inch welded machine chain, 6d and 8d common nails, drill with bit for screw eye starter holes, hammer, drill with bit for screw eye starter holes, adjustable wrench.

shopping

1. Get all lumber cut to the exact size needed.

preparation

1. Measure 14 inches up from the floor and locate wall studs. Mark the placement of the 72-inch-long 2×4 wall support (Fig. 9-44).

2. Measure 22 inches up from the top of the 2×4 wall support and mark placement of screw eyes in wall studs.

assembly

1. Fasten the four 1×6 tongue-and-groove boards together and nail the four 18-inch two-by-fours across to secure.

366

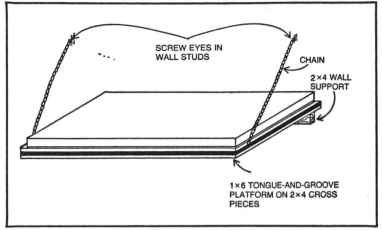

Fig. 9-44. Jail-cot bunk.

Start cross-pieces 1½ inches in from the back edge of the cot base to clear the 2×4 support piece along the wall.

2. Anchor the 72-inch 2×4 along the wall with 8d nails. Nail into the wall studs.

3. Drill starter holes for screw eyes in wall studs and insert the screw eyes. Turn them in with a wrench. Drill and insert screw eyes into the top outside edge of the cot base.

4. Place the cot base on a 2×4 ledge and fasten the chain from the wall screw eyes to the screw eyes on the cot base.

5. Nail back the section of the cot base to the 2×4 wall support with 6d nails.

finishing

1. Cover the cot base with a 4-inch-by-22-inch-by-72-inch foam rubber cushion covered with fabric to match the room decor.

2. Take aboard pillows to suit taste.

Ladder-and-Sling Magazine Rack

Lean it up against a wall within reach of your jail-cot bunk. Have all your favorite magazines and newspapers handy and in plain view (Fig. 9-45).

materials and tools

One 6 to 8-foot length of plain wooden ladder, four or five 1×2-inch lengths of muslin, heavy sewing thread, paint, metal eyelets, 4-yard cord, paintbrush, heavy needle, eyelet setter, ruler.

shopping

1. Get a nice old-fashioned round rung-type wooden ladder.

2. If you can't find a ladder, you can construct one very simply by buying two 7-foot-long 1×2s for the side rails and 10 1-inch-diameter dowels 14 inches long. Follow the assembly directions.

preparation

1. Measure and cut fabric into five 14×25-inch pieces (1½ yards of 54-inch material or 48-inch material).

2. Measure and fold over each 25-inch edge ½ inch and then ½ inch again to form hems.

3. Measure and fold first ½ inch and then 1 inch along the remaining edges to form hems.

4. Mark each wider hem ½ inch in from the edge and again every 1½ inches for eyelets, centering them in the hem.

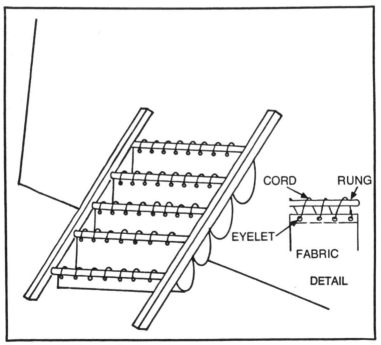

Fig. 9-45. Ladder and sling magazine rack.

assembly and finishing

1. Sew in all the hems.

2. Put in all the eyelets.

3. Lash the fabric to rungs by running the cord through eyelets and over rungs. Tie firmly at each end of the rung (Fig. 9-45).

ladder assembly

1. Drill 1-inch diameter holes partway through 1×2s starting 8 inches from the bottom on center.

2. Drill holes in the same manner at 8-inch intervals up the length of both 1×2s.

3. Glue dowels into holes.

1×2 Style Stow-It Rack

Here is a whole shelf system you can use for your hi-fi, books, or snacks and have it within easy reach of your jail-cot bunk, indoor hammock, or swinging bed. It goes together with glue and nails and is completely adjustable as to space between shelves (Fig. 9-46).

materials and tools

Eight 1×2s 62½ inches long, 36 1×2s 15 inches long, six pieces of ¾-inch plywood 30×15 inches, 3d casing nails, white glue, paint or varnish, hammer, nail set, ruler, blocks.

shopping

1. Have all lumber cut to exact dimensions.

preparation

1. Double-check all measurements to be sure the lumber was cut to exact dimensions.

assembly

1. Make the two sides by laying four of the long 1×2s side by side spaced exactly 3 inches apart. Nail and glue the short 1×2s across, spacing them exactly 2 inches apart.

2. Secure two of the ¾-inch plywood shelves to the top and bottom with glue and nails. The first and last 1×2 crosspieces on each side begin and end ¾ inch from top and bottom.

finishing

1. Paint or varnish including four loose shelves. When

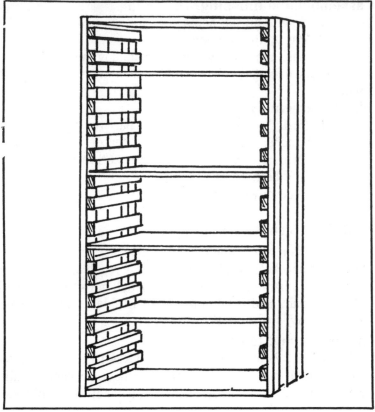

Fig. 9-46. The 1×2-style stow-it rack.

dry, fit shelves in on top of 1×2 crosspieces to suit the height of objects to be stored on shelves.

SCREENS FOR STORAGE AND PRIVACY

Here are some neat, quick-to-build screen/shelf systems.

Zigzag Shelf System

This room divider will provide you with plenty of shelf storage and give you a lot of hanging space.

materials and tools

Three pieces of ¾-inch plywood 15¾×60 inches, three pieces of ¾-inch plywood 15×60 inches, eight pieces of

¾-inch plywood cut to 14¼×14¼×20 inch triangles, two pieces of ⅛-inch pegboard 15×60 inches, 12 ⅜-inch spacers, 12¾-inch long roundhead wood screws, 3d casing nails, white glue, paint, four ¾-inch butt hinges, hammer, nail set, screwdriver, ruler.

shopping

1. Have all lumber and pegboard cut to exact size.

preparation

1. Measure ⅜ inch in from the edge of wider wood panels and mark the nail guideline.

2. Measure and mark nail guidelines on the backside of panels for the shelf arrangement suggested in Fig. 9-47.

assembly

1. Glue and nail each pair of panels together with butt joints at right angles to one another.

2. Glue and nail triangular shelves in place between two of the sets of panels.

3. Using spacers and screws, attach pegboard to the remaining two panels.

4. Hinge units together.

finishing

1. Paint or varnish.

Folding Storage

This folding storage screen complete with casters is ideal for a craft room. You can move your space about when necessity dictates. The screen is only 4 inches deep, but it can store tremendous amounts of craft supplies.

materials and tools

Four pieces ¾-inch plywood 15×72 inches, eight 1×4s 72 inches long, 18 1×4s 13½ inches long, six ¾-inch butt hinges and screws, metal ball-type flat plate furniture casters, 3d casing nails, glue, paint, hammer, nail set, screwdriver, ruler.

shopping

1. Get all lumber cut to exact sizes specified.

preparation

1. Measure ⅜ inch in from the edges of all plywood panels and draw nail guidelines.

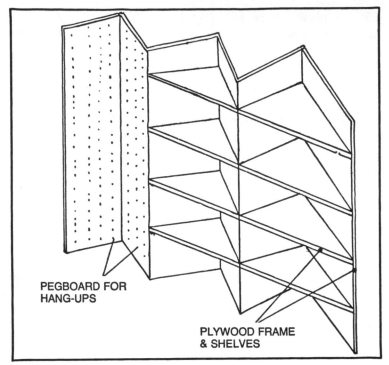

Fig. 9-47. Zigzag shelf system.

2. Using Fig. 9-48 as a guide, measure and mark nail guidelines for shelves.

assembly

1. Lay out two 72-inch 1×4s 13½ inches apart, then glue and nail two 13½-inch 1×4s between them—top and bottom.

2. Lay one 15×72-inch plywood panel on top. Nail and glue in place. Repeat the above step for all four sections.

3. Place remaining 1×4s inside sections as shelves or follow the suggestion in Fig. 9-48.

4. Add casters to the underside of the screen, two on each end section and one each on the two center sections.

finishing

1. Paint to suit.

Martian Sunset Screen

The scene for this screen is patterned after a picture sent back to earth by Viking I and reconstructed in color on corrugated cardboard. To create the desert landscape and rainbow sunset of Mars, cut out the pieces and layer them on the hardboard backing.

materials and tools

Three pieces ¼-inch hardboard 19×60 inches, six 1×2s 60 inches long, three 1×2s 17½ inches long, three panels corrugated kraft paper 17½×60 inches, 2d casing nails, white glue, four butt hinges with screws, hammer, screwdriver, scissors, ruler.

shopping

1. Get all lumber cut to exact sizes specified.

preparation

1. Enlarge patterns in Fig. 9-49 and draw onto corrugated kraft paper.

assembly

1. Frame the bottom and sides of the hardboard with 1×2s using 2d casing nails and glue.

2. Cut each piece of the pattern out from kraft paper and glue to the hardboard with white glue, layering them as you go. Be sure to cut all pieces with the "grain" of the cardboard.

3. Hinge the three panels together.

finishing

1. Spray paint as suggested on the color-coded pattern (Fig. 9-49). Overlap colors and color patterns on the frame, blending sunset and landscape into one unified picture.

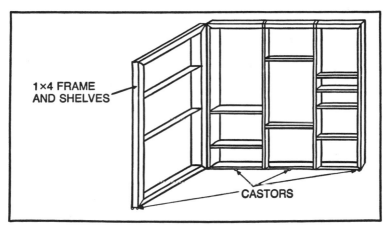

1×4 FRAME AND SHELVES

CASTORS

Fig. 9-48. Folding storage screen.

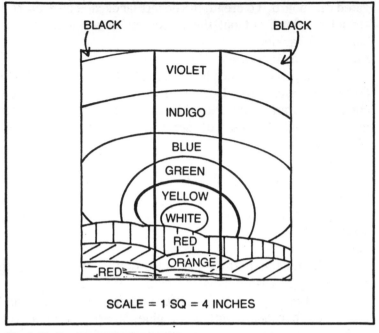

Fig. 9-49. Cardboard Martian sunset.

2. You may wish to place a few potted cactus plants near the screen to enhance the desert atmosphere.

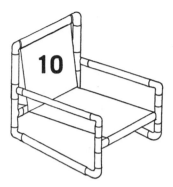

Comfort and Ease Projects

You can invest time in making projects that will contribute to your own comfort and ease. It is an investment that will pay off in more and better leisure time.

CARTS

Here's how to assemble a serving cart that a lumberyard worker can precut for you—including one of its three wheels.

Notch-Together Plywood Serving Cart

Figure 10-1 shows how the notch-together server is cut and assembled. It is cut from ¾-inch plywood—including the big third wheel and the back. Use plate-type furniture casters on the front to complete the set of tricycle rolling gear.

materials and tools

One piece ¾-inch plywood 48×60 inches cut according to sawing pattern (Fig. 10-2), two front legs 6×29 inches, two back legs 6×26 inches, two crosspieces 6×22 inches, one top 24×36 inches, one shelf 22×29 inches, one wheel 10 inches in diameter, one ½-inch dowel rod 8 inches long, two one-hole conduit straps (for ½-inch conduit), two plate-type casters, four mending plates (2-inch), 18½-inch flathead screws, four

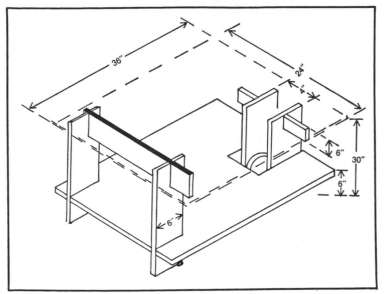

Fig. 10-1. Notch-together serving cart.

1½-inch flathead wood screws, putty, paint, sandpaper, sealer, screwdriver, small mallet or hammer, drill and small bits.

shopping

    1. Get all plywood parts cut to size and slotted.

    2. Conduit straps used for holding the dowel axle will be found in the electrical hardware department.

preparation

    1. On a large piece of butcher paper, reproduce the sawing pattern in Fig. 10-2 actual size for the person who will be making your cuts. Measure and draw in the notches accurately. They are all ¾ inch wide and 3 inches deep and should be centered and symmetrical.

    2. Wheel well cutout is 4 inches wide and 10 inches deep on the shelf piece. The handle on the top piece is a slot 2 inches wide and 18 inches long.

assembly

    1. Secure back legs to the shelf with mending plates (Fig. 10-3).

    2. Fit dowel axle into the wheel and secure to the underside of the shelf with one-hole conduit holders (Fig. 10-3).

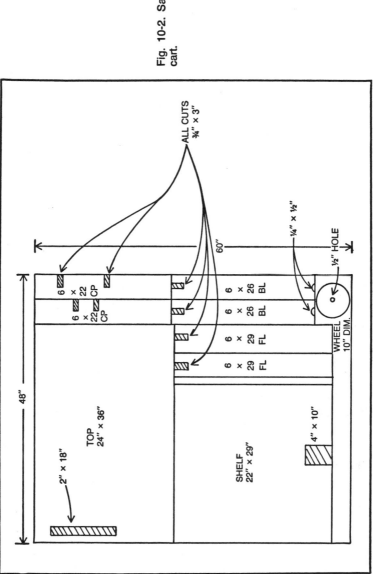

Fig. 10-2. Sawing pattern for the cart.

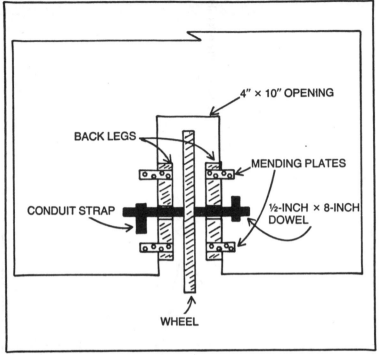

Fig. 10-3. Wheel assembly detail.

3. Fasten the casters to the two front legs.

4. Assemble the entire cart frame by sliding notches together using Fig. 10-1 as a guide.

5. Drill clearance holes in the top and pilot holes in both crosspieces. Screw the top to the crosspieces with four 1½-inch flathead wood screws.

6. Countersink and fill over screwheads with putty.

finishing

1. Sand, seal, and paint.

Tea and Coffee Cart

A new type of serving cart is presented in Fig. 10-4. It's an easy to serve from cart built on a triangular frame of 2×2s. An attractive section of plastic laminate is cemented to the ¾-inch plywood trays. Trays are trimmed with 1×2s tacked over 1-inch dowels. Axle dowels for the 6-inch plywood wheels are drilled and pegged for security.

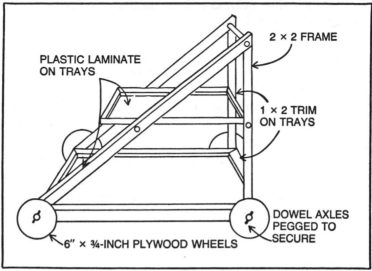

Fig. 10-4. Tea and coffee cart.

materials and tools

Two 2×2s 43½ inches long, two 2×2s 28¼ inches long, two 2×2s 17½ inches long, one ¾-inch piece of plywood 14½×15 inches, one ¾-inch piece of plywood 14½×30 inches, four ¾-inch plywood wheels 6 inches in diameter, five 1-inch dowels 19 inches long, four ¼-inch dowels 2 inches long, two 1×2s 32¾ inches, two 1×2s 16½ inches, four 1×2s 14½ inches, two pieces plastic laminate 14½×15 inches and 14½×30 inches, 3d and 6d nails, white glue, paint, sandpaper, sealer, hammer, small saw, drill, ¼-inch and 1-inch bits.

shopping

1. Shop for number one clear pine for your 2×2 frame and 1×2 trim.

2. The two trays and four wheels can be cut from a piece of plywood 30 inches square.

3. Pick paint to match or complement the laminate you select.

4. Get all pieces of lumber cut to size.

preparation

1. Measure and mark both ends of 43¼-inch frame members and one end of the 28¼-inch frame member to be cut at a 45-degree angle.

2. Measure and mark frame members for drilling 1-inch dowel holes (Fig. 10-5).

assembly

1. Cut frame members as marked with a small saw and glue each set together (Fig. 10-6). Use white glue and drive a corrugated fastener into the joint.

2. Drill dowel holes into frame members as marked.

3. Push two dowels through the bottom holes in the frame and slide on wheels.

4. Drill dowels and peg wheels on with ¼-inch dowels.

5. Twist the remaining three dowels into place.

6. Nail and glue 1×2 trim pieces to plywood trays.

7. Place trays on dowels and fasten them securely with 3d nails.

8. Cement laminates in place.

finishing

1. Paint to suit.

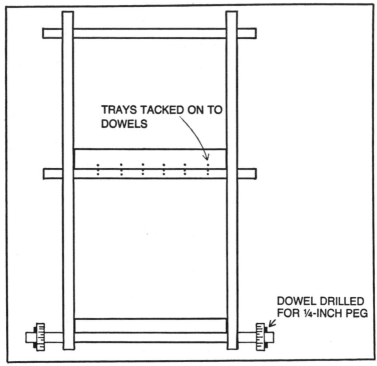

Fig. 10-5. End view of the tea and coffee cart.

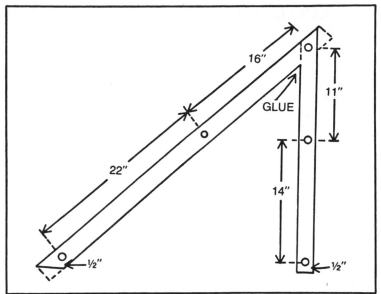

Fig. 10-6. Measuring and marking the frame for drilling.

Rugged Outdoor Cart for Your Barbecue

This attractive and rugged roll-around cart is easily assembled from 2×6 tongue-and-groove boards, with 1×2s for trim around the edges and sturdy 2×2 legs (Fig. 10-7).

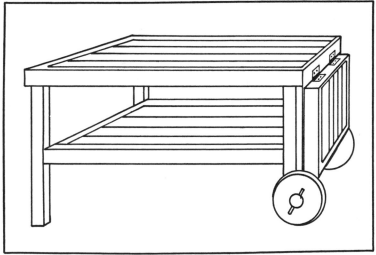

Fig. 10-7. Outdoor cart for barbecue.

materials and tools

Four 36-inch tongue-and-groove 2×6s, four 32-inch tongue-and-groove 2×6s, four 24-inch tongue-and-groove 2×6s, two 29-inch 2×2s, two 24-inch 2×2s, one 20-inch 2×10, one 28-inch 1-inch dowel, two 2-inch ¼-inch dowels, two 36-inch 1×2s, two 32-inch 1×2s, eight 24-inch 1×2s, two butt hinges, two table leaf braces, 3d casing nails, 6d casing nails, white glue, two chest handles, sandpaper, stain, polyurethane varnish, hammer, screwdriver, drill with 1-inch and ¼-inch bits.

shopping

1. Shop for an attractive wood that will take a natural finish.

2. Get all wood parts cut to exact size, including 10-inch diameter wheels cut from the 20-inch length of 2×10.

preparation

1. Locate the center of the wheels and mark for drilling 1-inch holes.

2. Mark 1-inch dowel ½ inch from each end for drilling a ¼-inch hole for pegging.

assembly

1. Assemble top, shelf, and drop leaf by pushing tongue-and-groove boards together.

2. Spread glue and nail 1×2 trim pieces with 3d casing nails around each side of the top, shelf, and drop leaf.

3. Nail the four legs to the top with 6d casing nails. Countersink heads and fill nail holes with putty.

4. Nail the shelf in place. Nail through the four legs with 3d casing nails. Countersink and fill holes.

5. Nail 1-inch dowel rod to the bottoms of short legs with 6d nails.

6. Drill holes in the center of wheels and drill small holes in the ends of 1-inch dowel.

7. Slide wheels on dowel and peg with ¼-inch dowels.

8. Install hinges on the underside of the top and drop leaf.

9. Install drop leaf brackets on the underneath side of the top and drop leaf (Fig. 10-8).

10. Finish with natural stain and liquid plastic protective

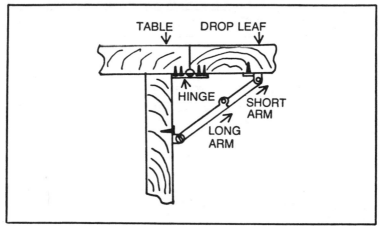

Fig. 10-8. Detail on installation of the table leaf brace.

coat. Install chest handles on the back edge of the top for moving.

11. Install a wine rack on the bottom shelf.

FLIP-DOWN TABLES

Even if you are cramped for space, one of these solutions will give you lots of extra eating and snacking space.

Storage/Work Space/Table Combo

You can use this idea with a storage unit you already have, or build the storage unit and attach the drop-leaf table to your new storage chest for a unit resembling Fig. 10-9.

materials and tools

One piece ¾-inch plywood 48×28 inches, two pieces ¾-inch plywood 48×24 inches, two pieces ¾-inch plywood 46½×23¼ inches, two pieces ¾-inch plywood 27¼×23¼ inches, two 1×2s 20 inches long, four butt hinges, two table-leaf braces, 3d casing nails, whilte glue, paint, sandpaper, sealer, hammer, screwdriver, ruler.

shopping

1. Get all lumber cut exactly to size.

preparation

1. Measure 12 inches up the side pieces and mark position for 1×2 cleats.

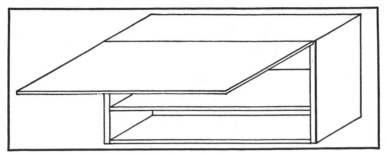

Fig. 10-9. Storage/work space/table combo.

2. Measure in ⅜-inch for the edges of plywood top and back pieces and draw nail guidelines.

assembly

1. Nail and glue sides fo the top of the storage box.

2. Nail cleats in place as marked. Nail the shelf and bottom in place.

3. Nail the back on the unit to complete the storage box.

4. Mount the hinges on the underneath side of the storage top and drop-leaf cover.

5. Mount table leaf brackets on each side of the storage box and to the underside of the drop leaf.

finishing

1. Sand well and seal.

2. Paint to match other room furnishings and enjoy your new storage/work space and flip-down eating space.

End-of-Counter or Island Flip-down

Figure 10-10 shows another way to acquire space for quick meals or extra company with a flip-down table attached to the end of a counter or kitchen island. Use plastic laminate to match counter tops and trim with 1×2s.

materials and tools

One 24×24-inch piece of ¾-inch plywood, one 24-inch 1×2, two 24¾-inch 1×2s, two butt hinges, two table leaf brackets, 3d nails, white glue, polyurethane varnish, sandpaper, hammer, screwdriver.

shopping

1. Get your lumber cut to exact dimensions.

preparation

1. Measure and mark carefully the placement of the flip-down table on the counter or island end. Mark position for hinges and table leaf brackets.

assembly

1. Glue and nail trim around three sides of the drop leaf tabletop.

2. Install table leaf brackets on each side of the drop leaf.

3. Install butt hinges on the underneath side of counter projection and drop leaf.

finishing

1. Sand well.

2. Install plastic laminate and varnish trim.

Wall Flip-Down Table

Even an unused wall in a hall or passageway can be used if you construct a flip-down table like the one in Fig. 10-11. Ours is 14×48 inches and seats two adults or three extra children.

materials and tools

Two 48-inch 1×2s, two 14-inch 1×2s, one 48×14-inch ¾-inch piece of plywood, two 14-inch lengths of link chain, 4 butt hinges, four small screw eyes, two magnetic latches, two

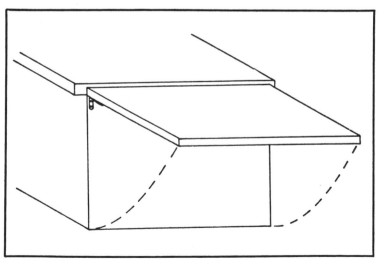

Fig. 10-10. End-of-counter-or-island flip-down.

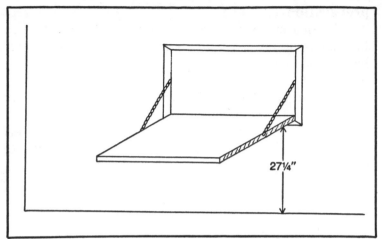

Fig. 10-11. Flip-down from wall.

wooden knobs, latex paint, liquid plastic for finish, 6d nails, sandpaper, screwdriver.

shopping

1. Get all lumber cut to exact size.

2. Shop for a good grade plywood with nice wood grain on both sides for an attractive flip-down top. Both sides will be exposed.

preparation

1. Measure carefully the placement of the frame of 1×2s, so the tabletop will be 28 inches from the floor or a few inches lower if the flip-down table is going to be used mostly by children. Remember that the narrow sides of the 1×2s face the front.

assembly

1. Locate studs in walls by knocking on the walls and marking areas where the sound is solid—not hollow.

2. Nail the frame to the wall so that the top edge of the bottom frame member is 27¼ inches from floor level or slightly less if step 1 under preparation applies.

3. Fit the tabletop into the frame and install hinges on the bottom underside.

4. Install screw eyes and attach link chain.

5. Install magnetic catches 1 foot from each side of the flip-down just inside the frame at the top.

6. Attach knobs on outside (underneath side when flipped down) opposite magnetic catches.

finishing

1. Sand.

2. Finish wood with a coat of latex paint and liquid plastic.

POLYVINYL CHLORIDE (PVC) PROJECTS

You can make many items of comfort and ease from PVC (polyvinyl chloride) pipe. Your pipe dreams can come true with a little time and the aid of a fine-toothed wood saw, some grit number 240-280 sandpaper, and a little epoxy or pipe cement.

Footstool

Figure 10-12 shows the basic items of pipe you will be working with—elbow joints and T-joints. Elbows come in 90

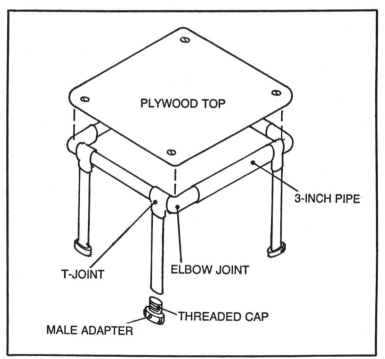

Fig. 10-12. Footstool.

and 45 degree angles in all sizes. In addition, there are reducers for changing from one pipe size to another and flanges for going through floors and ceilings. We will use flanges for other purposes. They make dandy fasteners for joining wood, plastic, or metal to the PVC framework or superstructure. For the first project you will use only straight pipe, 90-degree elbows, and T-joints with some threaded caps to protect your floors or floor coverings and to "cap off" the legs of the stool.

materials and tools

Four 18-inch lengths of 3-inch-diameter PVC pipe, four 12-inch lengths of 3-inch PVC pipe, four 3-inch PVC elbows, four 3-inch PVC T-joints, four 3-inch male adapters, four threaded caps, one piece of ¾-inch plywood 24 inches square with a 3-inch radius on each corner, epoxy or pipe cement, spray enamel of your choice, your favorite foot cushion, four 1¼-inch flathead wood screws, Fine-toothed wood saw, drill and bits for countersink, clearance and pilot holes, and a screwdriver.

shopping

1. If your pipe dealer does not cut to your specified lengths, you will need a total of 12 feet (120 inches) of straight PVC pipe. If you take sections that total this amount, be sure that the sections will cut evenly into four 12-inch and 4 18-inch lengths.

preparation

1. Measure and mark off the PVC pipe for cutting.

assembly

1. Cut the PVC pipe with a fine-toothed saw into four 18-inch and four 12-inch lengths.

2. Use pipe cement sparingly as you construct a rectangle by cementing one 18-inch length of pipe to one end of a T-joint. Cement an elbow into the other side of the T-joint and then another 18-inch length of straight pipe out of the elbow and into the next T-joint.

3. Cement the 12-inch pipe sections into the "bottom" end of each of the four T-joints.

4. Cement male adapters into each leg and screw on threaded caps.

5. Place a thumbtack upside down on each of the four T-joints. Lower the plywood square down gently on top of them with the same overhang on all sides. Press to pick up thumbtacks on the underside of the plywood. Tacks will mark the center of holes to be drilled for clearance and countersink of 1¼-inch flathead wood screws.

6. Drill clearance and countersink holes in plywood. Mark and drill pilot holes in the top of T-joints.

7. Secure the plywood to the pipe frame with wood screws.

8. Fill over screwheads with putty.

finishing

1. Spray with enamel. When dry, top with your favorite foot cushion.

Lamp Table Variation

The basic footstool frame in the preceding project lends itself to many variations for other kinds of furniture. Figure 10-13 illustrates a lamp table variation that can be dry-

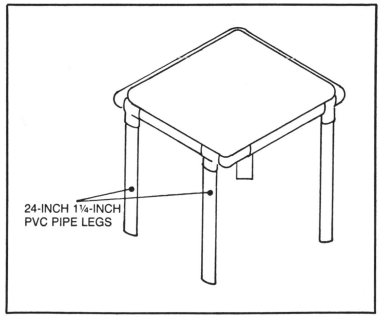

24-INCH 1¼-INCH
PVC PIPE LEGS

Fig. 10-13. Lamp table variation.

assembled in less than 10 minutes once you have your PVC pipe cut to length.

materials and tools

Four 18-inch lengths of 1¼-inch-diameter PVC pipe, four 24-inch lengths of 1¼-inch PVC pipe, four 1¼-inch PVC elbows, four 1¼-inch PVC T-joints, four 1¼-inch male adapters, four 1¼-inch threaded caps, one bronzed glass top ¼×24×24 inches with 3-inch radius on each corner, four rubber spacers, spray enamel of your choice, epoxy, fine-toothed wood saw if you cut your own pipe.

shopping

1. If you can get your pipe dealer to cut your pipe to length, it will be a time-saver.

2. The bronzed glass makes a very attractive tabletop. Other types of glass, Plexiglas or plastic can be used. Get the top in ¼-inch thickness, however, as you need the weight for stability and ruggedness.

preparation

1. Double-check to be sure your pipe lengths are the correct dimensions.

assembly

1. Dry-assemble by pushing one 18-inch length of straight pipe into one end of a T-joint and then into the elbow, and come out of the elbow with another piece of straight pipe (Fig. 10-12). Continue until the square frame is completed.

2. Push the 24-inch "leg" sections of pipe into the open end on the T-joints.

3. Push male adapters into the ends of pipe legs and screw on threaded caps.

finishing

1. Spray paint with enamel.

2. Epoxy rubber spacers on top of each T-joint and place the glass top on rubber spacers.

Coffee Table Variation

For the coffee table variation shown in Fig. 10-14, you may use either the 1¼, 1½, or 3-inch PVC pipe. We prefer the 3-inch pipe, but you can substitute the smaller diameter pipe in the materials list.

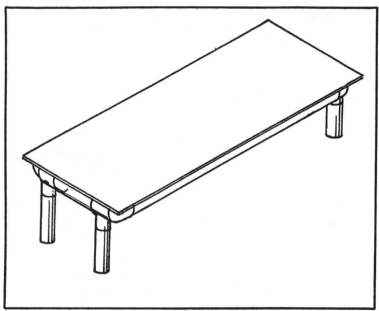

Fig. 10-14. Coffee table variation.

materials and tools

One bronzed glass top ¼×26×54 inches, four rubber spacers, two 24-inch lengths of 3-inch PVC pipe, two 18-inch lengths of 3-inch PVC pipe, four 14-inch lengths of 3-inch PVC pipe, four 3-inch PVC elbows, four 3-inch PVC T-joints, spray enamel, epoxy. No tools are needed if the pipe is precut.

shopping

1. Get PVC pipe cut to exact lengths.

preparation

1. Double-check measurements on pipe lengths.

assembly

1. Dry-assemble by pushing one 18-inch length of pipe into one end of a T-joint, then into the elbow, and come out of the elbow with a 24-inch length of pipe. Push it into the T-joint, push the elbow into the other end of the T-joint, and come out with the other 18-inch length of pipe. With the remaining pipe, T-joints and elbows complete the rectangular frame.

2. Push the 14-inch pipe sections into the T-joints, and your coffee table has its legs.

finishing

1. Spray paint the frame with enamel spray.
2. Epoxy rubber spacers to the tops of T-joints and place the glass top on the spacers.

Canvas Sling/PVC-Type Chair

The only tricky parts in making the chair are the sling and tie-to-tail. If you are handy at sewing, there will be no problem. If not, take your pattern and material to an awning shop. The people there will make the sling and tie it for you.

Square off pipe ends with sandpaper on a wood block as you deburr (remove flash from ends). Also, you might dry-fit your lengths of PVC pipe before cementing to insure accurate overall dimensions. Always cut a little on the long side and sand down to an exact fit.

You will be using a lot of epoxy or pipe cement, so work in a well-ventilated room. The fumes from epoxy-type cements are quite toxic. The epoxy sets very quickly—something less than 4 seconds—so you have to be right the first time you weld a piece together. This is why dry-fitting the chair before welding it together might be proper if you feel the least bit insecure about your craftsmanship.

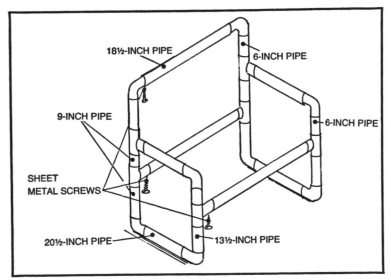

Fig. 10-15. PVC-type chair detail.

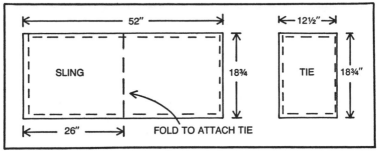

Fig. 10-16. Sling and tie patterns for the chair.

One trick that is helpful in making accurate fittings is to lay the basic assembly flat on a table or workbench. Always insert dummy pieces of pipe into any spare holes in T-fittings. This will help orient the fitting. We sometimes set up a large square of 1×4s, supported by clamps, and use the square as a guide to make quite accurate 90-degree turns.

Figure 10-15 will show you the details of chair construction. Notice that there are three joints not cemented together. Those joints are secured with screws turned into holes drilled through the fitting leg and inserted pipe. This will allow the removal and replacement of the canvas sling and tie. Figure 10-16 gives you the patterns for the sling and tie-to-tail. Figure 10-17 shows the finished chair. If you want to make cushions for your chair see Chapter 9.

materials and tools

Four 20½-inch lengths of 1½-inch PVC pipe, three 18½-inch lengths of 1½-inch PVC pipe, two 13½-inch lengths of 1½-inch PVC pipe, four 9-inch lengths of 1½-inch PVC pipe, four 6-inch lengths of 1½-inch PVC pipe, six T-joints of 1½-inch PVC, eight elbows, 90-degree PVC, one piece canvas 18¾ inches by 52 inches, one piece canvas 18¾ inches by 12½ inches, epoxy or solvent welding compound, spray enamel, three number 10 sheet metal screws, fine-toothed saw, sandpaper on wood block, drill and bits, screwdriver.

shopping

1. If you have pipe precut to lengths specified in the materials section, ask that it be cut a fraction long to give you "sanding room."

2. Buy grit number 240 to 280 sandpaper for removing

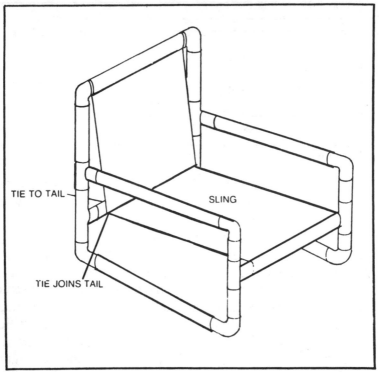

Fig. 10-17. Sling and tie-to-tail details for PVC chair.

printing from pipe, but get somewhat coarser paper for squaring off ends of pipe and smoothing burrs.

preparation

    1. Double-check pipe lengths with a good ruler and then dry-fit to make sure of the fit.

assembly

    1. Cut all straight pipe to proper lengths.

    2. Remove the imprint with sandpaper. Dampen the imprint before sanding.

    3. Square all cut ends of pipe with sandpaper and a wood block for an accurate fit.

    4. Using Fig. 10-15 as a guide, dry-fit all pipe components together.

    5. With a ⅛-inch-diameter bit, drill T-1, T-2, and E-1 as indicated (Fig. 10-15) for a number 10 sheet metal screw through connecting pipe.

6. Drive sheet metal screws into holes just drilled.

7. Disassemble all other joints.

8. Reassemble all joints using epoxy to secure them.

9. Spray paint the frame with enamel.

finishing

1. Using Fig. 10-17 as a guide, wrap the canvas sling around the front and back cross members and baste in place.

2. Wrap the tie around the bottom back member and baste.

3. Baste tie onto the sling at the fold (Fig. 10-17). Be sure to stretch the sling and tie tight before final basting.

4. Remove screws and pull chain members apart to remove the sling and tie.

5. Machine sew (or have machine sewn) all seams you have basted. Use double stitching.

6. Replace the sling and tie on the chair. Refit and screw joints back together. Pad with your favorite cushions, pull up your footstool and lamp table, and get comfortable.

SOLID WOOD COFFEE TABLES

A solid coffee table that can double as a game table (especially for floor sitters) and/or storage space for games, drinks, records, and tapes is an attractive piece of furniture.

Movable Coffee Table/Storage Unit

Essentially four boxes on a plywood base, this table/storage unit has three lift-off hinged tops on three of its cubes for lots of storage space. The fourth cube is quartered for holding your favorite reading material and/or potted plants. Figure 10-18 gives the general idea.

materials and tools

Eight pieces of ¾-inch plywood 18×14 inches, eight pieces of ¾-inch plywood 16½×14 inches, seven pieces of ¾-inch plywood 18×18 inches, two pieces of ¾-inch plywood 16½×14 inches, one piece of ¾-inch plywood 32×32 inches, three small piano hinges, four carpet casters, eight flathead wood screws 1¼ inches long, 3d casing nails, white glue, paint, sandpaper, sealer, hammer, small wood saw, screwdriver, drill with bit for starter holes.

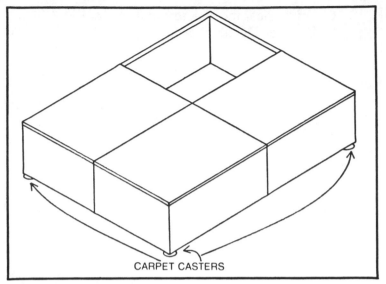

CARPET CASTERS

Fig. 10-18. Movable coffee table/storage unit.

shopping

    1. Shop for a good grade of plywood and have it cut to the exact sizes listed in the materials section.

    2. Pick a paint that will go with other furnishings and/or with big floor pillows if you plan to use them (see Chapter 9).

preparation

    1. For each of the 18-inch-square-by-14-inch-deep boxes, measure and mark your nail guidelines ⅜ inch in from all plywood edges.

    2. Measure and mark placement of hinges for the lids on three of the boxes. All four boxes have bottoms.

    3. Measure and mark the two 16½×14-inch pieces for the slot as shown in Fig. 10-19.

assembly

    1. Nail and glue all four boxes except for the lids.

    2. Place boxes on a 32-inch-square piece of plywood and secure with wood screws through the bottoms of boxes as shown in Fig. 10-20.

    3. Cut out the slots and insert in one of the boxes as shown by the dotted lines in Fig. 10-20.

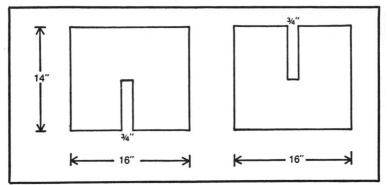

Fig. 10-19. Slots for dividers.

4. Secure lids with small piano hinges on the remaining three boxes.

5. Screw carpet casters to the bottom of the base.

finishing

1. Sand and seal.

2. Paint in a primary color to match the floor pillows or other room furnishings.

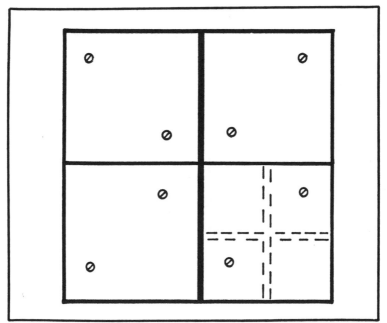

Fig. 10-20. Placement of screws and insert.

Sweet and Low Coffee/Storage Table

Figure 10-21 shows construction details for this table that will store your favorite art prints, records, etc. Basically, it is a low box on a pedestal base with one end of the box hinged for an opening. A magnetic catch keeps the end closed and stored items out of sight.

materials and tools

Two 36×36 inch pieces of ¾-inch plywood, two 36×12-inch pieces of ¾-inch plywood, two 34½×12-inch pieces of ¾-inch plywood, two 34½×34½-inch pieces of ½-inch plywood, six 30-inch 1×2s, two 28½-inch 1×2s, one piano hinge, one magnetic catch, 3d casing nails, white glue, paint, sandpaper, sealer, hammer, screwdriver.

shopping

1. Shop for a smooth grade of interior plywood and number 1 clear 1×2s for the pedestal base.

2. You will need a piano hinge about 34-35 inches long.

preparation

1. Measure in ⅜ inch from the edges of the plywood top bottom and side and back pieces. Mark the guideline for nails.

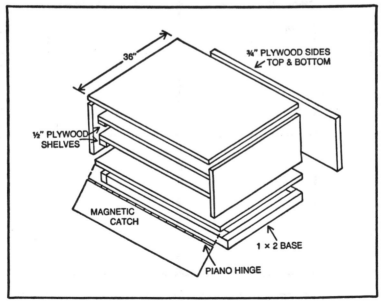

Fig. 10-21. Construction details for the coffee/storage table.

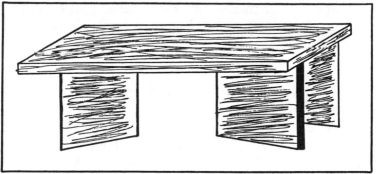

Fig. 10-22. Side view of the solid coffee table.

2. Measure and mark guidelines for the base on the bottom inset—3 inches on all sides.

3. Measure and mark placement of cleats for supporting ½-inch plywood shelves 4 inches apart and 4 inches from the top and bottom (12-inch vertical space is divided into three equal 4-inch sections).

assembly

1. Glue and nail shelf support cleats to the sides.

2. Assemble the box with glue and nails. Countersink nailheads with nail set and fill with putty stick.

3. Glue and nail 1×2 base strips to the bottom.

4. Secure leftover end to the bottom with the piano hinge.

5. Install a magnetic catch at the top center of the hinged end.

finishing

1. Sand and seal.

2. Paint to suit.

3. Install shelves by sliding them in on top of the cleats.

Solid Wood Coffee Table

materials and tools

Two 10×2×54 inch hardwood pieces, two 10×2×12½ inch hardwood pieces, two 8×2×12½-inch hardwood pieces, eight flathead wood screws 2-inch by number 10, white glue, sandpaper, 1 quart of linseed oil, ½-pint can of Japan drier, 1 quart of mineral spirits, cotton rags, 1 10d nail, screwdriver, drill with bits for countersink, clearance and pilot holes for number 10 screws (6/16, 3/16, and ⅛-inch), C-clamps.

shopping

1. Select your favorite hardwood. Choose pieces with good grain.

2. Have pieces cut exactly to size.

preparation

1. Lay the two 54-inch pieces of 10×2 side by side. Place smaller 10×2s and 8×2s on end in a V-formation exactly as in Fig. 10-23. Carefully outline the "V" after making sure all boards are tightly fitted together.

2. Remove leg pieces from top pieces and mark circles within rectangles for screw clearance holes (dotted lines, Fig. 10-23).

assembly

1. Drill clearance holes (3/16 inch) for number 10 screws. You are drilling from the underside of the tabletop, so clamp scrap wood to the top where the drill bit will emerge so as not to splinter the top.

2. Reassemble table pieces right side up and mark starter holes for pilot holes in leg pieces by using a 10d nail through the clearance holes.

3. Disassemble and drill pilot holes in legs and countersink holes in top.

4. Reassemble table pieces right side up. Apply white glue to all joining surfaces and drive home the eight screws that hold everything together.

5. Fill over screwheads with putty. Sand smooth.

finishing

If you want to finish this table quickly, you can give it a coat of polyurethane liquid plastic in about 10 minutes or go the conventional varnish route. Don't wax it. Wax softens the minute it comes into contact with anything greasy or oily. Because wax will not sink into hardwood, you will never get a durable finish no matter how many coats you try to put on. Another quick finish that works is a couple coats of shellac. Give the topcoat a good rubdown with linseed oil.

1. Scuff up the wood surface real good with your fine grain sandpaper. Remove dust.

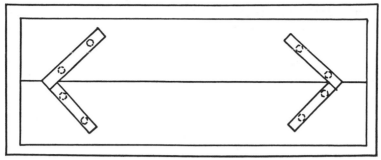

Fig. 10-23. Bottom view of the coffee table.

2. Mix 1 cup of linseed oil with ½ cup of mineral spirits. Add one heaping tablespoon of Japan drier.

3. Brush the mixture onto the wood until it will not absorb any more. Let the piece stand for one hour. If any dry spots show up, brush on some more. Let the piece stand for another hour. Wipe off any excess that has not been absorbed into the wood. Let the table stand for a week in a warm and dry place. Now you are ready to begin your finishing work.

4. Mix up the following in a container you can cover and keep for months: 1 cup linseed oil, 1¼ tablespoonfuls of mineral spirits, and, 1 teaspoonful of Japan drier.

5. Once a week for three months, spend about 30 minutes rubbing your table down with this mixture. Apply the mixture as you would a furniture wax or polish, but spend at least five minutes rubbing it in as hard as you can. When you have finished each rubbing session, use your cotton applicator cloth to wipe off the excess oil. Be sure to wring the pad out as hard as you can and then wipe down the surface again. Repeat and do it again, then one more time for good measure.

BINS AND TINS

Why not collect and use old Sonotubes? Sonotube is the brand name for a 7-foot-high laminated fiber cylinder used for making concrete pillars.

Sonotube Closet

You can build a closet for jogging togs, tennis shoes, and other recreational paraphernalia.

materials and tools

One Sonotube, one expansion closet rod with end hardware, 6 yards of 48-inch width fabric, 1 quart white paint, staples, linoleum knife, straightedge (metal), screwdriver, staple gun.

shopping

1. If you do not have a construction site nearby, you can contact any local contractor about the availability of Sonotubes. Used ones in good condition can usually be obtained, but even new and unused ones are not that expensive.

preparation

1. Mark the opening on one side of the tube 72 inches high and 36 inches wide. Leave approximately 9 inches at the top and a 3-inch "rim" at the bottom (Fig. 10-24).

assembly

1. Using a linoleum knife and metal straightedge, cut an opening in the Sonotube.

2. Paint the interior of the tube with white paint.

3. Staple fabric onto the outside of the tube, tucking edges under and around the edges of the opening (Fig. 10-25).

finishing

1. You may carpet the floor of your new storage bin with a shag rug carpeting that complements the fabric on the outside. It makes for a little touch of luxury.

2. Install a closet rod across the diameter of the tube.

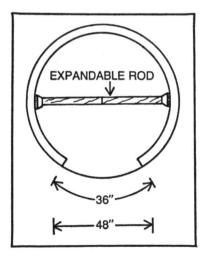

EXPANDABLE ROD

36"

48"

Fig. 10-24. Top view of the Sonotube closet.

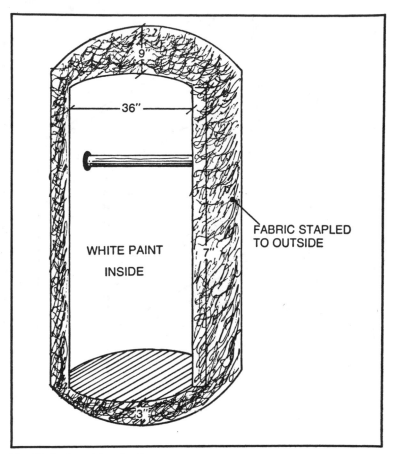

Fig. 10-25. Sonotube closet.

Storage Bins

Open cupboard storage is both handy and attractive in kitchens and bathrooms. Narrow spaces can often be found under counters too narrow for the usual storage bins, but just right for a drawer turned on end.

Figures 10-26, 10-27, and 10-28 illustrate open cupboard applications of salvaged drawers. Figure 10-26 shows a variation for using the drawer on end to slide in and out of a space only 5 or 6 inches wide. For this application you must add a track and guide for the drawer-cupboard unit. Figure 10-29 shows details of the track and guide. Here are details for one of the drawers (Fig. 10-28).

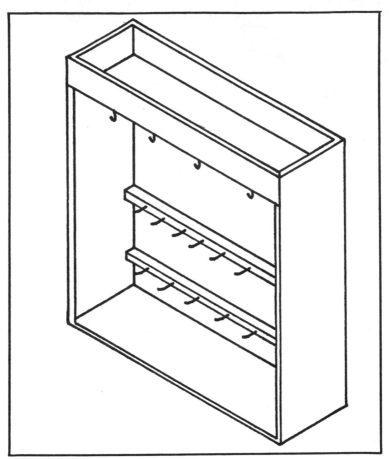

Fig. 10-26. Drawer cupboard with hooks for utensils.

materials and tools

One salvaged drawer in good condition (6×24×24 inches), three 24-inch sections of ½-inch dowels, three 24-inch sections of molding/trim, two 24-inch pieces of 1×6 lumber, 3d casing nails, 2d finishing nails, putty, paint, sandpaper, sealer, hammer, nail set, small handsaw.

shopping

1. Used furniture stores and salvage companies are the best places to shop for drawers. Usually they will be part of a damaged piece of furniture. Because there is little demand for drawers, you can usually get some in good condition for practically nothing

2. If you have your lumber cut to size, purchase your drawers first so you can get exact measurements for your lumber cuts. A small handsaw will still come in handy to do last minute trimming for an exact fit.

preparation

1. Measure and mark guidelines on the outside of the drawer for nail guides. Place shelves so that dishes or utensils to be stored will fit.

assembly

1. Secure shelves and dowel plate rails with glue and nails.

2. Using glue and finishing nails, fasten molding/trim to shelves and the bottom of the drawer side that now forms the bottom shelf of your cupboard.

3. Countersink all nailheads and remove all hardware from the drawer front.

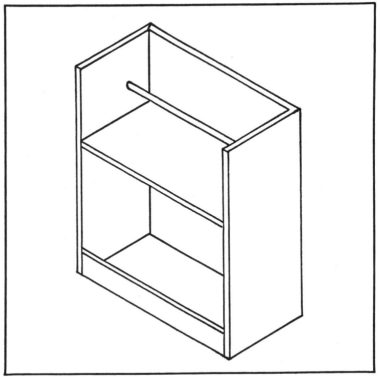

Fig. 10-27. Drawer cupboard for paper goods storage.

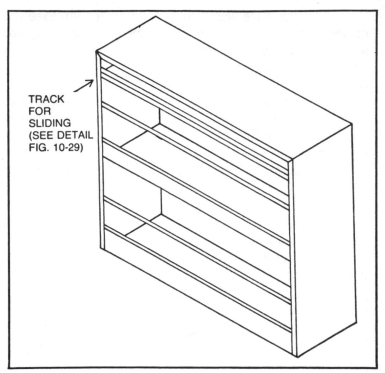

TRACK
FOR
SLIDING
(SEE DETAIL
FIG. 10-29)

Fig. 10-28. Drawer cupboard for plates and lids.

4. Fill all nail holes and holes left by hardware removal with putty. Sand smooth.

finishing

1. Paint and hang on wall studs or on the top of counters. For pull-out cupboard variation, salvage the drawer tracks and guides and install as shown in Fig. 10-29. You can make many variations on the salvaged drawers cupboard theme in addition to the ones illustrated. Remember that your design for any drawer-turned-on-end cupboard is always determined by the available drawer space in relation to the size and shape of the objects to be stored. A paper storage cupboard, like the one in Fig. 10-27, will need to be at least 8 inches deep to store large rolls of fluffy paper towels.

HANG-UPS

Most hang-ups make use of chain. The chain types available at hardware stores and discount outlets will be adequate for most hang-up chores and can be divided into two groups: decorative function and strength function. You will want to observe the working-load limit of any chain you use, even if it is primarily for decoration. All chain is tested for its working load limit, and your chain dealer will furnish you with this information. These dealers sell their chain off 100-foot reels and will cut it to length for you. These reels are often marked with the load-limit factor for the particular chain on that reel.

The load limit is a factor of the material and the thickness of the "wire" out of which the chain is made. A decorative brass jack chain with a ¼-inch diameter will have a working load limit of 10 pounds. You can get a ¼-inch diameter grade 30-proof coil chain that will have a working load limit of 1,250 pounds. When you shop for chain, be sure it will take the weight load to which you plan to subject it. Jack chain is usually the weakest chain you can buy, while machine chain is usually the strongest. If you need something stronger than machine chain, you will need to use Grade 30 proof coil chain. This 5/16-inch chain has a load limit of 1,900 pounds. If that doesn't suit, you can use high-test chain or grade 70. Our first hang-up project can be made with four strands of double jack

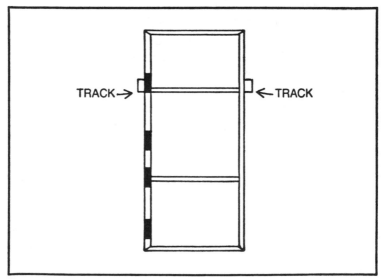

Fig. 10-29. Front view drawer cupboard for plates and lids.

chain. You may substitute whatever chain suits your fancy as long as it is strong enough to support the items placed on the shelves.

Chain and Pine Hang-Up

This hang-up is ideal for the middle of a room, by a window, or at the end of a kitchen counter top. It can be used for potted plants, pottery, a rock or pine cone collection, or a combination of these things.

materials and tools

Four 1×12 pine boards 24 inches long, four decorative screw eyes, four 72-inch sections of double jack chain, 16 cup hooks, four small cans of red, yellow, green, and blue spray enamel (one each), sandpaper, and a pair of pliers for turning hooks and screw eyes.

shopping

1. Shop for clear number 1 grade pine boards that are straight and true with no warp.

preparation

1. Measure and mark pilot holes for cup hooks 1 inch in from the end on the short edges of each pine board.

assembly

1. Sand boards.

2. Spray paint each board a separate color and let dry.

3. Insert cup hooks into the ends of each pine board. Use a nail to make the starter hole in the wood.

4. Insert decorative "sky hooks" into ceiling joists as shown in Fig. 10-30.

5. Hang the chain from the hooks.

6. Insert pine shelves into chain links over cup hooks.

finishing

1. Place your plants and collectibles on shelves.

Figure 10-31 suggests a variation on this theme using chain packaged for hanging porch swings and small screw eyes in place of cup hooks in the ends of the pine board shelves. You might make acrylic or Plexiglas shelves by welding brass cup hooks onto the edges with PVC pipe welding epoxy.

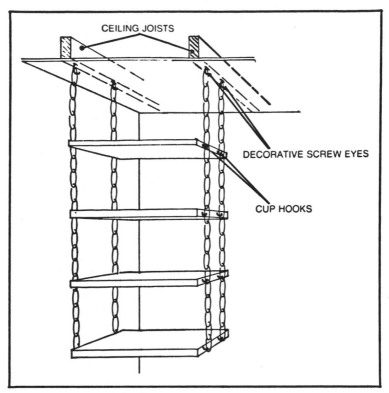

CEILING JOISTS

DECORATIVE SCREW EYES

CUP HOOKS

Fig. 10-30. Chain and pine hang-up.

Wall Shelf Hang-Up with Variations on the Theme

A simple wall shelf hang-up is shown in Fig. 10-32. Use dowel pegs under each shelf through the chain to hold the shelf in place. Holes are drilled in the shelf boards to pass the chain through.

materials and tools

Four 48-inch sections of ¼-inch brass single jack chain, two 1×12 pine boards 36 inches long, two decorative screw eyes, four ¼-inch dowels 2 inches long, small can of enamel spray paint, sandpaper, drill with ½-inch bit, pliers for turning screw eyes.

shopping

1. Buy number 1 clear pine boards for shelves and have them cut to size.

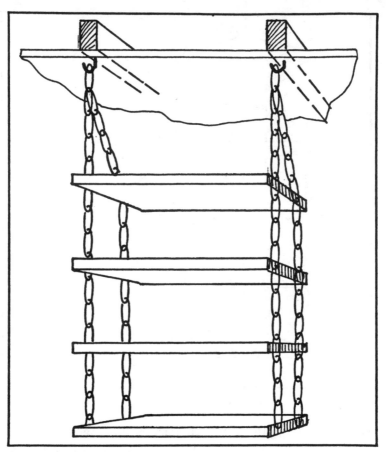

Fig. 10-31. Acrylic and chain hang-up.

preparation

1. Measure 1 inch in from each edge of the shelf and mark for the boring of the hole.

assembly

1. Bore holes in pine shelf boards.

2. Secure decorative screw eyes to wall studs.

3. Hang the chain from screw eyes and thread through holes in shelves. Secure the lower shelf with 2-inch lengths of ¼-inch dowels (Fig. 10-32).

finishing

1. Sand boards.

2. Spray paint.

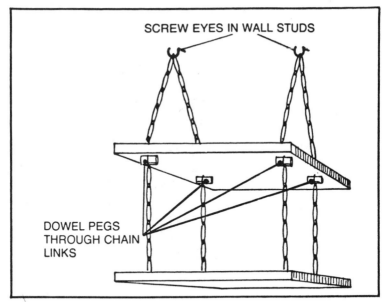

Fig. 10-32. Wall shelf hang-up.

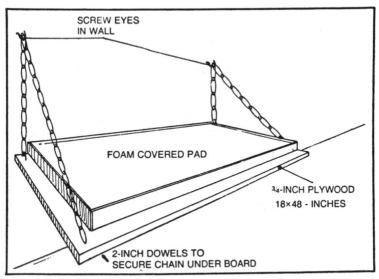

Fig. 10-33. Wall hang-up lounge.

Figure 10-33 shows a variation on this theme with a seat hung for the wall in like manner. It uses a single "shelf" 18×48 inches of ¾-inch plywood with a foam rubber cushion on top to make a comfortable seat.

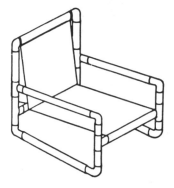

Index